AGRICOLA

AND

GERMANY

PUBLIUS CORNELIUS TACITUS is generally reckoned to have been the greatest of all Latin historians. It seems probable that his family came from southern Gaul (modern Provence) and that his father was the Cornelius Tacitus known to have been an imperial procurator at the time of Tacitus' birth, about AD 57. Tacitus studied at Rome and married the daughter of Julius Agricola, the famous governor of Britain, whose biography he was to write, in about 76. He became a senator, and held the standard magistracies at Rome, being successively quaestor, tribune of the plebs, and praetor, the latter in 88, in which year he also belonged to the prestigious senatorial priestly college, the *quindecimviri sacris faciundis*. Soon afterwards he was away from Rome for over three years, presumably holding appointments in the provinces. He was consul in 97, when he was already known as an outstanding orator. He and his friend the Younger Pliny successfully prosecuted a corrupt proconsul of Africa (modern Tunisia) in 99–100. His only other known public office was the proconsulship of Asia (western Turkey), in 112–13. He was almost certainly still alive and active in the reign of Hadrian (117–38), but it is not known when he died.

Tacitus' first works were *Agricola* and *Germany*, both composed in 98. His third short monograph, the *Dialogue on Orators*, probably followed soon afterwards. The first two survive complete, and the *Dialogue* with a short gap. Of his two major works, the *Histories*, covering the years AD 69–96, and the *Annals*, dealing with the period from Tiberius to Nero (14–68), only about a third and just over a half, respectively, survive.

ANTHONY R. BIRLEY was born in Northumberland in 1937 and educated at Clifton College and Magdalen College, Oxford. After posts at Birmingham and Leeds Universities he was Professor of Ancient History at Manchester from 1974 to 1990, and at present has a similar post at Düsseldorf. His publications include three books on Roman Britain, and biographies of Hadrian (1997), Marcus Aurelius (2nd edn., 1987), and Septimius Severus (2nd edn., 1988). He has also edited seven volumes of the writings of Sir Ronald Syme, whose pupil he was.

OXFORD WORLD'S CLASSICS

*For over 100 years Oxford World's Classics have brought
readers closer to the world's great literature. Now with over 700
titles—from the 4,000-year-old myths of Mesopotamia to the
twentieth century's greatest novels—the series makes available
lesser-known as well as celebrated writing.*

*The pocket-sized hardbacks of the early years contained
introductions by Virginia Woolf, T. S. Eliot, Graham Greene,
and other literary figures which enriched the experience of reading.
Today the series is recognized for its fine scholarship and
reliability in texts that span world literature, drama and poetry,
religion, philosophy and politics. Each edition includes perceptive
commentary and essential background information to meet the
changing needs of readers.*

OXFORD WORLD'S CLASSICS

TACITUS

Agricola
and
Germany

Translated with an Introduction and Notes by
ANTHONY R. BIRLEY

OXFORD
UNIVERSITY PRESS

OXFORD
UNIVERSITY PRESS

Great Clarendon Street, Oxford OX2 6DP

Oxford University Press is a department of the University of Oxford.
It furthers the University's objective of excellence in research, scholarship,
and education by publishing worldwide in

Oxford New York

Athens Auckland Bangkok Bogotá Buenos Aires Calcutta
Cape Town Chennai Dar es Salaam Delhi Florence Hong Kong Istanbul
Karachi Kuala Lumpur Madrid Melbourne Mexico City Mumbai
Nairobi Paris São Paulo Singapore Taipei Tokyo Toronto Warsaw

with associated companies in Berlin Ibadan

Oxford is a registered trade mark of Oxford University Press
in the UK and in certain other countries

Published in the United States
by Oxford University Press Inc., New York

British Library Cataloguing in Publication Data

Data available

Library of Congress Cataloging in Publication Data

Tacitus, Cornelius.
[Agricola. English]
Agricola; and Germany / Tacitus; translated with an
introduction and notes by Anthony R. Birley.
(Oxford world's classics)
1. Agricola, Gnaeus Julius, 40–93.   2. Statesmen—Rome—Biography.
3. Germanic peoples.   I. Birley, Anthony Richard.   II. Tacitus,
Cornelius, Germania, English.   III. Title.   IV. Series: Oxford
world's classics (Oxford University Press)
DG291.7.A2T313   1999   936.1'03—dc21   98–34569
ISBN 0–19–283300–6

3 5 7 9 10 8 6 4

Typeset by Best-set Typesetter Ltd., Hong Kong
Printed in Great Britain by
Cox & Wyman Ltd.
Reading, Berkshire

For Heide: *Britannica et Germanica*

CONTENTS

PREFACE

Tacitus' wonderful Latin style, striking not least for brevity, compression, and sometimes for ambiguity, is hard to imitate, and the present translation is not intended to do this. It is hoped that at least his meaning comes across clearly. (In places this depends on what he actually wrote, not always certain.) For the translation itself and for the interpretation I have relied most of all, in many passages, on the Oxford editions, the first thirty years old, the second twice that age: of *Agricola* by Ogilvie and Richmond, of *Germany* by Anderson, both models of their kind. In addition, a variety of literature which has been of help—on Tacitus, especially by Ronald Syme, whose pupil I was fortunate to be, on Britain, and on Germany—is indicated in the Select Bibliography and the Explanatory Notes. I must make special mention of the commentary on *Germany* by Allan A. Lund, whose improvements to the text I have in many cases gratefully adopted and acknowledged, and of the collected Roman–German studies by Dieter Timpe, which have shed new light on some of the most debated passages. It would have been improper not to refer to these two books. But, conscious that English-speakers would not derive much benefit from further references to works in German, I have not cited e.g. those monuments of *Wissenschaft*, Pauly–Wissowa's *Realencyclopädie* (completed in 1978) and the *Reallexikon der Germanischen Altertumskunde* (of which a second edition is in progress).

It is proper to note that my interpretation of Tacitus' career is new in some particulars, exploiting the fragmentary inscription from Rome recently identified as his, but taking a rather more radical view than its editor, my friend Géza Alföldy, on the early stages. To be specific, I believe that there is a good case for Tacitus having served as a military tribune in Britain for the first two or three years of his father-in-law Agricola's governorship.

As for Agricola's career, I have interpreted it largely as in my own *Fasti of Roman Britain* (1981). The dating of his governorship to AD 77–84 rather than 78–85 has since been supported by others,

notably by D. B. Campbell's arguments that he was consul in 76 and by M.-Th. Raepsaet-Charlier's re-examination of the whole *cursus honorum*.

On one point of detail in the translation, it should be mentioned that I have avoided the term 'tribe' to describe the native peoples or states of Britain and Germany, for which Tacitus uses a variety of terms, such as *civitas*, *gens*, *natio*. 'Tribe' is, I think, a misleading expression. It need hardly be added that the word 'race' has not been used either (as it once was). Instead I have used terms such as 'state(s)', 'people(s)', 'community', occasionally 'nation', according to the context. (For *civitas*, see the Glossary.)

Agricola and *Germany* were each divided into forty-six 'chapters' by an earlier editor, numbering which has no ancient authority. I have retained it simply so that readers may, for example, be able to find more easily here passages which they have found referred to elsewhere. In addition, I have supplied headings to the sections into which the two works seem to be divided, e.g. *Agricola's Life up to his Appointment as Governor of Britain*, *Britain and its Peoples*, or *Arms and Military Tactics*.

Helpful criticism and comments by Judith Luna of Oxford University Press, Julian Ward, the copy-editor, and Dr Christopher Pelling have much improved the text submitted in September 1997. For remaining imperfections I remain responsible.

A.R.B.

INTRODUCTION

Rome and the Northern 'Barbarians'

Tacitus' first two works, generally called *Agricola* and *Germany*, written nineteen centuries ago (AD 98), represent, among other things, respectively the first history of Britain, and the first detailed description of the ancient Germans, ancestors not only of the modern Germans and Austrians but also, among others, of the Danes, Norwegians, Swedes, Dutch—and the English or 'Anglo-Saxons'. To give some idea of how the two short pieces came to be written requires a rapid historical survey.

In the early fourth century BC the people of the Mediterranean world received a rude, indeed terrifying shock: an invasion of huge, strange, blond and blue-eyed warriors, called 'Celts' or 'Galatae' by the Greeks, Gauls ('Galli') by the Romans. One band, under Brennus, got as far south as Rome in 386 BC and captured the city: patriotic legend had it that the Capitol was saved by the sacred geese. Rome had to buy her survival with gold. Brennus' grim response to the senators' complaint when he added his sword to the scales became proverbial: 'Vae victis', 'Woe to the defeated!' The northern part of the peninsula, from the Alps to well south of the Po, became known as 'Gaul' ('Gallia'). It was later labelled 'Cisalpina', 'this side of the Alps', as the Romans became aware that the same Galli had occupied the entire country beyond the western Alps, which thus became 'Gallia Transalpina'. Other Celts burst into the Balkans a century or so later, ravaged as far as Delphi, and then fetched up in Asia Minor, where they were eventually penned into the territory called 'Galatia'.

The Greeks and Romans slowly became used to these fierce northerners. Rome eventually got the measure of them in the Cisalpina. In 42 BC this territory ceased to be a province and was incorporated into Italy. Meanwhile, since Rome was involved in Spain from the Hannibalic War (218–202 BC) onwards, Transalpine Gaul too became ever more familiar. From the 120s BC

Roman armies regularly campaigned there, beginning the process of annexation. A *colonia*[1] was even founded in 118 BC, effectively the first such settlement outside the Italian peninsula, at Narbo (Narbonne): it was to give its name to the province, Gallia Narbonensis.

Only a few years later came another shock, or series of shocks, comparable to that caused by the first appearance of the Gauls. This time it was all the more disturbing. Rome in the early fourth century BC had been relatively insignificant. By the late second century BC she was a great power, without a rival all across the Mediterranean. But when a new wave of northern invaders appeared in 113 BC, they defeated a Roman consul. Further Roman defeats followed (*Ger.* 37). The new enemy, the Cimbri and the Teutones, were thought at first to be a further horde of Gauls or Celts, for they were likewise very large, blond and blue-eyed warriors; and they had indeed Gauls in their ranks. But they were in fact Germans, the first to come into direct contact with the Romans. They had apparently left their home in Jutland because of severe floods, and on their southward trek had dislodged or temporarily absorbed a good many Celtic peoples living in what was later called—as much of it is now—'Germany'. The Germanic-speaking peoples, or the ancestors of what would become the Germans, had mostly up till then lived far from the Rhine and Danube (the Bastarnae at the Danube mouth were an exception).

The series of disasters inflicted by the Cimbri and their allies created panic in Rome, and special measures were needed to meet the emergency. Victory was won by a tough army commander of non-senatorial origin, Gaius Marius, a 'new man' in Roman parlance. He was elected to a series of consulships (104–100 BC), against all precedent, and by 101 had crushed the invaders: many were slaughtered, the rest enslaved, some isolated remnants, so it was later asserted, establishing themselves here and there in northern Gaul.

Some thirty years on, a further wave of Germanic invaders

---

[1] For *colonia* and certain other specific terms used below and in the Explanatory Notes, e.g. *auxilia*, *cognomen*, cohort, Commonwealth, consul, legion, *pontifex*, prefect, see the Glossary on pp. 136–42.

appeared, 'Suebians', led by Ariovistus. In 58 BC an ambitious new proconsul of Gaul, Gaius Julius Caesar, was confronted with a flood of Gallic refugees expelled by the Suebi. They were the Helvetii—who had earlier probably been driven out of what is now southern Germany by the Cimbri, or followed them south of their own free will, settling in what is now Switzerland. Ariovistus' people were seeking to occupy large tracts of land on the Gallic, or Roman, side of the Rhine.

The fact that Caesar, as well as being exceptionally able and exceptionally ambitious, was a nephew of the man who defeated the Cimbri certainly played a part in what followed. At all events, Caesar was able to assume the role of a new Marius, destroying the northern menace (*Ger.* 37). He conquered the whole of Gaul up to the Rhine; and in 55 BC he achieved two Roman 'firsts', crossing the Rhine and crossing the Channel to Britain (*Agr.* 13). The latter feat was repeated the next year in greater strength—and the Rhine was crossed again in 53. The Britons, so Caesar claimed, had helped the Gauls in all their wars against 'us', i.e. the Romans. The island was in effect an extension of Gaul, which would serve as a place of refuge unless it were subjugated.

Caesar's moves against Britons and Germans were largely for propaganda purposes, to increase his prestige at Rome. But they put both peoples firmly on the agenda. Britain as well as 'Germany'—a term by now almost equivalent to 'the land beyond the Rhine and Danube'—were now, quite suddenly, much more familiar to Rome. The Civil War which followed Caesar's proconsulship (49–45 BC), and then Caesar's murder in 44, with renewed internal conflict not ending until 30, inevitably put the northern peoples 'onto the back burner' (*Agr.* 13). The activity in the Rhineland in 38 by Marcus Agrippa, Octavian's son-in-law and principal supporter until his death in 12 BC, was, however, a portent. When Octavian had become Augustus (27 BC) and was the undisputed master of the empire and of twenty-eight legions, he could review priorities. Britain was not to be one of them (*Agr.* 13), but Germany was. After Agrippa's death Augustus had to rely on his stepsons, Tiberius and Drusus, and other trusted men linked to his dynasty to fight his wars. Drusus campaigned for four years,

from 12 until 9 BC, reaching the Elbe (*Ger.* 34, 37, 41). When he died from the effects of an accident in 9, it seemed that most of Germany had been conquered. This impression was confirmed in the years that followed, notably in AD 5 when Tiberius returned to the Elbe and his fleet unearthed remnants of the once dreaded Cimbri: they did homage to Augustus.

But in AD 6 things began to go wrong. A planned conquest of Bohemia and Moravia, to conquer the kingdom of Maroboduus, leader of the Marcomanni and of a considerable confederation (*Ger.* 42), had to be aborted when a great uprising began in Pannonia and the Balkans, lasting until 9—and a few days after that was suppressed came the appalling news that three entire legions had been wiped out by the Germans in the 'Teutoburgian forest'. The commander-in-chief in Germany, Quinctilius Varus, who took his own life, was made the scapegoat (*Ger.* 37). 'Germany's liberator' was Arminius, a young noble from the Cherusci (*Ger.* 36), who had been made a Roman citizen and an equestrian officer, commanding a regiment of his own people. He had suddenly changed allegiance and trapped the gullible Varus.

Rome never recovered the 'lost province', in spite of attempts to restore her prestige across the Rhine and split Arminius' coalition of anti-Roman peoples. Tiberius himself and then his nephew Germanicus (*Ger.* 37), who had inherited the name from his father Drusus, failed to restore Roman rule. In 16 the attempt was given up. When Germanicus' son Caligula became emperor he soon appeared to be reviving the conquest policy, not merely of Germanicus but of Caesar. But his plans to invade both Germany and Britain came to nothing (*Agr.* 13; *Ger.* 37).

As far as Britain was concerned, the unexpected elevation to the throne of Claudius, the neglected younger brother of Germanicus, made the difference. The invasion of Britain, reviving and bringing to fulfilment the policy of Julius Caesar, provided the ideal solution to Claudius' desperate need for military prestige (*Agr.* 13). But Claudius was not prepared to let others gain credit by a forward policy across the Rhine (cf. below, p. xix), which effectively remained the boundary. The Roman occupation of Britain was for the time being confined to the south. With the great rebellion in 60,

led by Boudicca, it must have seemed for a moment as if the disaster to Varus was going to be repeated. But Rome just won the day: Boudicca was not to be a female British Arminius (*Agr.* 14–16).

New Civil Wars (AD 68–70) led to a change of policy. The large Roman garrison in the Rhineland played a key role in this. Some kind of resentment, it seems, perhaps just opportunism, inspired a new German revolt, with what must have seemed a new Arminius at its head. This was Julius Civilis, from the royal stock of the Batavians, a German people about whom rather more needs to be said. The Batavian territory, the Rhine island, had remained within the empire when the conquests of Drusus were given up (in AD 16), and their men were particularly highly rated as soldiers (*Ger.* 29).[2] The German bodyguards of the Julio-Claudian emperors were mainly recruited from the Batavians. That unit was dissolved after Nero's death, but just when Tacitus was writing, Trajan, still in Germany, had formed a new 'Imperial Horse Guard', *equites singulares Augusti*, once again largely Batavian—indeed, this élite regiment was nicknamed 'the Batavians'.

The Batavians had also supplied units for the *auxilia* of the Roman army. Eight cohorts had been in Britain from the conquest onwards, although temporarily withdrawn under Nero. During the Year of the Four Emperors (AD 69), these cohorts launched the great uprising in the Rhineland, generally called the Batavian Revolt, under Civilis, who was prefect of one of the cohorts. Tacitus' comment in his *Histories* underlines their special status: 'long experienced in the German wars, their fame had been increased throughout Britain, for the cohorts, which, by an old-established practice, were commanded by the noblest among this people, had been transferred there' (*Hist.* 4. 12), and they were 'exempt from tribute' (ibid. 4. 17). Tacitus devotes much space to this rebellion in the *Histories*. Before they were defeated in autumn 70 by Petillius Cerialis—who went on a few months later to be governor of Britain (*Agr.* 8, 17)—the rebels had disturbing success. Not a few peoples on the Roman side of the Rhine, including the Batavians' Germanic neighbours the Tungrians, and the Gallic

[2] For what follows, cf. esp. M. P. Speidel, *Riding for Caesar* (London, 1994).

Treveri and Lingones, went over to them. A notable exception was the Romanized German Ubians of Cologne, who showed spirited loyalty. Yet in spite of their revolt, the Batavians retained their old privileges when it was over (*Ger.* 29). The remnants were reorganized and supplemented and new Batavian cohorts played a crucial role in Agricola's victory over the Caledonians (*Agr.* 36).

Fresh evidence for both Batavians and Tungrians in Britain is now available: writing-tablets from Vindolanda, the Roman fort midway between the Solway and the mouth of the Tyne, on the line that had effectively become the frontier after Agricola's Scottish conquests were abandoned. Between *c.* AD 90 and the 120s, several of these units, in particular the Ninth Cohort of Batavians and the First Cohort of Tungrians, left a wealth of written information behind them at Vindolanda, which illuminates the Roman army and the themes of both *Agricola* and *Germany*.[3] The mixture of names alone, Latin, Celtic, and Germanic, among the men, and the large number evidently able to write are striking. So too are some items which indicate contempt for native Britons by these garrisons.[4]

When the Civil Wars of 68–70 were over, it is not surprising that the new emperor, Vespasian, who had served in both Germany and Britain a quarter of a century earlier, ordered expansion in these areas. The change in Britain is stressed by Tacitus (*Agr.* 16–17): after a decade of stagnation following the revolt of Boudicca, with Vespasian's accession Britain was given a series of active governors who pursued a forward policy, extending Roman control over most of Wales and northern England and leaving for Agricola to

---

[3] For what follows, A. K. Bowman and J. D. Thomas, *The Vindolanda Writing Tablets* (*Tabulae Vindolandenses*, ii) (London, 1994). Various Vindolanda documents are cited in the Explanatory Notes.

[4] The number of equestrian officers called 'Flavius' revealed by the Vindolanda tablets, early in the reign of Trajan, at the very time Tacitus was writing and shortly afterwards, is a further point of interest. Clearly these Flavii were new citizens or sons of new citizens, enfranchised by the Flavian dynasty between AD 70 and 96, and taking the dynasty's family name. Flavius Cerialis, prefect of the Ninth Batavians, at least (the best-represented in these writing-tablets), was surely a Batavian noble, if not indeed of royal stock, perhaps born in 70, and given the *cognomen* of Petillius Cerialis. A child in his household, no doubt his son, was being set to learn Virgil *c.*100, surely an indication of a thoroughgoing identification with Rome and with Latin culture.

conquer, when he took over, Snowdonia and Anglesey in the west, and in the north Scotland.

In Germany, the advance under Vespasian is not documented by a comparable account. Tacitus mentions Vespasian (*Ger.* 8) only in connection with unfinished business east of the lower Rhine: the capture of the Bructeran prophetess Veleda, a figure-head of the Germans during the Batavian Revolt. But under Vespasian began the process of extending Roman control again beyond the upper Rhine and Danube, more than half a century after Germanicus' recall. The advance was to be taken further by Domitian in AD 83. But Tacitus loses no opportunity of denigrating this campaign. In *Agricola* 39, the triumph Domitian had celebrated for his victory over the Chatti is declared to have been a sham, while in *Germany* there is a series of disparaging remarks. The peoples who lived in the lands beyond the upper Rhine and Danube were not Germans at all (*Ger.* 29)—hence, by implication, Domitian could not have conquered Germans. Nothing at all is said about Domitian in the section on the Chatti (30–1), although they were Domitian's principal opponents. Finally, Tacitus expresses the view that 'in recent times the Germans have been the objects of triumphs rather than victories' (*Ger.* 37): thus, this time without naming him, the charge levied against Domitian in the *Agricola* is repeated.

In the mean time, Domitian had largely abandoned the conquests made by Agricola in Britain. Clearly taking the view that the occupation of Scotland was of dubious value, Domitian withdrew a legion and some auxiliary troops, *c.* AD 86, to reinforce the Danube front (where, as Tacitus notes, *Agr.* 41, there were certainly major problems). By the time of his death in 96 he had effectively brought back the frontier in Britain to where it had been when Agricola became governor nearly twenty years earlier. Tacitus was clearly disgusted: 'Britain completely conquered—and then let go', as he summarizes the events there at the start of his *Histories* (1. 2).

Just before Tacitus began to write, Germany had become very topical again. 'Over sixty thousand [Germans from the people of the Bructeri] were killed, not by Roman swords or spears, but what was far more splendid, to gladden Roman eyes' (*Ger.* 33). They had in fact been attacked by other German peoples, while the Romans

were simply 'spectators of the battle'. This encounter was apparently very recent, and must be associated with what the Younger Pliny relates (*Letters* 2. 7): his elderly friend Vestricius Spurinna 'was awarded a triumphal statue on the proposal of the emperor', evidently Nerva in AD 97, because he had 'installed the king of the Bructeri in his kingdom by force of arms, and by the mere threat of war had completely subdued an extremely fierce people'.[5]

Tacitus' comment on the massacre is grim: 'Long may the barbarians continue, I pray, if not to love us, at least to hate one another'—he adds the words, 'as fate bears remorselessly on the empire'. The three Latin words, 'urgentibus imperii fatis', are among the most discussed in Tacitus' works. Most take them as a sign of Tacitus' anxiety and foreboding about Rome's future, as here, hence 'remorselessly', which slightly exaggerates the sense— 'bears down on' would suffice. Tacitus' language echoes that in Livy (5. 36. 6, cf 5. 22. 8 and 22. 43. 9), 'all three passages [dealing with] a threatening calamity'.[6] Others take the words in an 'optimistic, imperialist' sense, meaning 'since the destiny of the empire is driving us onwards'—to universal conquest.[7] A radical new interpretation is offered by D. Timpe: the three words are neutral and mean no more than 'since destiny will have it so for the empire'. What Tacitus is driving at can only be understood from the rest of the sentence, 'fortune can offer no greater boon than discord among our enemies'. The stress must be on 'discord', 'discordiam'—as in *Annals* 2. 36. 2, Tiberius' view that it was better to let the Germans tear each other apart in internal 'discordiis' than to wage war against them, and 2. 44. 2, where Tiberius sends his son to stir up such 'discordias' among the Germans. Tacitus would

---

[5] The two episodes are surely connected. The massacre of '60,000' Bructeri (the actual number probably exaggerated) could have preceded Spurinna's installation of the new king, even though Pliny called the Bructeri 'an extremely fierce people'. 'If only a broken remnant . . . received a chieftain from Spurinna's hands, Pliny saw no reason for impairing the fame of an old friend—and cheap laurels had been the aim of a weak or enfeebled government.' J. G. C. Anderson (ed.), *Cornelii Taciti De Origine et situ Germanorum* (Oxford, 1938), 161, is supported by R. Syme, *Roman Papers*, vii (Oxford, 1991), 545 (here quoted), revoking his previous scepticism (id., *Tacitus*, 2 vols. (Oxford, 1958), ii. 634 f.) about connecting the two episodes.

[6] Thus Anderson, *De origine*, 163; Syme, *Tacitus*, i. 46 f.

[7] A. A. Lund (ed.), *P. Cornelius Tacitus: Germania* (Heidelberg, 1988), 202.

rather have seen Roman generals and armies conquering Rome's enemies, but under the principate this had become increasingly difficult, a major theme of *Agricola*: Timpe compares *Agricola* 17, 'a great man—in so far as it was then possible to be great', and quotes Corbulo's sigh after Claudius stopped him campaigning across the Rhine, *Annals* 11. 20: 'Roman generals in the old days [i.e. in the Republic] were fortunate [to have had the chance of winning glory]'. In other words (to simplify a complex discussion), Tacitus' thought is merely that 'given the present-day circumstances, with campaigns of conquest scarcely being permitted any more, the best we can hope for is that our enemies destroy one another'.[8]

The Life of the Historian Tacitus

The Batavian Revolt of AD 69–70 and the new forward policy in the north must have made a deep impression on contemporaries. This applies not least to the young Tacitus, probably a boy of about eleven or twelve in 69, whose father had served as a high official in the Rhineland. Much of what is known about Publius Cornelius Tacitus derives from his own writings. In *Agricola* 9 we learn that he was married, 'being then a young man', to the daughter of Agricola, just after the latter's term as consul, probably in 76, ended. Towards the end of *Agricola* (ch. 45), he mentions that he and his wife had been away from Rome for four years at the time of Agricola's death in August 93. In his third work, the *Dialogue on Orators*, the dramatic date of which is AD 75 (*Dial*. 17), Tacitus purports to recall a discussion he attended 'when still a very young man' (*Dial*. 1). Exactly the same expression ('iuvenis admodum') is applied to the future emperor Domitian when the latter was aged just over 18 (*Agr*. 7). At the beginning of the *Histories* (1. 1), his first extended piece of writing, he insists on his impartiality in dealing with the Flavian dynasty, even though he owed his rank—as a senator—to Vespasian and was promoted by Titus and much further by Domitian. Finally, in the *Annals*, his last work, he mentions in

---

[8] D. Timpe, *Romano-Germanica: Gesammelte Studien zur Germania des Tacitus* (Stuttgart and Leipzig, 1995), 203 ff.

passing (11. 11) that in 88 he had been serving as praetor and also as a member of the 'Fifteen Men to deal with sacred matters' (*quindecimviri sacris faciundis*), one of the most prestigious colleges of 'priests' in Rome.

Further information is supplied in the *Letters* of Tacitus' friend and contemporary the Younger Pliny, in particular that Tacitus was consul in 97 and already regarded then as an outstanding orator (*Letters* 2. 1. 6). Finally, an inscription from Mylasa in the province of Asia registers Tacitus as proconsul of that province (*L'Année épigraphique* 1890. 110). It is not dated, but comparison with careers of other proconsuls indicates that Tacitus probably held the office—for the normal twelve months' term—from summer 112 to summer 113.

The regulations, as revised by the first emperor, Augustus, on the age at which the old 'Republican' magistracies at Rome could be held, allow inferences to be made about Tacitus' date of birth.[9] The praetorship could normally be held at 29, the consulship at 41. Certain conditions—a year's exemption for each child—or imperial favour could reduce these age limits. Hence, if praetor in AD 88, Tacitus should have been born *c.*58. If so, he would have been consul at 39, slightly below the regular minimum. Further, he will have married when only 18, slightly younger than usual for men. This fits well his statement in the *Dialogue*, referred to earlier, that at the time of the discussion reproduced in that work, i.e. AD 75, he was 'still a very young man'. His 'four years' absence' from Rome up to the time of Agricola's death, 90 to 93, were presumably spent on imperial service in the provinces, probably commanding a legion.

As the *cognomen* 'Tacitus' was uncommon, it is likely that another Cornelius Tacitus, mentioned by the Elder Pliny (who died in AD 79) in his *Natural History* (7. 76), was the historian's father. This other Tacitus was equestrian procurator of Belgica and the two Germanies, and thus paymaster-general of the Rhine legions. The historian would then, as son of an *eques Romanus* or 'knight', have been a 'new man', the first member of his family to

---

[9] For discussion of senatorial careers, see A. R. Birley, *The Fasti of Roman Britain* (Oxford, 1981), 4 ff.

enter the senate, a body only six hundred strong, the tiny imperial élite. Where the family's home was can only be conjectured. A story Tacitus himself told the Younger Pliny, reported in one of the latter's *Letters* (9. 23), may give a clue: 'I have never felt such pleasure as recently from a conversation with Cornelius Tacitus. He told me how at the latest Circus races he had sat next to a Roman knight. After discussing various learned topics this man asked him: "Are you an Italian or a provincial?" Tacitus replied: "You know me from your reading." To which the man said: "Are you Tacitus or Pliny?"' Pliny himself came from Como in the far north-west of Italy, which had once belonged to the province of Gallia Cisalpina. It may be inferred that he and Tacitus shared a slight 'Celtic' accent, and that Tacitus came from a Celtic part of the empire, either northern Italy or, perhaps more likely, southern Gaul, the old *provincia*—Provence—which, as the Elder Pliny remarked (*Natural History* 3. 31), was more like Italy than a province. Tacitus' ancestors had very likely been non-Roman, receiving the citizenship in the late Republican period through the intervention of a Roman office-holder called Cornelius.

A few further details can be added, if we accept the recent identification by Géza Alföldy of a fragmentary text on marble from Rome as part of Tacitus' funerary inscription.[10] The stone comes from the south side of the Via Nomentana, close to the barracks of the Praetorian Guard on the north-eastern side of the city. When complete, the inscription had evidently been some four metres long and up to ninety centimetres high (13 ft. by 3 ft.), and belonged to an elaborate monument.

After '[Ta]cito', in the dative, comes apparently the start of another name, so the historian may have had more than the 'standard' three Roman names.[11] After the names follows a summary

---

[10] G. Alföldy, 'Bricht der Schweigsame sein Schweigen? Eine Grabinschrift in Rom', *Mitteilungen des deutschen archaeologischen Instituts. Roemische Abteilung*, 102 (1995), 251–68.

[11] It had become common in high society to add on extra names to the basic three—an example is Agricola's predecessor as governor of Britain, whose full style was Q. Petillius Cerialis Caesius Rufus, called 'Petillius Cerialis' for short. Tacitus' (first) additional name on this inscription begins 'Ca['. Perhaps he was called P. Cornelius Tacitus Ca[ecina Paetus], for the Caecina family was also commemorated close to this monument and a Caecina in the third century AD had the name Tacitus.

listing of the offices held: first the consulship and 'priesthood', then the remaining posts in 'ascending order', beginning with the lowest listed. The first can be restored as 'X]viro stlitib[us iudicandis': the decemvirate was one of the minor magistracies in the 'vigintivirate'. What comes next is lost, but may be assumed to have been a military tribunate in a legion, not compulsory, but none the less very frequently held before entry to the senate. The remainder of the surviving text may be restored as '[quaesto]ri Aug. tribun[o plebis]'. Tacitus was thus 'quaestor of Augustus', one of the two quaestors (out of the total of twenty each year) attached to the emperor (their duties included reading out the emperor's speeches before the senate), and then tribune of the plebs.

One may infer that Tacitus was _decemvir_ in AD 76, aged 18 or so, and that this, or perhaps the award of senatorial status, the 'broad stripe', _latus clavus_, is the benefit conferred by Vespasian to which he refers in the _Histories_. Commissions as military tribune were in practice at the disposition of the provincial governor. There are numerous examples of tribunes serving under their father or father-in-law.[12] Why not suppose that Tacitus served in Britain, in one of the four legions in Agricola's army? He could well have stayed there for two to three years, from 77 to 79. It might then not be coincidence that the account of Agricola's first three years in _Agricola_ 18–22 is considerably fuller than that of the two immediately following seasons (chs. 23–4). On this reconstruction, Tacitus would have returned to Rome in autumn 79, to be elected quaestor in 80 and hold office in 81, at the age of 22—younger than the normal minimum age, either because he already had children or because he was favoured by the emperor Titus. The 'increase' in his status conferred by Titus, mentioned in the _Histories_, would mean that he was quaestor of that emperor in 81. One may assume, too, that he was retained in the position by Domitian when he succeeded in September that year.

By 88 (if not before) Tacitus had Domitian's favour. Not only was he praetor, probably at the 'normal' age, his membership of the _quindecimviri_, prestigious enough at any stage in a man's career, had

---

[12] Birley, _Fasti_, 9 ff.

come early. Often senators did not get into this élite 'priestly' college or one of the other three of equal status until after being consul. Further, in 88 the *quindecimviri* had a particularly important role: supervising the Secular Games. As praetor Tacitus probably had to preside over one of the permanent courts in the capital and to put on games at his own expense (cf. *Agr.* 6). From the beginning of 89, as an ex-praetor, he was qualified for a wide range of posts. He evidently left Rome with his wife in 90 not to return for over three years, until after the death of Agricola on 23 August 93 (*Agr.* 45). He must have been away in public service, probably a legionary command, for some three years. A legion on the Rhine or Danube is statistically likelier than one elsewhere. At all events, by autumn 93 Tacitus was, to judge from his language in *Agricola* 45 ('we ourselves led Helvidius to prison'), back at Rome, and had to attend the treason trials in the senate. He may be conjectured to have obtained another appointment from Domitian soon afterwards, probably the governorship of an imperial 'praetorian' province for two or three years, *c.*94 to 96 or 97, with the prospect of the consulship when it ended (as with Agricola in Aquitania, *Agr.* 9).

Domitian's murder on 18 September 96 and his replacement by Nerva did not cause any interruption in Tacitus' career. He may, indeed, have been designated to the consulship by Domitian. If so, Nerva confirmed it. Nerva himself opened the year 97 as consul with, as colleague, a relic of a previous generation, the 83-year-old Lucius Verginius Rufus, both holding office for the third time. Rufus was rehearsing his speech of thanks for the appointment when he fell and broke his hip. It did not mend properly and the old man died. He was given a state funeral, at which 'the speech was given by the consul Cornelius Tacitus, a most eloquent orator, whose tribute put the crowning touch to Verginius' good fortune', as Pliny related (*Letters* 2. 1). In other words, Tacitus was holding office as one of the suffect consuls in 97, not necessarily in the pair that had replaced Nerva and Verginius. There were several pairs of suffects in 97, and Verginius may not have died until the autumn.

At all events, the duty of composing and delivering this speech may be supposed to have had two effects on Tacitus. First, it will

have reminded him that he had been unable to give such a funeral speech for Agricola four years earlier. Secondly, in relating the career of Verginius Rufus he must have had to recall the fall of Nero and the struggle for power that followed—Verginius had been offered the throne more than once by the army in 68–9, but had declined each time, and yet survived. His career was thus unique. If that had not been enough to spark Tacitus' interest in the events of those years, what happened in October 97 will have been a further stimulus. The Praetorian Guard mutinied and forced Nerva to hand over Domitian's murderers to be lynched. Nerva's position uncannily resembled that of Galba in January 69. Like Galba old and childless, Nerva too reacted to a mutiny by adopting a son and heir. But his choice was happier than Galba's, or at least more likely to succeed: instead of a young aristocrat with no military experience, Nerva chose Trajan, then governor of Upper Germany, who was in a position to give the new regime armed support.

Tacitus' First Literary Steps

This was the background against which Tacitus composed his biography of Agricola, a tribute to the dead man, whom he loved, and thus a substitute for the funeral address or encomium Agricola should have had in AD 93. Tacitus indeed states that he would have needed permission (from Domitian, evidently) to compose such a biography then (*Agr.* 1). Throughout the fifteen years of Domitian's reign Tacitus and others had been obliged 'to keep silence' and not to write or publish anything.

'Publication' in ancient Rome meant, in the first instance, a reading or recitation before an invited audience. Such occasions are frequently mentioned by the Younger Pliny in his *Letters* (e.g. 1. 13, 3. 18, 4. 27, 5. 12, 8. 12). In one case (9. 27) he mentions the impact when an historian (not named) 'had begun a reading of a work of exceptional candour, and had left part to be read another day'. He was then requested by some of those whose deeds were treated in the history to cancel the next reading. The author complied, but, Pliny adds, 'the book, like their deeds, remains and will remain, and will always be read.' Authors often circulated a draft among friends

and asked for comments (cf. Pliny, *Letters* 3. 15, 4. 14). Booksellers (*bibliopolae*) would then act as publishers (1. 2)—even outside Rome. In another letter (9. 11) Pliny is glad to hear that his work is on sale at Lugdunum (Lyons).

Now Tacitus looks forward 'to putting together a record of our former servitude and a testimony to our pleasant blessings' (*Agr.* 3). In other words, shortly after Domitian's assassination he was already planning the work which would become his *Histories*—his initial conception, the reign of Domitian and its immediate aftermath, i.e. the years 81–97/8, was of course to be modified. 'For the time being,' he adds, at the end of his Preface, 'this book, intended to honour Agricola, my father-in-law, will be commended, or at least excused, as a tribute of dutiful affection.'

Agricola incorporates a personal political credo. Tacitus was defending the choice which men like his father-in-law, or the new emperor-designate Trajan and, not least, he himself, had made: to serve Rome even under the despotic Domitian, rather than, like the Stoic opposition, to seek a martyr's end 'with no benefit to the Commonwealth' (*Agr.* 42). By insisting that Agricola had forecast and prayed for Trajan's coming to power (*Agr.* 44), Tacitus makes the link between the two men even stronger.

Agricola's principal claim to fame was that he had completed the conquest of Britain, four decades after it had begun. Yet, as Tacitus bitterly remarks at the beginning of the *Histories* (1. 2), the newly conquered territory had been 'let go'—by Domitian, soon after Agricola's recall. Knowing the martial qualities of Trajan, Tacitus may well have hoped that he would put this right, i.e. reconquer Scotland. There was a further point: the governor of Britain just appointed by Nerva was one of the Stoics, Avidius Quietus, hardly the right man, Tacitus may have thought, to resume the active policy of Agricola and restore his conquests.[13] This was a further incentive to remind the new emperor and the public at Rome about what had been won and then abandoned. In any case, Agricola was so intimately bound up with Britain—he spent up to a quarter of his life on the island and had conquered the far north—that a

---

[13] Birley, *Fasti*, 85 ff.

discussion of Britain's physical and human geography and of its history under Roman rule was an essential part of the biography.

In a Preface (chs. 1–3), Tacitus justifies the composition of a laudatory biography, noting that this was once regarded as a natural and legitimate type of writing, but that the age he lives in prefers invectives. In fact, two recent biographies had been banned and burned and their authors sentenced to death. But the despotism—of Domitian, not named at this stage of the work—is now over. There is a new dawn of freedom under Nerva and his designated successor Trajan.

The biography proper begins with Agricola's birth, parentage, and upbringing, and his career up to his appointment as governor of Britain (AD 40–77), (chs. 4–9). As Agricola had also held two junior appointments there, as tribune and legionary legate, some detail is already provided on the island in this first section (chs. 5 and 7–8).

More about Britain follows in the next two parts. The first is a brief account of land and peoples (chs. 10–12): this allows Tacitus to offer general observations on the geography of the island, stressing that the remotest parts were only discovered 'then', i.e. by the governor Agricola. Next comes a history of Rome's dealings with Britain from Julius Caesar to Agricola (chs. 13–17): Caesar's foray, the policy of Augustus, Tiberius, and Caligula, and the conquest under Claudius, emphasizing the role of Vespasian, one of the legionary commanders in the invasion army. The achievements of each of the ten governors before Agricola are summarized. The first two, Plautius and Scapula, the fifth, Paulinus, and Agricola's two immediate precedessors, Cerialis and Frontinus, are praised, the others are portrayed more or less negatively. The lion's share is devoted to the rising of Boudicca (chs. 15–16), already briefly treated in connection with Agricola's service as tribune (ch. 5).

The main part is devoted to the governorship (chs. 18–40). The first six years are treated relatively concisely (chs. 18–28), concentrating on the military activities, but with important passages on Agricola's stamping out of abuses in the administration (ch. 19) and his measures to encourage 'Romanization' (ch. 21). The climax

comes with the seventh season, the great victory against the peoples of Caledonia at the battle of the Graupian Mountain (chs. 29–38). Within this long section come the speeches of the opposing leaders, the Caledonian Calgacus (chs. 30–2) and Agricola (chs. 33–4).

The account of the victory is followed by a section on Agricola's recall and last years (chs. 40–3). An Epilogue (chs. 44–6), sums up Agricola's life and character, with reflections on what he managed to escape by his timely death, a consolation for those he left behind, and a forecast of immortal fame.

Compared with *Germany*, there is less detail about Britain and the Britons in *Agricola*. In the second work he would name over fifty different German states, giving their geographical location and in many cases a good deal on their individual characteristics. *Agricola* names just the Silures, Ordovices, and Brigantes out of the two dozen or so British states that were to remain Roman for centuries, together with the otherwise unknown Boresti of northern Scotland. Tacitus does not give many British place-names either: only Mona (Anglesey), Orcades (Orkneys), Thule (Shetland), Clota (Clyde), Bodotria (Forth), Taus (Tay), Caledonia (for Scotland north of the Forth–Clyde line), the site of the final battle, at Mons Graupius, the 'Graupian Mountain', and, finally, a Roman naval station, Portus Trucculensis (of which the name may be garbled in transmission). Three individual Britons are mentioned, the client king Cogidumnus (perhaps really called Togidubnus) and the resistance leaders Boudicca and Calgacus. Still, even in *Germany*, entirely devoted to the land and its inhabitants, only four Germans are named, the prophetesses Veleda and Albruna and the kings Maroboduus and Tudrus.

The characteristics of the Britons are given much more concisely than those of the Germans. This is perhaps partly because the Britons—at least those of the south—closely resembled the Gauls (*Agr.* 11), by then well known to the Romans, in appearance, religion, and language, and less needed saying. Religion, indeed, unlike in *Germany*, is not treated at all. Exceptional cases, the red-haired Caledonians, more like Germans, and the swarthier Silures, perhaps deriving from Spain, are singled out. The Britons'

qualities, stressed repeatedly, serve, of course, to highlight Agricola's achievement: they are still fierce—as the Gauls used to be before Rome tamed them—and fight to retain or regain their freedom, although prone to chronic disunity. The disparaging comments on British weather and the correspondingly limited nature of the island's agricultural products are closely matched by those in *Germany*.

Agricola does provide the fullest surviving account of the early Britons and, as much of the work is cast in the form of an historical narrative—hence the speeches before the final battle in Caledonia, a traditional feature of ancient historiography—it also supplies a connected history of Britain from 55 BC to AD 83. Still, it remains first and foremost a biography, a tribute to a beloved older kinsman whose achievement had not been adequately celebrated. At the same time, *Agricola* is a political statement. Certain themes recur, freedom and glory in particular—and moderation. Not merely are Agricola's qualities as a general praised. Attention is drawn again and again to his self-restraint. He deserved more glory than he got, for the imperial system restricted the freedom once enjoyed by the élite. But he did his duty, refusing to opt out: 'there can be great men even under bad emperors' (*Agr.* 42).

The pages that Tacitus wrote about Britain and its peoples perhaps gave him a taste for this kind of topic. At all events, *Agricola* 10–12 foreshadows what he began immediately afterwards, *Germany*. This was in a sense even more topical. When Tacitus wrote, Trajan had just succeeded to the throne and was still in the Rhineland, where he remained for some months. Delegations were going to and fro not only from Rome but from all the provinces to the new emperor's court at Cologne.

In any case, Tacitus had—or certainly developed—a keen interest in Germany. A substantial part of what survives from the *Histories* deals with events in the Rhineland. The very starting-point, 1 January AD 69, was probably selected because the Rhine legions on that day declined to swear allegiance to Galba, thus setting in train the events which led to 69 becoming the Year of the Four Emperors. Further, the Batavian Revolt which began in 69 demonstrated the fragility of Roman rule there and the power

that the Germans had if they could only unite against Rome. The opening of the *Annals*, too, focuses on events in the Rhineland—the mutinies that followed Tiberius' accession in AD 14 and Germanicus' campaigns.

In *Agricola* (ch. 39) Tacitus had just commented with bitter mockery on the falsity of Domitian's triumph after his war against the Chatti in 83, contrasted with Agricola's real victory. Tacitus' friend the Younger Pliny repeats the charge two years later in his *Panegyric* on Trajan, who will hold a genuine triumph, not one with the 'images of a sham victory' (*Pan.* ch. 16). Domitian had taken the name 'Germanicus', conqueror of the Germans, and this 'conquest' had been repeatedly portrayed on the imperial coinage. He had later held a further triumph 'over the Germans' (AD 89). In his second work Tacitus reflects (*Ger.* 37) that Rome had been 'conquering' the Germans for two hundred and ten years. The free Germans are, in his view, a more dangerous foe than Rome's supposed only real rival, the Parthians in the east, under their despotic monarchy. Yet in recent times (i.e. under Domitian) there had been more triumphs over the Germans than real victories. Tacitus, like others at Rome, may have expected—indeed hoped—that Trajan would soon put this right with a real campaign of conquest. In such an atmosphere, *Germany* would have been especially appropriate.

It would be rash to suppose that Tacitus' information about Germany and the Germans was all second-hand. He may even have been born on the Moselle, close to the land and the peoples he was to describe in this work. He could easily have inherited from his father the procurator the role of patron for some of the communities in the Rhineland. If, as suggested above, Tacitus was military tribune in Britain in the late 70s he could have travelled through the Rhineland on his way there and back. He might well have commanded a legion in Germany in the early 90s. All the same, it is clear enough that he used written sources, in particular Caesar's *Gallic War* and the monograph by the Elder Pliny (now lost) on Rome's wars in Germany.

Germany is almost exactly the same length as *Agricola*, but very different in character, even if some turns of phrase and thought

patterns recur. It falls into two parts: in the first there is a discussion of the Germans, the origin of the people, their country, and their characteristics (chs. 1–27), in the second (27–46) a presentation of information about the individual peoples of Germany, in geographical order, from west to east. In chapters 1–4, following the traditions of ancient ethnography, at which Tacitus had just had some practice on a miniature scale with Britain (*Agr.* 10 ff.), he first addresses the question of the origins of the people of Germany, concluding that they were not immigrants—unlike the Britons— but had always been there; and further, that they had not intermarried with other peoples, but were 'pure' and uncontaminated. (For the influence of this and other passages on modern thinking, see below, p. xxxvii.) Tacitus' discussion of the name 'Germani' (ch. 2) has provoked endless scholarly debate.

From chapter 5 onwards the theme that is dominant is that the Germans are a primitive people, 'noble savages', with, to be sure, faults such as laziness and drunkenness, but endowed with desirable qualities of simplicity and uprightness that the Romans had lost. On the other hand, in many places what is portrayed is a strange world where everything, for better or for worse, is just the opposite of what happened at Rome. German land is poor and they have no silver and gold—but take no interest in them. Freedom is something that they prize and most of them, even those peoples ruled by kings, are still free-spirited (e.g. chs. 7, 11). They show great respect for women and even treat them as holy, but not as goddesses (8)—an implicit contrast with Rome, where even women had been deified. Their religion is simple—although human sacrifice does occur (chs. 9, 39). They are thoroughly warlike, of course, as is constantly repeated. The chastity of their women is particularly held up for praise, as is their refusal to practise abortion, or to use wet-nurses (chs. 18 ff.). The contrast with decadent Roman morality is here particularly pronounced. Germans are open-hearted and hospitable, inclined to excessive drinking, but with only one simple, old-fashioned form of entertainment, the sword-dance (chs. 21 ff.). Their form of slavery is very restricted and basic, and (in unspoken contrast to Rome) freedmen have little influence; they know nothing of moneylending; even their funerals

are very plain, with none of the extravagance that had developed at Rome (chs. 25 ff.).

The second part begins with exceptions to Tacitus' general rule that the Germans are the ones who had migrated southwards and westwards, and he also particularly stresses the loyalty of the Ubians, who prefer to be called 'Agrippinensians', having become citizens of the Roman *colonia* (i.e. Cologne). He moves on at once to the Batavians, 'the most notable for their bravery' (ch. 29). Tacitus did not need to remind his readers or listeners that the Ubians and Batavians had been the major German participants, on opposing sides, in the war of AD 69–70, the Batavian Revolt. He then takes the chance to debunk Domitian's claims to conquest: the 'Ten-Lands', which are, in effect, the territory Domitian had annexed, are not even inhabited by Germans but by an immigrant riff-raff from Gaul.

From chapter 30 onwards Tacitus surveys about a dozen peoples in the north-west and west, at varying length, presumably partly a reflection of the differing sources available as well as of the special interest e.g. of the Chatti (chs. 30–1), against whom Domitian had fought and who were thus still topical. A comment he makes on the Bructeri having recently been virtually wiped out by other German peoples, while the Romans watched (ch. 33, cf. discussion above, p. xviii), is another source of dispute: at all events, whatever exactly he meant by 'fate' and the 'empire', he prays that 'the barbarians may continue, if not to love us, at least to hate one another'. In chapter 37 he comes to the Cimbri, which gives the chance for a brief historical retrospect of the two hundred and ten years during which Rome has been fighting the Germans—ending with another swipe at Domitian's 'sham triumphs'. Most of the rest of the work is devoted to Germans beyond the Elbe as far as Scandinavia and the east coast of the Baltic, and down through Poland to Bohemia and Moravia. He classes these Germans collectively as 'Suebians', the same name as that of Ariovistus' Germans whom Caesar had driven out of Gaul. The exact relationship of all these peoples to one another or their group identity is not entirely clear, and some of those included are in any case clearly non-Germanic, e.g. the Aestii (ch. 45).

Finally, in chapter 46, come the easternmost Germans, the Bastarnae, who have degenerated by intermarriage with non-Germans, and two doubtful cases: Venethi, 'probably German', and Fenni, obviously not, for they are the extreme in primitive savagery—only exceeded by the tailpiece, the fabulous Hellusii and Oxiones, supposedly half man, half beast.

Tacitus' sources certainly included Caesar, whom he quotes in chapter 28, and clearly also the lost monograph by the Elder Pliny on Rome's wars in Germany. He may have heard tales from traders and travellers, he may have personally talked to Germans, auxiliary soldiers—or their officers. German aristocrats from the Rhineland, men like Arminius and Julius Civilis, but of a new generation, were still commanding auxiliary regiments drawn from peoples like the Batavians and Tungrians, mentioned in both *Agricola* and *Germany*, as was probably also the case for units recruited from other, smaller Germanic peoples on the left bank of the Rhine, such as the Baetasii, Frisiavones, or Sunuci. People like this could have proved valuable informants on Germany and the Germans for Tacitus, if only for western Germany. Tacitus could well have met men like the prefect of the Ninth Cohort of Batavians, Flavius Cerialis, and other equestrian officers whose letters have been found at Vindolanda.[14]

Tacitus' Later Career and Other Writings

If Tacitus hoped that Trajan would launch a new expansion across the Rhine, he was mistaken. But he had perhaps rightly assessed the new ruler's intentions in a more general way. Three years after his accession, in AD 101, Trajan declared war against the powerful Dacian kingdom of Decebalus north of the lower Danube. At its conclusion in 102 vast tracts of land beyond the river were annexed and added to the Moesian provinces. War was resumed in 105 and ended the next year with the total incorporation of Dacia as a Roman province.

[14] At all events, the letters and documents they have left behind throw interesting new light on the writings of their great contemporary, and are referred to in several places in the Explanatory Notes.

How Tacitus was occupied after writing *Germany* is revealed, in part, by Pliny's *Letters* (2. 11–12). The two men jointly prosecuted the corrupt proconsul of Africa, Marius Priscus, with the emperor himself presiding over one session. During the trial, completed in 100, Tacitus spoke 'with all the majesty which characterizes his style'. Appropriately enough his next work was the *Dialogue on Orators*, cast in the form of a discussion which he purports to have attended in the reign of Vespasian (*Dial.* 1, 17). He dedicated the work to his friend Fabius Justus, who was consul early in 102. 'The practice of dedicating a composition to a friend or patron when he entered upon public office was not uncommon', as Syme observes and the *Dialogue* may therefore belong to this year.[15] But in a letter written in about 107 (8. 7) Pliny refers to Tacitus having submitted a work to him for comment, 'as one orator to another'. Perhaps he was revising the *Dialogue* then. Tacitus may in the mean time have been away from Rome again. In 104 or 105 Pliny wrote to Tacitus expressing pleasure that he had returned to Rome safely (*Letters* 4. 13). It is not implausible that he had been away governing a consular province such as Upper or Lower Germany for two or three years, *c*.101–4.

On his return Tacitus devoted himself to his *Histories*. Pliny himself, as a letter of 105 (5. 8) shows, toyed with the idea of writing history, following his uncle's example, but decided against. He probably knew that his friend was already at work. By the next year Tacitus was clearly well ahead with his preparations, had indeed, perhaps, already finished his account of AD 69 and the reign of Vespasian. At Tacitus' request, Pliny supplied him with an account of the eruption of Vesuvius, which took place in 79, soon after Vespasian's death (*Letters* 6. 16 and 20). A year later, Pliny was prophesying that 'your histories will be immortal' (7. 33); he offered further material on the events which led to the treason trials of 93 (cf. *Agr.* 45 for Tacitus' first brief account)—and expressed the hope that Tacitus would, without going beyond the facts (for 'history should always confine itself to the truth'), give proper weight to his (Pliny's) conduct at that time.

---

[15] Syme, *Tacitus*, i. 112.

At the opening of the *Histories*, Tacitus announces (1. 1) that, if he lives long enough, he intends to go on in his next work, reserved for his old age, to make good what he had already promised (*Agr.* 3), to write about 'our present blessings', i.e. to cover the principate of Nerva and the reign of Trajan, 'a period of rare felicity, in which one may think what one wishes and say what one thinks'. Instead, he went further back, to the period from the death of Augustus up to the reign of Nero, to produce the work known today as the *Annals*. When he began it, and how long he lived, remain uncertain. The odds are that he lived on into the reign of Hadrian.

The question must be asked: how conscientious and accurate was Tacitus as an historian—and how impartial was his judgement? A startling recent discovery has gone a long way towards vindicating his reputation for diligent research and sober assessment of evidence. In books 2 and 3 of his *Annals* Tacitus narrates in detail the downfall of Gnaeus Calpurnius Piso after his conflict with Germanicus in the east, Germanicus' death, Piso's suicide, and the debate in the senate at Rome. The complete text (175 lines) of the senatorial decree of 10 December AD 20 which concluded the affair was found on bronze tablets in southern Spain in the late 1980s, and has now been published with full commentary.[16] It demonstrates, among much else, that Tacitus really had done research in the 'Acts of the Senate', the Roman 'Hansard' (which had often been doubted), and that he was able to read between the lines of the official version of events.

Of course, Tacitus' famous claim at the beginning of his *Annals* (1. 1) that he wrote 'without either hostile prejudice or partisan favour' ('sine ira et studio') has never been taken seriously. His presentation of Tiberius, Claudius, and Nero, most of which survives, paints these emperors in the darkest of shades. Certain others, such as Sejanus and Tigellinus, also come off very badly, whereas, by contrast, a limited number of figures such as Germanicus and Corbulo are treated favourably—more so than they deserved, it may be. In his *Histories*, too, the first three emperors of AD 69, Galba, Otho, and Vitellius, as well as many of their

---

[16] W. Eck, A. Caballos, and F. Fernández, *Das senatus consultum de Cn. Pisone patre* (Munich, 1996).

supporters and others, especially time-serving senators, receive a very negative portrayal. So too does the youthful Domitian. His elder brother Titus, on the other hand, is depicted as the perfect prince. Yet Suetonius (*Titus* 7) makes a convincing case for Titus having been hated and feared—until he became emperor. Tacitus' aim here, as in *Agricola* and *Germany*, was not least to demolish the grossly flattering accounts of Domitian's achievements that circulated in the emperor's lifetime.

In both *Agricola* and *Germany* hostility to Domitian is ever present, and the work of some of Agricola's predecessors is minimized or perhaps even distorted to enhance the great man's role. Some of the details in *Germany* were probably compiled hastily and both works seem to contain minor errors of fact (cf. the notes on *the Brigantes, with a woman as their leader*, in *Agr.* 31, and *Raetia's splendid colonia* in *Ger.* 41). But they remain a precious, largely reliable, and extremely readable source of information on Britain, Germany, and a great deal else.

Tacitus' Style and Influence

Tacitus' writings (with the exception of the *Dialogue*) are characterized by a markedly individual style, very different from the smooth cadences of Livy. In particular, Tacitus affects the same brevity and concision of expression at which Sallust had aimed. But his thought is even more compressed than Sallust's, and his sentences often deliberately abrupt and sometimes obscure. He favoured archaic and poetic words and frequently uses metaphor. These characteristics reached their high point in the *Annals*, but are already present in *Agricola* and *Germany*. Both these works have a fair number of epigrams, brief and often biting comments, generally placed in a telling position. From *Agricola*, for example: 'he retained from philosophy the hardest lesson of all, a sense of proportion' (ch. 4); 'he understood the age of Nero: indolence was then a kind of philosophy' (6); 'their courage has been lost along with their liberty' (11); 'Bolanus . . . had contrived to win popularity as a substitute for authority' (16); 'the Britons, who had no experience of this, called it "civilization", although it was a part of

their enslavement' (21); 'everything unknown is given an inflated worth' and 'they make a desert and call it "peace"' (30). From *Germany* come more examples: 'the same people love idleness as much as they hate peace' (ch. 15); 'good morality is more effective there than laws elsewhere' (19); 'they will be as easily defeated by their vices as by force of arms' (23); 'speed and timidity go together' (30); 'where force is decisive, restraint and uprightness are labels applied only to the stronger side' (36); 'defeat in battle always begins with the eyes' (43); 'they have reached a state that is very difficult to attain: they do not even need to pray for anything' (46).

Both Tacitus' earliest works are, as chance would have it, unique specimens of their respective genres: no other biography of a Roman senator of the imperial period survives,[17] no other example of an ancient ethnographical monograph. That Tacitus' writings did survive is something of a miracle. The manuscripts of *Agricola* and *Germany* all go back to a single original, written in the Benedictine monastery at Hersfeld (or at nearby Fulda) in Germany shortly before the middle of the ninth century. This was taken to Rome in the fifteenth century. It was made public in 1455, and copies were made, which resulted in the works becoming well known and influential, especially *Germany*. The manuscript from Hersfeld was soon split up, however, and vanished. Part of it (so most scholars believe), containing much of *Agricola*, was rediscovered at Jesi in Italy in 1902. Sadly the precious relic disappeared again in the Second World War.

What Tacitus wrote about the early Germans was no doubt appreciated by the medieval scribes. This was certainly the case with the German humanists in the early modern period. One of them, Conrad Celtis, produced an edition of *Germany* which was reprinted over fifty times in the sixteenth century. Early on there were attempts to make political capital out of the work: in 1501 Jakob Wimpfeling claimed that Tacitus supported the case for Alsace having always been German. Throughout the sixteenth

---

[17] Among lost specimens of this genre one may note Arulenus Rusticus' biography of Thrasea and that of Helvidius Priscus by Herennius Senecio, see *Agr.* 2. Cf. also Pliny, *Letters* 7. 31: an equestrian friend of the Younger Pliny wrote the life of a senator called L. Annius Bassus (who had commanded a legion in AD 69, *Tac. Hist.* 3. 50, but is otherwise unknown).

century stress was laid on the second chapter, as demonstrating that the Germans were a pure and unmixed race. Tacitus' testimony to the Germans' courage and love of freedom, their moral rectitude and generous hospitality, their freedom from greed and their loyalty was, it is no surprise, also repeatedly quoted and applied to the ancient Germans' descendants. Thereafter interest diminished for a while. In the Age of Enlightenment such attitudes were less attractive.

There was a new perspective in the eighteenth century: Montesquieu attributed the excellence of the English constitution to the Anglo-Saxons having inherited the division of powers invented in the forests of ancient Germany (*Ger.* 11). In the early nineteenth century nationalism emerged as a force in Germany, as elsewhere. Johann Gottlob Fichte, in his 'Speeches to the German Nation' (1807–8), inspired by Tacitus' work, urged that the German people had retained its characteristics unchanged from Roman times and must fight to preserve its national identity. Remarkably, Fichte avoided the 'biological' or racial argument. It was left to the French writer, Count Arthur Gobineau, in his *Essay on the Inequality of the Human Races* (1853–5) to proclaim the superiority of the Germanic or Nordic race, again and again basing his case on Tacitus (although also criticizing him for his excessively negative portrayal of the Germans). The process was taken further by a naturalized German of English origin, Houston Stewart Chamberlain (1855–1927), who enjoyed considerable success with his *Foundations of the Nineteenth Century* (1898): Tacitus' *Germany* was again exploited to demonstrate that the 'Aryans' were responsible for all that was great and creative in European culture. From here it was a short step to the glorification in the Third Reich of the ancient Germans as forerunners of the National Socialist racial ideas. Writing on the origin and ethnic history of the Germans (in 1935), the leading Nazi race theorist H. F. K. Günther went well beyond the usual list of qualities vouched for by Tacitus: racial purity, love of freedom, moral rectitude, loyalty (the origin of the *Treue* stressed so much by the SS), and the rest. Günther could even find in chapter 12 of *Germany*, on the old Germanic death penalty, justification for eliminating degenerate elements from society: bizarre as it may seem, Tacitus was being misused to justify

the policy which culminated in genocide. Given the approval of Tacitus' *Germany* expressed by Rosenberg, Himmler, and others, it is no surprise that the work has been described as 'among the hundred most dangerous books ever written' (by A. Momigliano in 1956).

Agricola has had its influence, too, albeit of a more beneficent nature. Initially its appeal was mainly as a source for national history. It was used in the early sixteenth century by the Scottish scholar Hector Boethius as the basis for his *Scotorum historiae* (1527), the original being greatly embroidered and expanded. Fifty years later Ralph Holinshed incorporated a translation of much of *Agricola* into his *Chronicles of England, Scotland, and Ireland* (1577), and the Queen's Antiquary, William Camden, likewise used it extensively for his *Britannia* (1586).

Agricola was cited approvingly by Montaigne in the sixteenth century. Then, in 1605 Francis Bacon commended Nerva's combination of monarchy and freedom at Rome to James I—but he misqoted the passage from *Agr.* 3: 'principatum ac libertatem' became 'imperium et libertatem'. Bacon's version evidently misled Henry St John, Viscount Bolingbroke in his *Idea of a Patriot King* of 1738, where 'imperium et libertas' also appears. Another passage, the comment on chronic British disunity (*Agr.* 12), was used by Benjamin Franklin to warn his American fellow rebels not to quarrel in 1776. Disraeli revived Bacon's misquotation in the House of Commons in 1851, in a speech on the agricultural distress: England, he said, 'has achieved the union of those two qualities for combining which a Roman Emperor was deified, *Imperium et Libertas.*' Near the end of his political career, at the time of the Third Afghan War, Disraeli produced the phrase again, the context this time his own invention, in his speech at Guildhall on 10 November 1879. The citizens of London, he proclaimed, would not 'be beguiled into believing that in maintaining their Empire they may forfeit their liberties. One of the greatest of Romans, when asked what were his politics, replied, *Imperium et Libertas.* That would not make a bad programme for a British Ministry. It is one from which Her Majesty's Ministers do not shrink.' Gladstone retorted that Disraeli meant 'Liberty for ourselves, Empire over the rest of

mankind', and shortly afterwards, at the start of his first Midlothian campaign, drove this message home. All the same, after Disraeli's death, when his admirers founded the Primrose League to propagate Conservative and Imperial values, they chose *Imperium et Libertas* as its motto. This now forgotten body could be described in 1920 as 'one of the most numerous and most efficient political organisations in existence'.[18]

Gladstone could easily have cited another passage of *Agricola* against the Conservatives, the famous epigram denouncing Roman 'imperialism' put into the mouth of the Caledonian Calgacus: 'They make a desert and call it "peace"' (*Agr.* 30). This was left to an unexpected critic of British policy in the Boer War, Field Marshal Sir Neville Chamberlain, denouncing Kitchener's blockhouses, farm-burning, and 'concentration camps' (the first of their kind). The octogenarian veteran of the Indian Army, however, while quoting Tacitus' words, attributed them to Byron. The poet had indeed made use of Tacitus, though in adapted form: 'He makes a solitude—and calls it—peace!' (*The Bride of Abydos* (1813), canto ii, line 431). The Field Marshal's nephew, the already mentioned naturalized German, H. S. Chamberlain, quoted this attack on British imperialism with relish in 1919.[19]

In the mean time, especially in Scotland, *Agricola* was the inspiration for unpolitical, if no less passionately pursued debate, with the search for the battlefield of Mons Grampius, as the name was still incorrectly spelt (cf. the note to *Agr.* 29, *the Graupian Mountain*), to the fore. Walter Scott's fictional *Antiquary*, Jonathan Oldbuck, has had a host of real-life fellows, determined to establish 'the local situation of the final conflict between Agricola and the Caledonians'.[20]

---

[18] W. F. Monypenny and G. E. Buckle, *The Life of Benjamin Disraeli, Earl of Beaconsfield*, iii (London, 1914), 283; vi (1920), 495, 631.

[19] H. S. Chamberlain, *Lebenswege meines Denkens* (Munich, 1919), 25. The passage was written in October 1916. It should be added that these Chamberlains were not related to Joseph Chamberlain, Colonial Secretary at the time of the Boer War, whose son was the better known Neville Chamberlain.

[20] See G. Maxwell, *A Battle Lost: Romans and Caledonians at Mons Graupius* (Edinburgh, 1990), esp. 72 ff.

NOTE ON THE TEXT

The most widely used modern texts of Tacitus' 'minor works' are the Teubner edition by E. Koestermann (1970) and that by M. Winterbottom and R. M. Ogilvie (1975) in the Oxford Classical Texts series (in which the text of *Agricola* is largely based on Ogilvie's 1967 edition). In significant cases where they differ from one another, or where a third version seems preferable, I have based this translation on the following readings (in the case of *Germany*, those marked* are owed to A. A. Lund, cf. Select Bibliography below):

	Oxford World's Classics	Koestermann	Winterbottom
Agr.			
5	intersaepti exercitus	intercepti exercitus	intersaepti exercitus
10	oblongae scapulae	oblongae scutulae	oblongae scutulae
20	nova pars ⟨pariter⟩ inlacessita	nova pars ⟨pariter⟩ inlacessita	nova pars inlacessita
29	Initio ⟨insequentis⟩ aestatis	Initio ⟨insequentis⟩ aestatis	Initio aestatis
31	⟨bel⟩laturi	laturi	†laturi
33	ex quo ⟨vestra⟩ virtute	ex quo ⟨vestra⟩ virtute	ex quo virtute
34	quadraginta annis	quinquaginta annis	quinquaginta annis
36	cum aegre in gradu stantes	cum aegre clivo adstantes	cum aegre in gradu stantes
45	visus ⟨adflixit⟩	visus	visus ⟨adflixit⟩
46	obruet	obruit	obruet
Ger.			
3*	et apud eos Herculem	apud eos et Herculem	apud eos et Herculem

	Oxford World's Classics	Koestermann	Winterbottom
Ger.			
5*	utilitate	vilitate	vilitate
8	Albrunam	Albrunam	Auriniam
12*	reddant	reddunt	reddunt
15*	magna arma	magn⟨ific⟩a arma	magnifica arma
21*	nemo discernit: victus inter hospites communis. abeunti . . . obligantur.	nemo discernit. abeunti . . . obligantur. [victus inter hospites communis.]	nemo discernit. abeunti . . . obligantur. [victus inter hospites comis.]
26*	ab universis in usum	ab universis in vicem	ab universis †vices†
30*	nec nisi rationi et disciplinae concessum	nec nisi Romanae disciplinae concessum	nec nisi Romanae disciplinae concessum
31*	pretia ⟨ag⟩noscenda	pretia nascendi	pretia nascendi
35	recedit	redit	recedit
43*	ceterum animis super vires, quibus enumeratos paulo ante populos antecedunt, truces: insitae feritati	ceterum Harii super vires, quibus enumeratos paulo ante populos antecedunt, truces, insitae feritati	ceterum Harii super vires,quibus enumeratos paulo ante populos antecedunt, truces, insitae feritati
45. 2*	id pro armis omnium: quae tutela	id pro armis omniumque tutela	id pro armis omniumque tutela
45. 5*	crediderim: quae	crediderim, quae	crediderim, †quae†

	Oxford World's Classics	Koestermann	Winterbottom
Ger. 46*	—sordes omnium— at corpora procera conubiis mixtis	sordes omnium ac torpor procerum. conubiis mixtis	sordes omnium ac torpor procerum; conubiis mixtis

SELECT BIBLIOGRAPHY

Editions of the Latin Text of *Agricola* and *Germany*

Koestermann, E. (ed.), *Cornelius Tacitus*, ii. 2: *Germania. Agricola. Dialogus de Oratoribus* (Leipzig, 1970).

Winterbottom, M., and Ogilvie, R. M. (eds.), *Cornelii Taciti Opera Minora* (Oxford, 1975).

Commentaries

Anderson, J. G. C. (ed.), *Cornelii Taciti De origine et situ Germanorum* (Oxford, 1938; repr. London, 1997).

Lund, A. A. (ed.), *P. Cornelius Tacitus: Germania* (Heidelberg, 1988).

Ogilvie, R. M., and Richmond, I. A. (eds.), *Cornelii Taciti De vita Agricolae* (Oxford, 1967).

Translations into English

Fyfe, W. H., *Tacitus: Dialogus, Agricola, and Germania* (Oxford, 1908).

Hutton, M., and Peterson, W., Tacitus, *Tacitus*, i: *Agricola, Germania, Dialogus*, rev. R. M. Ogilvie, E. H. Warmington, and M. Winterbottom (London and Cambridge, Mass., 1970).

Mattingly, H., *Tacitus: The Agricola and the Germania*, rev. S. A. Handford (Harmondsworth and New York, 1970).

Background Material on Tacitus and on Britain and Germany up to *c.* AD 100

Alföldy, G., 'Bricht der Schweigsame sein Schweigen? Eine Grabinschrift in Rom', *Mitteilungen des deutschen archaeologischen Instituts. Roemische Abteilung*, 102 (1995), 251–68.

Benario, H. W., 'Tacitus' *Germania* and Modern Germany', *Illinois Classical Studies*, 15 (1990), 163–75.

—— 'Recent Works on Tacitus: 1984–1993', *Classical World*, 89 (1995), 91–162.

Birley, A. R., *The Fasti of Roman Britain* (Oxford, 1981).

Burn, A. R., 'Tacitus on Britain', in T. A. Dorey (ed.), *Tacitus* (London, 1969), 1–18.

Dorey, T. A. (ed.), *Tacitus* (London, 1969).

—— '*Agricola* and *Germania*', in id. (ed.), *Tacitus* (London, 1969), 1–18.

Hanson, W. S., *Agricola and the Conquest of the North* (London, 1987).

—— 'Tacitus' 'Agricola': An Archaeological and Historical Study', in W. Haase (ed.), *Aufstieg und Niedergang der römischen Welt*, II. 33. 3 (Berlin and New York, 1991), 1742–84.

Jones, B., and Mattingly, D., *An Atlas of Roman Britain* (Oxford, 1990).

Raepsaet-Charlier, M.-T., 'Cn. Iulius Agricola: Mise au point prosopographique', in W. Haase (ed.), *Aufstieg und Niedergang der römischen Welt*, II. 33. 3 (Berlin and New York, 1991), 1808–57.

Rivet, A. L. F., and Smith, C., *The Place-Names of Roman Britain* (London, 1979).

Syme, R., *Tacitus*, 2 vols. (Oxford, 1958).

—— *Roman Papers*, i–vii (Oxford, 1979–91).

Timpe, D., *Romano-Germanica: Gesammelte Studien zur Germania des Tacitus* (Stuttgart and Leipzig, 1995).

Wells, C. M., *The German Policy of Augustus* (Oxford, 1972).

CHRONOLOGICAL TABLE
OF EVENTS COVERED IN *AGRICOLA* AND *GERMANY* AND IN TACITUS' LIFE

113 BC	The invading Cimbri and other German and Celtic peoples defeat a Roman army in Noricum.
109	Cimbri defeat another Roman army in the Rhone valley.
105	Cimbri defeat Romans at battle of Arausio (Orange).
102	Teutones and Ambrones, allies of Cimbri, defeated by Gaius Marius at Aquae Sextiae (Aix-en-Provence).
101	Marius destroys Cimbri at Vercellae in Po valley.
c.71	Ariovistus, king of the German Suebi, invades Gaul at the invitation of Sequani and defeats Helvetii.
59	Ariovistus recognized as a 'friend of the Roman People'.
58	Julius Caesar becomes proconsul of Gaul and defeats Helvetii, who invaded the Roman province under pressure from Suebian Germans; Caesar goes on to defeat Suebi.
57–55	Further campaigns of Caesar in Gaul.
55	Caesar crosses the Rhine and launches first invasion of Britain.
54	Caesar's second invasion of Britain.
53	Caesar's second crossing of the Rhine.
49	Caesar crosses the Rubicon and begins the Civil War.
48	Caesar defeats Pompey.
44	Caesar assassinated by Brutus, Cassius, and others.
42	Battle of Philippi: Brutus and Cassius defeated by the Triumvirs Antony and Octavian.
38	Agrippa crosses the Rhine, resettles the German Ubii on the left bank, and founds a centre for them, the later Cologne.
31	(2 September) Battle of Actium; Octavian defeats Antony and Cleopatra.

30	(1 August) Octavian captures Alexandria. End of the Civil War.
27	(13 and 16 January) Octavian 'restores the Republic' and takes the name Augustus.
12–9	Campaigns of Drusus, stepson of Augustus, beyond the Rhine, ending with Drusus' death.
8–7	Further campaigns by Tiberius beyond Rhine.
AD 4	Tiberius adopted by Augustus.
4–6	Renewed campaigns by Tiberius beyond Rhine.
5	Naval expedition led by Tiberius discovers remnants of Cimbri in Jutland.
6	Campaign by Tiberius against Maroboduus, to annex Bohemia and Moravia, abandoned owing to uprising in Pannonia.
9	Romans under Varus defeated by Arminius at battle of Teutoburgian forest; three legions destroyed, and Romans withdraw to Rhine.
10–12	Further campaigns by Tiberius in Germany.
14	(19 August) Death of Augustus; Tiberius emperor.
14–16	Campaigns beyond Rhine by Germanicus, Tiberius' nephew.
16	Germanicus recalled by Tiberius. End of Roman attempt to recover Germany up to Elbe.
37	(16 March) Death of Tiberius; Caligula emperor.
39–40	Grandiose plans of Caligula for campaigns beyond Rhine and across Channel come to nothing.
40	(13 June) Birth of Agricola.
41	(24 January) Caligula murdered; his uncle Claudius emperor. Gabinius campaigns beyond the Rhine and recovers the last legionary eagle from the disaster of AD 9.
43	Claudius orders invasion of Britain, led by Aulus Plautius.
44	Claudius holds a triumph for the conquest of Britain and names his young son Britannicus.
47	Plautius succeeded in Britain by Ostorius Scapula. Domitius Corbulo's campaign beyond the Rhine halted by Claudius.

49	First Roman *colonia* in Britain founded at Camulodunum (Colchester).
50	Pomponius Secundus campaigns against the Chatti in Germany. The British resistance leader Caratacus defeated by Scapula, flees to the Brigantes, whose Queen Cartimandua hands him over to Rome. Veteran legionaries settled at Cologne, which is made a *colonia* named after Agrippina.
51	Caratacus and family are paraded in a ceremony before Claudius and the Younger Agrippina at Rome.
52	Death of Scapula in Britain; his successor, Didius Gallus (52–7), not very active.
54	(13 October) Death of Claudius, succeeded by his stepson Nero.
57	A new governor of Britain, Quintus Veranius, begins a forward policy in South Wales but dies within a year.
between 47 and *c*.58	Elder Pliny serves as officer in Germany; he meets Tacitus' presumed father, procurator of Belgica.
58	Suetonius Paulinus campaigns in Wales. Agricola appointed military tribune in Britain.
c.58	Tacitus born, perhaps at Trier (Augusta Treverorum).
60	As Paulinus prepares to attack Mona (Anglesey), an uprising led by Boudicca destroys Camulodunum (Colchester), Verulamium (St Albans), and Londinium; suppressed by Paulinus.
61	Paulinus replaced by Petronius Turpilianus, who adopts a mild policy.
61	Agricola marries Domitia Decidiana.
62	Agricola's son born but dies in infancy.
63	Petronius replaced as governor of Britain by Trebellius Maximus, who carries out no campaigning.
63–4	Agricola quaestor in Asia; birth of his daughter.
c.65	The legion XIV Gemina and Batavian cohorts withdrawn from Britain for a planned campaign by Nero.
66	Agricola tribune of the plebs.
68	Agricola praetor. The army of Upper Germany, under Verginius Rufus, defeats Gallic uprising against Nero,

	which was supported by Galba, governor of Hither Spain, but Nero panics and commits suicide; Galba becomes emperor (*c*.8 June).
69	Renewed Civil War: the Year of the Four Emperors. (1–3 January) The Rhine legions proclaim Vitellius emperor. Galba murdered at Rome (15 January) and replaced by Otho. (March) Agricola's mother murdered by Otho's fleet in Liguria. (14 April) Vitellius' army defeats Otho in northern Italy. The governor of Britain, Trebellius, expelled by his own army, replaced by Vettius Bolanus. (1–3 July) Vespasian proclaimed emperor in the east. Agricola joins Flavian side and levies new troops. Batavian Revolt in the Rhineland begins, led by Julius Civilis. Queen Cartimandua of the Brigantes rescued by the governor Bolanus. The legion XIV Gemina returns to Britain. Flavian armies defeat the Vitellians in northern Italy, 24–5 October, and capture Rome, 20 December.
70	Agricola appointed legate of the Twentieth legion in Britain. The legion XIV Gemina withdrawn from Britain again to assist Petillius Cerialis suppress the Batavian Revolt, which he ends in autumn.
71	Cerialis becomes governor of Britain, bringing a further legion, II Adiutrix, and the reorganized Batavian and Tungrian cohorts to rejoin British garrison; he campaigns in northern England.
c.73	Cornelius Clemens campaigns beyond the upper Rhine; extension of the empire in this region.
73	Roman fort at Luguvalium (Carlisle) founded. Cerialis replaced by Julius Frontinus.
73–6	Agricola governor of Aquitania; followed by his consulship, probably in autumn 76.
73–7	Frontinus governor of Britain; he campaigns against the Silures of South Wales.
c.76	Tacitus marries Agricola's daughter.
c.77	Rutilius Gallicus campaigns against the German Bructeri and captures their prophetess Veleda.
77	(midsummer) Agricola succeeds Frontinus as governor of Britain and campaigns against the Ordovices in North

Wales, going on to capture Mona (Anglesey); the legionary fortress at Lindum (Lincoln) is vacated at latest in this year; the legion, II Adiutrix, moves to Deva (Chester); the empty Lincoln fortress is in due course converted into a *colonia* for veterans, perhaps by Agricola, at the latest before the death of Domitian (AD 96).

78   Agricola campaigns in northern England and southern Scotland.

79   (23 June) Death of Vespasian, his elder son Titus becomes emperor. Agricola reaches the estuary of the Tay (Taus). For Agricola's successes Titus takes an 'acclamation' (his fifteenth). (24 August) Eruption of Vesuvius; death of Elder Pliny. Winter: Agricola's 'romanization' measures.

80   Agricola strengthens newly conquered regions in Scotland with forts.

81   Agricola campaigns against hitherto unknown peoples in Scotland (beyond the Clyde (Clota)) and draws up his troops facing Ireland. (13 September) Death of Titus; Domitian becomes emperor.

82   Agricola campaigns beyond the Forth (Bodotria). He narrowly fails to win complete victory over the Caledonian peoples. Mutiny of the cohort of Usipi. Agricola's wife bears him a son.

83   Domitian increases army pay. He launches a major expedition against the Chatti beyond the upper Rhine; new frontier line established with watch-towers. Domitian celebrates triumph 'over the Germans' at Rome and takes the name 'Germanicus'. Agricola's infant son dies (spring). Agricola's seventh campaign: he defeats the Caledonians at the battle of the Graupian Mountain (September).

84   (spring) Recall of Agricola from Britain. He receives an 'honorary triumph'. His successor begins building a legionary fortress at Inchtuthil.

85   Heavy Roman losses in Danube area; Domitian, based in Moesia, directs Roman counter-offensive.

86   The Guard Prefect Cornelius Fuscus defeated and killed by the Dacians; Domitian returns to the Danube.

87   One of the four legions in Britain, II Adiutrix, withdrawn
          to strengthen the Danube army; newly conquered area
          in Scotland given up and new legionary fortress at
          Inchtuthil dismantled before it is fully completed.

88   Tacitus praetor and *quindecimvir*; Secular Games held.

89   (January) Antonius Saturninus rebels against Domitian
          in Upper Germany but is quickly suppressed; Domitian
          campaigns against the Chatti again and then on the upper
          Danube.

92–early 93   Domitian campaigns on the Danube.

93   (23 August) Death of Agricola. Tacitus returns to Rome.
          Treason trials, executions of Helvidius, Rusticus, and
          Senecio.

96   (18 September) Domitian murdered, replaced by Nerva.
          Trajan appointed governor of Upper Germany.

97   Tacitus consul, delivers funeral speech for Verginius
          Rufus. (October) Mutiny of Praetorian Guard against
          Nerva. A Roman general wins minor success against
          eastern (Suebian) Germans. Nerva adopts Trajan as
          his son and successor, *c*.27 October. Both take the title
          'Germanicus'. Trajan, now 'Caesar', remains on the
          Rhine, at Cologne. Tacitus begins writing *Agricola*. An
          elderly Stoic, Avidius Quietus, becomes governor of
          Britain. A third *colonia* founded in Britain, at Glevum
          (Gloucester).

98   (27 January) Death of Nerva; Trajan succeeds as emperor
          and remains in the north, not returning to Rome until 99.
          Tacitus finishes *Agricola* and composes *Germany*.

99–100   Tacitus and the Younger Pliny prosecute Marius Priscus
          before the senate.

101–2   First Dacian War. Trajan annexes territory north of the
          lower Danube.

102?   Tacitus writes the *Dialogue on Orators*.

c.102–4?   Tacitus perhaps governs an imperial province. He begins
          writing the *Histories*?

105–6   Second Dacian War. The Kingdom of Dacia annexed.

c.105?   First part of the *Histories* completed.

c.110	*Histories* completed.
c.110–112	Younger Pliny governor of Pontus-Bithynia, where he dies.
c.111	Tacitus begins research on the *Annals*.
112–13	Tacitus proconsul of Asia.
113	(October) Trajan leaves Rome for the East.
114–17	Parthian War. Tacitus begins writing the *Annals*.
117	(9 August) Death of Trajan. (11 August) Hadrian proclaimed emperor in the East.
117–38	Hadrian emperor.
121	Hadrian orders the erection of a palisade on German frontier.
122	Hadrian orders the beginning of his Wall in Britain. Some time during this reign Tacitus presumably dies, his *Annals* perhaps not quite completed.

0   300   600 km

Luguvalium
Eburacum
BRITANNIA
Deva Lindum
Isca
Londinium
GERMANIA INF Colonia Agrippinensis
BELGICA Moguntiacum
LUGDUNENSIS Carnuntu
GERMANIA SUP RAETIA NORICUM Aquincum
GALLIA PANNONIA
Lugdunum
AQUITANIA DALMATI.
TARRACONENSIS NARBONENSIS
HISPANIA ITALY
Tarraco
LUSITANIA CORSICA Rome
Emerita SARDINIA
Corduba
BAETICA
SICILY
Tingi
Caesarea Carthage
MAURETANIA MAURETANIA M e d i t e
CAESARIENSIS TINGITANA
NUMIDIA
AFRICA

MAP 1. THE ROMAN EMPIRE IN THE FIRST AND EARLY SECOND CENTURIES A

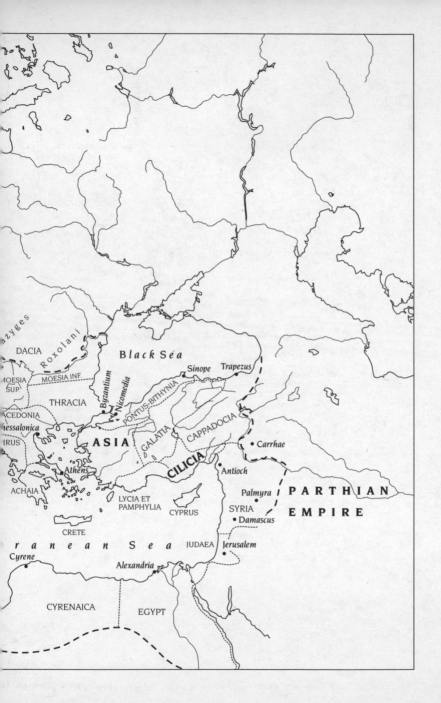

MAP 2. GERMANY AND NORTHERN GAUL, IN THE TIME OF TACITUS

0   300   600 km

Mellusii

Sithones

Fenni

Aestii

Gotones

R. Vistula

undiones

Venethi

R. Dnieper

Manimi

R. Dniester

Harii

Buri

Cotini

Osi

Sarmatae
Jazyges

Bastarnae (Peucini)

Aquincum

R. Theiss

Daci

Sarmatae
Roxolani

Black Sea

R. Danube

MOESIA

Names that occur in the Latin text of 'Tacitus' Agricola are over shaded.

Possible locations of battle of *MONS GRAUPIUS* (the Graupian Mountain)

THULE

Portus Trucculensis?

ORCADES

Cornovii

Cuereni Lugi

Smertae

Vacomagi

Carnonacae Decantae

Creones

? Boresti

Venicones Taexali

Taus

Inchtuthil (Victoria?)

Bodotria

CALEDONIA

Oceanus

Epidii

Selgovae

Votadini

Clota

Vindolanda

Coria

Novantae

Tina

Luguvalium

Ituna

Eburacum

BRITANNIA

Brigantes

HIBERNIA

Mona

Deva

Lindum

Ordovices

Cornovii

Coritani

Ratae

Iceni

Viroconium

Trinovantes

Catuvellauni

Camulodunum

Demetae

Silures

Verulamium

Colonia

Isca

Glevum

Londinium

Dobunni

Cantiaci

Portus

Atrebates

Rutupensis ?

Durotriges

Gesoriacum

Dumnonii

Oceanus

'States granted to King Cogidumnus' (?Togidubnus)

Civitates Cogidumno regi

[or: Togidumno regi]

GALLIA

0   100   200   300km

MAP 3. ROMAN BRITAIN, *c.* AD 98

AGRICOLA

THE LIFE OF AGRICOLA

Preface

1. It was the custom in past times to relate famous men's deeds and
characters for posterity. Even our present age, though indifferent
to its own affairs, has not abandoned it, at least whenever some
great and noble virtue has overcome and surmounted the vice that
is common to small and great states alike: ignorance of what is right
and jealousy.

Yet in former generations the path to memorable achievements
was less uphill and more open. Further, the most distinguished
writers were attracted to publish accounts of meritorious achievement, without partiality or self-seeking. Their sole reward was in
doing what they knew to be right. Indeed, many considered that to
compose a record of their own life showed confidence about their
conduct rather than conceit. Rutilius and Scaurus did so and were
neither disbelieved nor criticized. Of course, excellence can best be
appreciated in those ages in which it can most readily develop. But
in these times I needed permission when I intended to relate the life
of a dead man. I should not have had to request this if I had been
planning an invective. So savage and hostile to merit has this age
been.

2. We have read how Arulenus Rusticus' eulogy of Paetus
Thrasea and that of Priscus Helvidius by Herennius Senecio were
treated as capital offences; further, that savage punishment was
inflicted not only on the authors themselves but on their books.
The Board of Three was delegated with the task of burning, in the
Comitium and Forum, the biographies of distinguished men of
genius. No doubt they thought that in that fire the voice of the
Roman People, the liberty of the senate, and the conscience of
mankind could be wiped out—over and above this, the teachers of
philosophy were expelled and all noble accomplishments driven
into exile, so that nothing honourable might anywhere confront
them.

We have indeed provided a grand specimen of submissiveness. Just as the former age witnessed an extreme in freedom, so we have experienced the depths of servitude, deprived by espionage even of the intercourse of speaking and listening to one another. We should have lost our memories as well as our voices, were it as easy to forget as to be silent.

3. Now at last spirits are reviving. At the first dawning of this most fortunate age, Nerva Caesar at once combined principles formerly incompatible, monarchy and freedom. Day by day Nerva Trajan is enhancing the happiness of our times. Public security has not merely inspired our hopes and prayers but has gained the assurance of those prayers' fulfilment and, from this, strength. And yet, by the nature of human frailty, remedies take longer to act than diseases. Our bodies, which grow so slowly, perish in an instant. So too you can crush the mind and its pursuits more easily than you can recall them to life. Indolence indeed has a charm of its own, to which we gradually yield, and we end up by loving the inaction that we at first hated. After all, in the space of fifteen years, a large portion of a human life, many have died by the intervention of chance, and all the most mentally active as victims of the emperor's cruelty. The few of us that are left have outlived not only the others but, so to speak, our own past selves. So many years have been stolen from the middle of our lives, years in which those of us who were youths have become old men and the old men have reached almost the end of their allotted span—in silence.

None the less, it will not be an unpleasant task to put together, even in a rough and uncouth style, a record of our former servitude and a testimony to our present blessings. For the time being, this book, intended to honour Agricola, my father-in-law, will be commended, or at least excused, as a tribute of dutiful affection.

Agricola's Life up to his Appointment as Governor of Britain

4. Gnaeus Julius Agricola came from the ancient and famous *colonia* of Forum Julii [Fréjus]. Both his grandfathers were procurators of the Caesars, the equivalent of nobility for equestrians. His father Julius Graecinus belonged to the senatorial order and was

noted for his devotion to eloquence and philosophy. By these very accomplishments he incurred the wrath of Gaius Caesar [Caligula], for he was ordered to prosecute Marcus Silanus and, because he refused, was put to death. His mother was Julia Procilla, a woman of exceptionally pure character. Brought up under her tender care, he passed his boyhood and youth in a complete training in liberal studies. Apart from his own natural integrity, the fact that he lived and went to school from his very early years at Massilia [Marseilles] kept him away from the temptations of bad companions. It is a place where there is a well-blended mixture of Greek culture and provincial thrift. I remember that he used to tell how in his early youth he would have imbibed the study of philosophy more deeply than is permitted for a Roman and a senator, had not his mother sensibly restrained his burning enthusiasm. It is clear that his lofty and aspiring nature was attracted, with more passion than is prudent, to the fair image of great and exalted glory. In time, discretion and age assuaged these feelings, and he retained from philosophy the hardest lesson of all, a sense of proportion.

5. His first lessons in military life he learned to the satisfaction of Suetonius Paulinus, a conscientious and circumspect commander. Agricola had been selected to be tested on Paulinus' staff. He did not regard his rank of tribune and his inexperience as an excuse for idle pleasure-seeking and going on leave, like those young men who irresponsibly turn military service into self-indulgence. Instead he got to know the province and made himself known to the army, learned from the experienced men, and chose the best models to follow. He never applied for a task as a chance for self-advertisement and never declined one through cowardice. He performed with both caution and alertness.

Britain has certainly never before or since been in a more disturbed or dangerous state. Veterans had been massacred, *coloniae* burned down, armies cut off. They had to fight for their lives first, before they could think of victory. All these operations were, to be sure, carried out under the direction and leadership of another, and the supreme command and the glory of recovering the province went to the general. Still, this all gave the young man additional skill and experience and a passion for military glory entered his

soul—not welcome in those days, when distinction aroused unfavourable reactions and a great reputation was no less dangerous than a bad one.

6. From Britain he returned to the city to enter the career of office and married Domitia Decidiana, who was of illustrious parentage. This union brought him both distinction and material support when he was seeking advancement. They were an unusually united pair. Their affection was mutual, each putting the other first. Still, a good wife deserves more than half the praise, just as a bad one deserves more than half the blame.

For the quaestorship the lot of the draw assigned him the province of Asia and as proconsul Salvius Titianus. He was not corrupted by either, although the province is rich and wide open to wrongdoers, while the proconsul, who was prone to all forms of greed, was only too ready to guarantee a mutual cover up of illegal conduct. While he was there he was blessed with a daughter, which was both a consolidation of his position and a consolation—for shortly afterwards he lost the son who had been born previously.

He then spent the year's interval between the quaestorship and the tribunate of the plebs, and the actual year as tribune as well, in quiet inactivity. He understood the age of Nero: indolence was then a kind of philosophy. His praetorship ran the same silent course, for no presidency of a court had fallen to him. He conducted the games and the empty shows of his office with a compromise between economy and excess; while being far from extravagant, he came near to popular approval. He was at that time selected by Galba to take an inventory of temple treasures. As a result of his extremely thorough scrutiny it was as though the Commonwealth had never experienced sacrilege at the hands of anyone but Nero.

7. The following year dealt a grievous blow to his heart and to his family. Otho's fleet, which was roaming about out of control, plundered the Intimilian district of Liguria as though it was enemy territory. They murdered Agricola's mother on her estate and looted the estate itself and a large part of the family property, which had been the motive for killing her. Agricola had accordingly set out for the ceremonies required of filial duty when he was over-

taken by the news of Vespasian's bid for the imperial power. He at once went over to his party.

The early stages of the reign and the government of the city were in the hands of Mucianus, Domitian then being a very young man who was using his father's success only as an opportunity for dissolute conduct. Mucianus appointed Agricola, who had been sent to conduct a levy and had carried this out with integrity and energy, to the command of the Twentieth legion. It had been late in coming over to swear allegiance and the previous commander was reported to have behaved treasonably. Indeed, the legion had been too strong and formidable even for the consular legates, and the praetorian legate was impotent to control it. It is not clear whether this was because of his character or that of the troops. Hence the chosen successor was at the same time to mete out punishment. Agricola, with a most rare moderation, preferred to let it appear that he had found the men well disciplined, not that he had made them so.

8. The man then governing Britain was Vettius Bolanus, with a gentler hand than was appropriate for an untamed province. Agricola reined in his own energy and restrained his eagerness in case it became too strong. He knew how to obey and had learned to combine expedience with propriety. Shortly afterwards Britain acquired as consular Petilius Cerialis. There was now scope to display talents. But to start with it was only hard work and danger that Cerialis shared with him. In due course a share in the glory came too. Often, as a test, Cerialis assigned him part of the army. Sometimes, on the strength of the result, he put him in command of larger forces. However, Agricola never boasted of his achievements to enhance his own reputation. He attributed his success, as a subordinate should, to his general, who had made the plans. Thus his quality of obedience and his modesty in reporting his achievements ruled out any jealousy but did not rule out some glory. 9. As he was returning from his legionary command, the Deified Vespasian enrolled him among the patricians, and then appointed him to govern the province of Aquitania. It was a particularly splendid post and carried the prospects of the consulship, for which the emperor had marked him out.

Many believe that the military temperament lacks discrimination, because the proceedings of a court martial, being not subject to control, rather blunt, and often high-handed, give no scope for the finesse of the lawcourts. Agricola, with his innate good sense, although now in a civilian milieu, performed his duties both readily and equitably. Furthermore, he made a clear division between his periods of work and relaxation. When the assizes and the courts demanded his attention, he was serious and attentive, strict but often merciful. When he had completed his official duties, he no longer wore the mask of power. Sullenness and arrogance and greed he had cast aside. And in his case, what is very rare, his familiar manner did not lessen his authority nor did his strictness reduce his popularity. To mention incorruptibility and self-restraint in such a man would be an insult to his excellent character. He did not court fame either, which is a temptation even for good men, by parading his virtues or by intrigue. He avoided rivalry with colleagues and disputes with procurators, for he considered it no kind of glory to win and demeaning to be worsted.

After being kept in this governorship for less than three years, he was recalled with the immediate prospect of a consulship. He was accompanied by a rumour that Britain was to be given him as his province. There had been nothing in his own conversation on this subject, rather it was because he seemed the right man. Rumour is not always wrong. Sometimes it even determines the choice. As consul he betrothed his daughter, then a girl of outstanding promise, to myself, then a young man, and after his consulship gave her in marriage. His appointment to govern Britain followed immediately afterwards, coupled with the priestly office of *pontifex*.

Britain and its Peoples

10. Britain's position and its peoples have been described by many writers. I shall offer my own account, not to compete with their diligence and literary talent, but because Britain was then for the first time completely conquered. Hence matters formerly uncertain,

which my predecessors embellished in eloquent fashion, will be reported on the evidence of the facts.

Britain is the largest of the islands known to the Romans. As regards its extent and situation, it faces Germany on the east and Spain on the west, while on the south side it is actually visible to the Gauls. Its northern parts, with no solid land confronting them, are battered by the harsh and open sea. The most eloquent authors, Livy among the older ones, Fabius Rusticus among the moderns, have compared Britain's shape to an elongated shoulder-blade or to an axe. That is indeed what it looks like on this side of Caledonia, which is why the description has been applied to the whole island. Those who have gone past this point have found a huge and irregular expanse of land, projecting beyond the apparently outermost shore and tapering into a wedge-like shape.

It was then that a Roman fleet for the first time circumnavigated this coast of the remotest sea and established that Britain is in fact an island. Then too it discovered the islands, hitherto unknown, which are called the Orcades [Orkneys], and subjugated them. Thule [Shetland] was thoroughly viewed, as well, but no more, for the fleet's orders were to go no further, and winter was approaching. It is reported, however, that the sea there is sluggish and difficult for the rowers, and is not even stirred up by the winds as happens elsewhere. The reason is, I believe, that land and mountains, which create and feed storms, are further apart there, and the deep mass of unbroken seawater is set in motion more slowly. It is not the purpose of the present work to investigate the physical properties of the Ocean and the tides, which have in any case been dealt with by many writers. I would add only one point. Nowhere is the dominance of the sea more extensive. There are many tidal currents, flowing in different directions. They do not merely rise as far as the shoreline and recede again. They flow far inland, wind around, and push themselves among the highlands and mountains, as if in their own realm.

11. As to what human beings initially inhabited Britain, whether native-born or immigrants, little has been established, as is usually the case with barbarians. Be this as it may, their physical

appearance is varied, which allows conclusions to be drawn. For example, in the case of the inhabitants of Caledonia, their red-gold hair and massive limbs proclaim German origin. As for the Silures, their swarthy features and, in most cases, curly hair, and the fact that Spain lies opposite, provide evidence that Iberians of old crossed over and settled this territory. Those nearest to the Gauls also resemble that people. Either their common origin still has some effect or, since the two countries converge from opposite directions, shared climatic conditions produce the same physical appearance.

All the same, it is plausible on a general estimate that the Gauls occupied the adjacent island. You can find their rites and their religious beliefs. The language is not much different, likewise the same boldness in seeking out danger—and, when it comes, the same timidity in facing it. Still, the Britons display more ferocity, having not yet been made soft by prolonged peace. We are told, indeed, that the Gauls, as well, used to be warriors of repute. Then decadence set in, hand in hand with peace: their courage has been lost along with their liberty. The same has happened to the Britons long since conquered. The rest are still like the Gauls once were.

12. Their infantry is their main strength. Some of their peoples also engage in battle with chariots. The nobles are the charioteers, their clients fight for them. In former times the Britons owed obedience to kings. Now they are formed into factional groupings by the leading men. Indeed, there is nothing that helps us more against such very powerful peoples than their lack of unanimity. It is seldom that two or three states unite to repel a common threat. Hence each fights on its own, and all are conquered.

The climate is miserable, with frequent rain and mists. But extreme cold is not found there. The days last longer than in our part of the world, the nights are bright and in the most distant parts of Britain so short that you can hardly distinguish between evening and morning twilight. If clouds do not block the view, they say that the sun's glow can be seen by night. It does not set and rise but passes across the horizon. In fact, the flat extremities of the earth, casting a low shadow, do not project the darkness, and night falls below the level of the sky and the stars.

The soil bears crops, apart from the olive and the vine and other natives of warmer climes, and has an abundance of cattle. The crops ripen slowly but shoot up quickly. The cause is the same in both cases, the abundant moisture of land and sky. Britain contains gold and silver and other metals, the booty of victory. The Ocean also produces pearls, but they are dusky and mottled. Some attribute this to the divers' lack of skill, for in the Red Sea the oysters are torn from the rocks alive and breathing, in Britain they are collected as and when the sea casts them up. For myself, I would find it easier to believe that the pearls are lacking in quality than that we are lacking in greed.

Roman Rule in Britain before Agricola's Governorship

13. The Britons themselves submit readily to conscription and taxes and the obligations imposed by the empire, so long as there are no abuses. These they are not willing to tolerate: they have now been broken in to obedience, but not yet to slavery. At any rate, the Deified Julius, the first of all the Romans to enter Britain with an army, intimidated the inhabitants by a successful battle and gained control of the coast. But he can be considered to have pointed it out, not handed it over, to future generations. The Civil Wars followed, with the leading men turning their arms against the Commonwealth. Britain was long forgotten, even in peace. The Deified Augustus called that 'prudence', Tiberius made it an 'injunction'.

That Gaius Caesar [Caligula] entertained thoughts of invading Britain is clear enough. But his impulsive character was quick to think better of it, and his grandiose undertakings against Germany had come to nothing. The Deified Claudius was responsible for carrying out the mighty task. Legions and *auxilia* were shipped across and Vespasian was given a role in the enterprise, the first step towards his future greatness. Peoples were subdued, kings captured, and destiny pointed to Vespasian.

14. The first of the consulars to be placed in command was Aulus Plautius, soon followed by Ostorius Scapula, both of them outstanding soldiers. The part of Britain nearest to us was gradually shaped into a province and was given a *colonia* of veterans as

well. Certain states were granted to Cogidumnus as king: he remained most loyal up to the time I can myself remember. It is an ancient and now long-established practice of the Roman People to use even kings as instruments of enslavement.

The next governor, Didius Gallus, held on to what his predecessors had acquired. Some forts, but very few, were pushed into the outlying regions, so that he could get the credit of having expanded the task assigned to him. Veranius succeeded Didius, but he died within a year. After this Suetonius Paulinus had two years of success: peoples were conquered and garrisons consolidated. Relying on these, he attacked the island of Mona [Anglesey], which, he thought, was a source of support to the rebels. He thus laid himself open to an assault from the rear.   15. For, their fears removed by the absence of the legate, the Britons began to discuss the evils of their slavery, to compare their wrongs and inflame their feelings by putting a worse construction on them.

'All that is achieved by submissiveness is that heavier burdens are imposed, as if we found them easy to bear. In former times we each had a single king, now two are imposed: the legate to wreak his fury on our lifeblood, the procurator on our property. Whether our masters quarrel or agree, it is equally fatal for us their subjects. One has centurions as his instruments, the other slaves, to inflict a mixture of violence and insults on us. Nothing is any longer exempt from their greed and lust. In battle it is the braver who takes the spoils. As things are now, it is mostly cowards and weaklings that plunder our homes, kidnap our children, and impose conscription on us—as if it were only for our own country that we do not know how to die.

'Yet what a small handful of soldiers has crossed over here, if we Britons count our own numbers! Thus did the Germanies throw off their yoke, and yet they have only a river, not the Ocean, to protect them. We have our country, our wives, and our parents to fight for; the Romans have nothing but greed and self-indulgence. They will withdraw, as the Deified Julius withdrew, if only we can match the courage of our ancestors. We must not lose heart by the loss of one battle or even two. The successful may have a more aggressive spirit but those who suffer have the staying power. Now even the

gods are taking pity on us Britons: they are keeping the Roman general away, keeping his army in exile on another island. We ourselves have undertaken the most difficult step: we have begun to plan. Besides, it will be more dangerous if we are detected planning in this way than if we dare to act.'

16. Stirred up by mutual encouragement of this kind, with Boudicca, from royal stock, a woman, as their leader—for they do not distinguish between the sexes when choosing commanders—the whole people launched a war. Hunting out the soldiers dispersed among the forts and taking their defences by storm, they burst into the *colonia* itself, which they saw as the seat of their enslavement. No form of the savagery common to barbarians was omitted: they were enraged, and they had conquered. Had not Paulinus rapidly come to the rescue as soon as he heard of the uprising in the province, Britain would have been lost. A single successful battle restored it to its old submissiveness. But many retained their weapons. They were influenced by consciousness of their guilt as rebels and by their personal fear of the legate—in case this otherwise excellent man would take high-handed measures against those who surrendered and would punish every offence with undue severity, as if it were a personal affront.

Petronius Turpilianus was therefore dispatched: it was thought that he would be less inflexible and, being a stranger to the enemy's crimes, milder towards those who repented. He pacified the previous turbulence but ventured nothing further, and handed the province over to Trebellius Maximus. Trebellius was even less active. He never inspected the camps and governed the province as an affable administrator. Now the barbarians, as well, learned to condone seductive vices; and the intervention of the Civil Wars provided a legitimate excuse for inactivity. But there was a serious mutiny, for the soldiers, who had been accustomed to campaigning, were growing unruly through doing nothing. Trebellius escaped the anger of his army by taking flight and hiding. Disgraced and humiliated, he remained in command on sufferance for the time being. It was as if a bargain had been struck: the general's life was spared in return for allowing the army a free hand. Thus the mutiny ended without bloodshed.

Nor did Vettius Bolanus trouble Britain by imposing discipline—the Civil Wars were still going on. There was the same lack of action against the enemy, the same sort of disorderly conduct in the camps, the only difference being that Bolanus, himself an upright man and not hated for any misdeeds, had contrived to win popularity as a substitute for authority.

17. But when, together with the rest of the world, Vespasian recovered Britain as well, there came great generals and outstanding armies, and the enemies' hope dwindled. Petilius Cerialis at once struck them with terror by attacking the state of the Brigantes, which is said to be the most populous in the whole province. There were many battles, some not without bloodshed; and he embraced a great part of the Brigantes within the range either of victory or of war. Cerialis, indeed, would have eclipsed the efforts of any other successor. Julius Frontinus, a great man, in so far as it was then possible to be great, took up and sustained the burden; and he subjugated the strong and warlike people of the Silures, overcoming not merely the courage of the enemy but the difficulties of the terrain.

Agricola's Governorship of Britain

18. Such was the situation of Britain and these the vicissitudes of war that Agricola found when he crossed over, it being already midsummer. The soldiers, on the assumption that there would be no campaigning, were turning their thoughts to relaxation; the enemy, by the same token, were turning theirs to seizing the opportunity. The state of the Ordovices, not long before his arrival, had virtually wiped out a cavalry regiment operating in its territory and this initial stroke had excited the province. Those who wanted war welcomed the lead and were waiting to test the temper of the new legate. The summer was over, the army units dispersed throughout the province, and the troops had taken it for granted that there would be no fighting that year; in fact the season was late and unfavourable for one intending to launch a war, and many thought it preferable simply to garrison the suspected districts.

But Agricola decided to go out and meet the threat. He concentrated the legionary detachments and a modest force of *auxilia* and, as the Ordovices did not venture to come down into the plain, led his men up into the hills, himself at the head of the column so as to impart his own courage to the rest by sharing the danger. Almost the entire people was cut to pieces.

Well aware that he had to build on this prestige and that the outcome of his first operations would determine how much fear his later actions would inspire, he took the decision to reduce the island of Mona. I have previously recorded how Paulinus had been recalled from occupying it by the rebellion of the whole of Britain. But, as happens in enterprises undertaken at short notice, there were no ships available. However, the general's resource and resolution got the troops across. Auxiliaries, specially selected from those who knew the fords and whose national practice was to swim while carrying their weapons and controlling their horses, were told to discard all their equipment. Then he launched them into attack so suddenly that the enemy were dumbfounded. They had been expecting ships and an attack by sea; now they believed that for men who came to war in this way nothing was difficult or insuperable.

So, after they had petitioned for peace and surrendered the island, Agricola was now regarded as a famous and a great man: on his entry into the province, a period which others spend in pageantry and soliciting attention, he had preferred toil and danger. Agricola did not exploit his success to glorify himself but described his campaign and victory as 'keeping a conquered people under control'. He did not even use laurel-wreathed dispatches to report on his actions. But the very fact that he disguised his fame actually made him more famous. People gauged his hopes for the future by his reticence about such great deeds.

19. None the less, he was aware of the feelings of the province, and at the same time he had learned from the experience of others that force achieves little if followed by undue harshness. He determined to root out the causes of the war. Beginning with himself and his staff, he first enforced discipline on his own household, a

task which many find no less difficult than governing a province.
He made no use of freedmen or slaves for official business. He was
not influenced by personal likings or by recommendations or peti-
tions when choosing centurions or soldiers for staff appointments.
He reckoned that the best men would prove the most trustworthy.
He knew everything that went on, but did not always inflict punishment: he condoned minor offences, major ones he dealt with
strictly. He did not always impose a penalty, but was often content
to accept an expression of remorse. He preferred to appoint to staff
and administrative posts men who would not transgress rather
than to have to punish those who had transgressed.

He alleviated the levying of corn and taxes by distributing
the burden fairly, cutting out the devices for profit which were
more bitterly resented than the tax itself. It turned out that people
were being forced to go through the charade of waiting outside
locked grain-depots and, what is more, had to buy the corn and pay
a high price for it. Roundabout routes and far distant regions were
being prescribed, in such a way that communities had to deliver
their consignments not to the nearest permanent forts but to
remote and inaccessible places. The result was that a service which
should have been easy for all was becoming a source of profit for a
few men.   20. By clamping down on these abuses at once in his
first year, he gave peace a good name: it had been feared no less than
war through either the negligence or the arrogance of previous
governors.

But when summer came, he concentrated the army, and was present everywhere on the march, praising discipline and keeping
stragglers up to the mark. He chose the sites for pitching camp
himself and reconnoitred estuaries and forests personally. And all
the while he gave the enemy no rest, by launching sudden plundering raids. When he had done enough to inspire fear, by acting with
clemency he showed them, as a contrast, the attractions of peace.
As a result, many states which up to that moment had operated
on equal terms abandoned violence and gave hostages. They were
also surrounded by garrisons and forts, with such skill and thor-
oughness that no new part of Britain ever came over with so little
damage.

21. The following winter was taken up by measures of a most beneficial kind. His intention was, in fact, that people who lived in widely dispersed and primitive settlements and hence were naturally inclined to war should become accustomed to peace and quiet by the provision of amenities. Hence he gave encouragement to individuals and assistance to communities to build temples, market-places, and town houses. He praised those that responded promptly and censured the dilatory. As a result they began to compete with one another for his approval, instead of having to be compelled. Further, he educated the sons of the leading men in the liberal arts and he rated the natural talents of the Britons above the trained skills of the Gauls.

The result was that those who just lately had been rejecting the Roman tongue now conceived a desire for eloquence. Thus even our style of dress came into favour and the toga was everywhere to be seen. Gradually, too, they went astray into the allurements of evil ways, colonnades and warm baths and elegant banquets. The Britons, who had had no experience of this, called it 'civilization', although it was a part of their enslavement.

22. The third year of campaigns opened up new peoples with the ravaging of the territories up to the Taus [Tay] (that is the name of the estuary). This action so intimidated the enemy that they did not dare to challenge the army, although it was harassed by wild storms. There was even time to spare for establishing forts. Experts commented that no other general selected suitable sites more wisely. No fort established by Agricola was ever taken by the enemy by storm or abandoned either by capitulation or by flight. In fact, they could make frequent sallies, for they were assured against long sieges by supplies to last for a year. Hence winter there had no terrors; the garrisons were self-sufficient. The enemy were baffled and in despair, because they had been used to making good the summer's losses by successes in winter and now they were under pressure in summer and winter alike.

Agricola was never greedy to steal the credit for others' achievements. Whether centurion or prefect, each had in him an honest witness to his deeds. According to some accounts he was rather harsh in delivering reprimands. He was courteous to good men, but

equally he could be unpleasant towards those who behaved badly. But his anger left no hidden traces, so that you did not need to fear his silence: he thought it more honourable to give offence than to harbour hatred.

23. The fourth summer was spent in securing what he had over-run. And, if the spirit of the army and the glory of the Roman name had permitted it, a frontier had been found within Britain itself. For the Firths of Clota [Clyde] and Bodotria [Forth], carried far inland by the tides of opposite seas, are separated by a narrow neck of land. This was now being securely held by garrisons and the whole sweep of country on the nearer side was secured: the enemy had been pushed back, as if into a different island.

24. In the fifth year of the campaigns he crossed in the leading ship and defeated peoples up to that time unknown in a series of successful actions. He lined up his forces in that part of Britain that faces Ireland, an expression of hope rather than of fear. For, in fact, Ireland, which lies midway between Britain and Spain, and is also within easy reach of the Gallic Sea, would have united the strongest parts of the empire with great mutual advantage. Its size, if compared to that of Britain, is small, but it is larger than the islands in our sea. Its soil and climate and the character and way of life of the people do not differ greatly from Britain. The routes of approach and the harbours are known through trade and mer-chants. Agricola had given refuge to one of the minor kings from this people, who had been expelled in a family quarrel. He treated him like a friend, keeping him in case an opportunity arose. I have often heard him say that Ireland could be conquered and held with a single legion and modest numbers of *auxilia*. That would, he thought, be advantageous against Britain as well, if Roman arms were everywhere and freedom were, so to speak, removed from sight.

25. To resume the story, in the summer in which he began his sixth year in post, he enveloped the states situated beyond the Bodotria. Because there were fears that all the peoples on the fur-ther side might rise and the land routes be threatened by an enemy army, Agricola reconnoitred the harbours with the fleet. It had been brought in by Agricola for the first time to form part of his

forces and was making an excellent impression as it followed along: the war was being pushed forward simultaneously by land and sea. Men from the infantry, cavalry, and navy were often in the same camp, sharing supplies and high spirits. Each stressed their own exploits and their own dangers: as they boasted, in the way soldiers do, the ravines in the forests and mountains were compared with the dangers of storm and tide, victories on land against the enemy with the conquest of the Ocean.

Besides this, the Britons, as was learned from prisoners, were dumbfounded at the sight of the fleet, as though, now that the secret places of their own sea had been opened up, the last refuge for the vanquished was closed. The peoples who inhabit Caledonia turned to armed struggle. Their preparations were on a large scale, exaggerated, as the unknown usually is, by rumour. Further, by attacking some forts, they had added to the alarm, as if they were throwing out a challenge. There were cowards, posing as men of prudence, who began to urge withdrawal to this side of the Bodotria and that it was better to retire rather than be driven back. Meanwhile he learned that the enemy were about to attack in several columns. To avoid encirclement by superior forces familiar with the country, he himself divided his army into three divisions and advanced.

26. When the enemy discovered this, with a rapid change of plan they massed for a night attack on the Ninth Legion, as being by far the weakest in numbers. They cut down the sentries and burst into the sleeping camp, creating panic. Fighting was already going on inside the camp itself when Agricola, who had learned of the enemy's route from his scouts and was following close on their tracks, ordered the most mobile of his cavalry and infantry to charge the combatants from the rear and then the whole army was to raise the battle-cry. At first light the standards gleamed. The Britons were terrified at being caught between two fires, while the men of the Ninth regained their spirits and now that their lives were safe began to fight for glory. They even ventured on a break out and a fierce battle followed in the narrow passage of the gates. Finally the enemy were driven back before the rival efforts of two armies. The one wanted to show that it had come to the rescue, the

other that it had not needed help. Had not marshes or forests covered the retreating enemy, that victory would have ended the war.

27. Consciousness of this success, or the report of it, emboldened the army. 'Nothing can stand in the way of courage,' they roared, 'we must go deep into Caledonia, and, fighting battle after battle, we must find the furthest limit to Britain at last.' Even those who had just before been cautious and prudent were now, after the event, keen and boastful. This is the unfairest aspect of warfare: all claim for themselves the credit for success, failure is blamed on a single man.

The Britons, however, reckoned that they had not been defeated by superior courage but by the opportune actions and skill of the general. They lost none of their haughty spirit, in fact they armed their young men, moved their wives and children to places of safety, and ratified the alliance between their states by meetings and sacrifices. Thus spirits on both sides were stirred up as they parted.

28. That same summer a cohort of Usipi that had been conscripted in the Germanies and sent across to Britain ventured to carry out a major crime, which deserves to be set on record. They murdered a centurion and some soldiers, who had been incorporated in their ranks to inculcate discipline by showing an example and were treated as instructors. Then they boarded three small warships, dragging the pilots with them by force. One operated the steering-oar, the other two fell under suspicion and were killed. The news had not yet spread and they began sailing past like an apparition. Then, when they had landed to seize water and supplies, they came into conflict with groups of Britons, who tried to defend their property. Though often successful, they were in the end driven back and hence were reduced to such extremity of hunger that first they ate the weakest in their own number and then victims chosen by lot. In this way they sailed round Britain and after losing their ships through lack of navigational skill were taken for pirates and captured, first by the Suebi, then by the Frisii. Some were sold into slavery and passed from one owner to another until they finally reached our bank of the river and won notoriety by the story of this remarkable adventure.

The Battle of the Graupian Mountain

29. At the start of the next summer Agricola suffered a family blow by losing a son that had been born the previous year. He bore this misfortune without the show of endurance many brave men put on, but, again, not with the loud expressions of grief that belong to women either. Besides this, the war provided relief from his sorrow.

Accordingly, he sent the fleet ahead to plunder at various points in order to spread general panic and uncertainty. The army was marching light, reinforced by the bravest of the Britons and those whose loyalty had been tested in a long period of peace. So he came to the Graupian Mountain. It had already been occupied by the enemy.

The Britons were, in fact, in no way broken by the outcome of the previous battle: they were awaiting either revenge or enslavement. They had at last learned the lesson that a common danger could only be warded off by a united front. By means of embassies and alliances they had rallied the forces of all their states. Already more than thirty thousand armed men could be observed and still all the young men and famous warriors, whose 'old age was still fresh and green', each man wearing the decorations he had won, were flowing in. Now one outstanding among their many leaders for his valour and nobility, Calgacus by name, faced the assembled multitude as they clamoured for battle. He is reported to have spoken in words like these:

30. 'Whenever I consider the causes of the war and our desperate position, I have great confidence that today, the day on which you are of one mind, will mark the beginning of freedom for the whole of Britain. For all of you have united together, and you have not tasted servitude. There is no land beyond us and even the sea is no safe refuge when we are threatened by the Roman fleet. Thus battle and arms, which brave men honour, are the safest recourse even for cowards. Battles have been fought against the Romans before, with varying success. But our forces were the Britons' hope and their reserve, for we, the noblest in all Britain, who dwell in her innermost sanctuary and do not look across at any subject shores,

had been keeping even our eyes free from the defilement of tyranny. We are the last people on earth, and the last to be free: our very remoteness in a land known only to rumour has protected us up till this day. Today the furthest bounds of Britain lie open—and everything unknown is given an inflated worth. But now there is no people beyond us, nothing but tides and rocks and, more deadly than these, the Romans.

'It is no use trying to escape their arrogance by submission or good behaviour. They have pillaged the world: when the land has nothing left for men who ravage everything, they scour the sea. If an enemy is rich, they are greedy, if he is poor, they crave glory. Neither East nor West can sate their appetite. They are the only people on earth to covet wealth and poverty with equal craving. They plunder, they butcher, they ravish, and call it by the lying name of "empire". They make a desert and call it "peace".

31. 'Nature has willed it that each man should love best his children and his own kin. These are now being torn away by conscription to be slaves in another land. Wives and sisters, even if they escape being raped by Romans as enemies, are seduced by men posing as friends and guests. Goods and possessions are consumed by taxation, the fields and their harvests by the grain-requisition, men's very bodies and hands by building roads through forests and marshes, under the lash and subject to insults. Those born to be slaves are sold once and for all and, what is more, are fed by their masters. Britain pays for its own enslavement every day, feeds its masters every day. In a private household the latest newcomer among the slaves is the object of derision even to his fellow slaves. So too, in this slave-household, to which the whole world has long belonged, we are the new ones, the cheap ones, who are picked out to be destroyed. For we have neither fertile lands nor mines nor harbours in which we might be kept to work. Besides, courage and an untamed spirit in its subjects are not welcome to the imperial power. Even our remoteness and our very seclusion, while they have kept us safer, have also made us more suspect.

'Abandon then, any hope of mercy, take courage at last, whether it is life or glory which you hold most dear. The Brigantes, with a

woman as their leader, set a *colonia* in flames and stormed a fortress. If their success had not made them careless, they could have thrown off the yoke. We, who are still unimpaired and unconquered, will be going to war to defend our freedom, not to regain it after second thoughts. Let us show straightaway in this first encounter what manner of men Caledonia has kept in reserve. 32. Or do you believe that the Romans' bravery in war matches their licence in peace? It is by our quarrels and disunion that they have gained fame. They have exploited the faults of their enemies to win glory for their own army. That army has been put together from peoples that are very different from one another. Success has kept it together, but it will fall apart in defeat. Or can you really suppose that Gauls and Germans and—it is shameful to mention them—many Britons too are bound by loyalty and goodwill? They may be lending their lifeblood to a foreign tyranny, but they have been enemies for longer than they have been slaves. Terror and intimidation are no strong bonds of affection. When you break these bonds, fear will end and hatred begin. Everything that can inspire to victory is on our side.

'The Romans have no wives there to fire them, no parents to taunt them if they flee. Most of them have no home country, or an alien one. They are few in number, scared and bewildered, staring round at the sky itself and the sea and the forests, all strange to them—they are in a way like men imprisoned and chained, and the gods have delivered them into our hands. Do not let their outward show alarm you, it means nothing, the gleam of gold and silver that can neither shield them nor wound us. Even in the enemy lines we shall find forces of our own. The Britons will recognize our cause as their own, the Gauls will remember their lost liberty, the rest of the Germans will desert them exactly as the Usipi have just done. There is nothing beyond them to fear: just empty forts, *coloniae* of old men, towns sick and disunited between unwilling subjects and unjust rulers. Here is your general, here is your army; on the other side, taxes, mines, and the other punishments imposed on slaves. Whether we endure these for ever or take quick vengeance will be decided on this field. On then into battle and as you go think both of your ancestors and of your descendants.'

33. They reacted to the speech with enthusiasm, expressed in the barbarian fashion with roaring, singing, and inarticulate cries. Now columns of men began to move and arms flashed as the boldest darted before the ranks. The battle-line was already being drawn up when Agricola, thinking that the soldiers, although cheerful and scarcely kept back within their defences, needed to be encouraged still further, addressed them as follows:

'Fellow soldiers, it is now the seventh year that, thanks to your bravery, under the auspices of the Roman empire, together with my own loyal service, you have been conquering Britain. In so many campaigns, in so many battles, whether courage against the enemy or endurance in the face of Nature herself was needed, I have had no complaint to make of my men nor you of your general. Thus I have gone beyond the limits reached by former legates and you have exceeded those reached by previous armies. The furthest point of Britain is no longer a matter of report or rumour: we hold it, with forts and with arms. Britain has been discovered and subjugated.

'Many a time on the march, when marshes or mountains and rivers were wearing you out, I have heard the bravest among you exclaim: "When will we get at the enemy? When shall we have a battle?" They are coming, we have dug them out from their lairs, and your prayers and your courage have a fair field. Everything is in our favour if we win. But in case of defeat the same conditions would be against us. To have accomplished such a long march, to have passed through forests, to have crossed estuaries, on our forward advance, all this redounds to our credit and our renown. But in retreat today's success could become most dangerous, for we lack their knowledge of the country and their abundant supplies. But we have our own hands and weapons and everything depends on them. As for myself, I long ago decided that neither an army nor a general can safely turn their backs. Hence, while an honourable death is preferable to a life of dishonour, safety and honour go together. And it would not be inglorious to die at the very place where the world and nature end.

34. 'If these had been new peoples, and an unknown force stood

to face you, I would quote the example of other armies to encourage you. Instead, just think back on your own battle-honours, simply question your own eyes. These are the men who last year attacked one legion like thieves in the night—and you defeated them by raising the battle-cry. They are the greatest runaways of all the Britons and that is why they have survived so long. When we were plunging into the forests and gorges just now, all the bravest wild animals charged against us, the timid and slothful ones were driven back by the mere sound of our march. So too now: all the bravest Britons have fallen long since, what is left is a band of frightened cowards. You have found them at last. They have not made a stand, they have been trapped. Their extremity and their deadly fear have paralysed them on the ground on which they stand, ground on which you may win a great and memorable victory. Have done with campaigning; crown forty years with one great day and prove to the Commonwealth that her army was never to blame for wars dragging on or for causing rebellions.'

35. Even while Agricola was still speaking, the eagerness of the soldiers was apparent and a tremendous outburst of enthusiasm greeted the end of his speech. At once they ran to take up their arms. While they were inspired and eager to charge, he deployed them in battle-line. Of the auxiliaries, he put the infantry, which numbered eight thousand, in the centre, with the three thousand cavalry spread out on the flanks. The legions were stationed in front of the rampart: victory in a battle where no Roman blood was shed would be a tremendous honour; if the *auxilia* were driven back, the legions were a reserve.

The Britons' line was posted on the heights, both to make a show and to intimidate: their front ranks were on the flat ground, the remainder were packed together on the slopes of the hill, rising up as it were in tiers. The charioteers filled the middle of the plain, making a din as they rode back and forth. At this point, Agricola was anxious, in view of the enemy's superior numbers, that they might attack his front and flanks simultaneously, so he opened out his ranks. Although the line was going to be rather extended and many were urging him to bring up the legions, he was always ready

to hope for the best and resolute in the face of difficulties. So he sent away his horse and took up his position on foot in front of the colours.

36. The battle opened with fighting at long range: the Britons not only stood firm but displayed skill in parrying the javelins of our men with their massive swords or catching them on their short shields, while hurling a great rain of spears themselves. Then Agricola exhorted the four Batavian and two Tungrian cohorts to fight hand to hand at sword's point. This was what they had been trained for in their long service, whereas it was awkward for the enemy with their small shields and enormous swords—for the swords of the Britons, having no points, were unsuited for a cut-and-thrust struggle and close-quarters battle. So the Batavians rained blows indiscriminately, struck with their shield-bosses, and stabbed in the face. When they had cut down those posted on the plain, they started to push their battle-line up the hillsides. The other cohorts, in eager competition, pressed forward to attack, and cut down the nearest of the enemy. In the haste of victory a good many were left half-dead or untouched.

Meanwhile—for the charioteers had fled—the cavalry squadrons joined in the infantry battle. But though they had created panic by their first onslaught, they began to stick fast in the solid ranks of the enemy and the uneven ground. The battle bore little resemblance to a cavalry action: our men could hardly keep their footing and were at the same time jostled by the horses' flanks. Often, too, runaway chariots or terrified, riderless horses with nothing but fear to direct them careered into the ranks from the side or head on.

37. The Britons stationed on the hilltops had as yet taken no part in the battle, and, not being involved, were regarding our small numbers with contempt. Now they began gradually to descend and to work their way round the rear of the winning side. But Agricola, who had feared this very move, sent four regiments of cavalry, which had been reserved for the emergencies of battle, to block them as they came on. The more ferociously they charged, the more vigorously he drove them back and scattered them in flight.

Thus the Britons' tactics recoiled on themselves. The cavalry regiments, on the general's command, wheeled round from the front of the battle and charged the enemy in the rear. Now indeed a vast and grim spectacle unfolded on the open plains: the cavalry pursued, inflicted wounds, took captives, and, as fresh foes appeared, butchered their prisoners. On the enemy side each man behaved according to his own character: whole crowds of armed men turned tail before inferior numbers, but some unarmed individuals deliberately charged and exposed themselves to certain death. Everywhere could be seen weapons, bodies, mangled limbs, and bloodstained earth. Sometimes even the vanquished displayed their fury and their courage. For when they reached the woods, they grouped together and, knowing the ground, began to ambush the first incautious pursuers. But Agricola was everywhere at once. He ordered strong light-armed cohorts to form a kind of huntsmen's cordon, part of the cavalry to dismount and scour the forest where the trees were dense, the remainder to range through the clearings—otherwise, over-confidence might have led to serious casualties. As it was, when the enemy saw their pursuers coming forward again in good order with closed ranks, they turned to flight. They did not keep in column of march, as before, each waiting for the other, but scattered, avoiding each other, and headed for distant and inaccessible retreats.

Nightfall brought an end to the pursuit—and our men had had enough. Some ten thousand of the enemy had been killed; on our side three hundred and sixty fell, among them Aulus Atticus, prefect of a cohort, whose youthful eagerness and spirited horse had carried him into the enemy's ranks.   38. Of course, the night was a cheerful one, with delight at the outcome and the booty, for the victors. The Britons dispersed, men and women mingling their cries of grief, dragging off the wounded, calling out to survivors, abandoning their homes and in their rage even setting fire to them, choosing hiding-places, and leaving them again at once. They met to make some sort of joint plan, then split up again. Sometimes the sight of their loved ones made them break down, more often it roused them to fury. There was good evidence that some of them laid violent hands on their wives and children, as though in pity.

At dawn next day the scale of the victory was more apparent: the silence of desolation on all sides, the hills lonely, homesteads smouldering in the distance, not a man to encounter the scouts. They were sent out in every direction and reported that the fugitives' tracks were random and that the enemy were not massing at any point. As the summer was already over and the war could not be extended further, he led the army down into the territory of the Boresti. There he took hostages and instructed the prefect of the fleet to sail round Britain: forces were allocated for the purpose, and panic had gone before. He himself, marching unhurriedly, to intimidate new peoples by the very delay with which he traversed their territory, settled the infantry and cavalry in winter quarters. At the same time the fleet, with a favourable wind and reputation behind it, occupied the Trucculensian harbour, from which it had set out to coast along the adjacent shore of Britain, and to which it had now returned intact.

Agricola's Recall

39. Agricola's dispatches on this course of events, although not exaggerated by boastful language of any kind, produced a characteristic reaction on the part of Domitian: his expression was one of delight, but in his heart he was uneasy. He was well aware that his recent sham triumph over Germany had aroused ridicule—slaves had been purchased in the market, who could, with suitable clothing and their hair treated, be made to look like prisoners of war. But now he saw a genuine and great victory, with so many thousand enemy dead, winning unrestrained praise from the public. What he dreaded most of all was for the name of a subject to be exalted above that of the emperor.

In vain had public eloquence and distinction in civilian professions been brought to silence if someone other than himself were to snatch military glory. Other talents could be more easily ignored; good generalship belonged to the emperor. Tormented by such anxieties, he brooded over his resentment in silence—and this was a sign of his sinister intentions—and decided it was best to store up his hatred for the present and wait for the first burst of popular

applause and the enthusiasm of the army to wane. For besides, Agricola still held Britain. **40.** Triumphal decorations, a public statue, and all the insignia that go with an honorary triumph were therefore decreed by the senate on the emperor's command, coupled with a flattering speech. Further, the impression was to be conveyed that the province of Syria was intended for Agricola, it being then vacant through the death of Atilius Rufus the consular and reserved for senior men. Many people believed that a freedman from one of the senior palace departments had been sent to Agricola, bearing an imperial letter of appointment to the Syrian command, under instructions to hand it to Agricola if he should still be in Britain. The freedman, it was said, met Agricola actually in the Channel crossing and, without even speaking to him, returned to Domitian. The story may be true, or it may be a fiction invented to suit the emperor's character. Agricola handed over to his successor a province peaceful and secure.

Agricola's Retirement and Last Years

So that his entry would not attract attention by crowds flocking to welcome him, he avoided the friends who wanted to pay their respects and came into the city by night, and by night also, just as he had been instructed, to the Palace. He was greeted with a perfunctory kiss and then dismissed without a word, into the crowd of courtiers.

From now on, to play down his military reputation, distasteful to civilians, he departed into the depths of calm retirement. His style of life was modest, he was courteous in conversation, with only one or two companions in public. As a result, most people, who always measure great men by their display, when they saw or noticed Agricola, asked why he was famous. A few understood. **41.** He was often accused in his absence before Domitian, but in his absence was found not guilty. The reason why he was under threat was not any actual charge or a complaint from someone that he had been harmed, but simply the emperor's hostility to merit, the man's glory, and—the worst sort of enemy—those who sang his praises.

Indeed, in those years that ensued for the Commonwealth, Agricola could not be passed over in silence. So many armies had been lost, in Moesia and Dacia, in Germany and Pannonia, by the folly or cowardice of their generals, so many military men, with so many cohorts, had been defeated in battle and taken prisoner. It was no longer the frontier of the empire and the river-bank that were in question, but the permanent fortresses of the legions and Roman territory. So, with loss following on loss and every year marked by funerals and disasters, public opinion began to demand Agricola as general. Everyone contrasted his energy, resolution, and proven courage in war with the inaction and timidity of others. There is evidence that Domitian's own ears were stung by the lash of such talk. In this the best of his freedmen were motivated by loyalty and affection, the worst, out of malice and jealousy, worked on the feelings of the emperor, who always inclined to take the worse advice. Thus, alike because of his own virtues and because of the failings of others, Agricola was being driven to the precipice of glory.

42. The year had now come round for him to ballot for the proconsulship of Africa or Asia. The recent murder of Civica was both a warning for Agricola and for Domitian a precedent. Certain men privy to the emperor's thinking approached Agricola and asked of their own accord whether he was going to go to a province. At first just dropping hints, they praised the life of quiet retirement. Then they offered their help in supporting a request to decline. Finally, throwing off the mask, using persuasion and threats at the same time, they dragged him before Domitian. The latter had prepared his hypocrite's part, put on a majestic air, listened to the plea to be excused, and, after consenting, was graciously pleased to accept thanks for conferring a favour, without a blush for its invidious nature. However, he did not give Agricola the proconsular salary that is usually offered and that he had himself granted in some cases. It may be that he was offended that it was not requested, or perhaps he was ashamed to appear to have paid out money for something that he had forbidden.

It is part of human character to hate someone you have hurt. In fact, Domitian was by nature a man who plunged into violence and the more he concealed his feelings the more implacable he was.

However, he was mollified by the self-restraint and good sense of Agricola, who was not one to court renown and ruin by defiance and an empty parade of freedom. Those whose habit is to admire what is forbidden ought to know that there can be great men even under bad emperors, and that duty and discretion, if coupled with energy and a career of action, will bring a man to no less glorious summits than are attained by perilous paths and ostentatious deaths that do not benefit the Commonwealth.

43. The end of his life was a source of grief for us and sad for his friends. Even outsiders and strangers were affected. The common people, too, and the population of the city, usually otherwise occupied, kept coming to his house and talked about him in the market-places and at social gatherings. No one when they heard of Agricola's death was glad and no one immediately forgot it. The sympathy that was felt was increased by the persistent rumour that he had been poisoned. I would not venture to assert that we have any definite evidence. All the same, all through his last illness there were more visits from leading freedmen and court physicians than is usual with emperors who pay their visits by proxy, whether that meant anxiety or espionage. In fact, on the last day, as he was dying, it was known that the critical stages were being reported on by relays of messengers. No one believed that news that the emperor would have been sad to hear would have been speeded up like this. However, he did put on an outward show of grief in his manner and expression. He was relieved of the need for hatred, and he was one who could hide joy more easily than fear. It was no secret that when Agricola's will was read out, in which he named Domitian as joint heir with his excellent wife and most dutiful daughter, the emperor was delighted, taking it as a deliberate compliment. His mind was so blinded and corrupted by incessant flattery that he did not understand that a good father would only make a bad emperor his heir.

Epilogue

44. Agricola was born on the Ides of June in the year when Gaius Caesar was consul for the third time [13 June AD 40]. He died in his

fifty-fourth year, on the tenth day before the Kalends of September, when the consuls were Collega and Priscinus [23 August 93]. Should posterity wish to know something of his personal appearance too, he was a good-looking, if not particularly tall man. There was no trace of aggressiveness in his features, kindliness abounded in his expression. You would readily believe him a good man, and be glad to think him a great one. He himself, although, to be sure, in his middle years, in the prime of life, when he was snatched from us, in terms of glory had completed the longest of spans. For he had attained to the full those true blessings which depend on a man's own virtues. He had been consul and had been awarded the triumphal insignia: what more could fortune have added? He did not enjoy excessive wealth, though he had a handsome fortune. His daughter and wife survived him, and he can even be regarded as fortunate, his rank unimpaired, at the height of his fame, his family and friends secure, to have escaped what was to come.

He was, it is true, not permitted to live to see the dawn of this most fortunate age and Trajan's principate, which he used to predict, observing the signs and praying for their fulfilment, in our hearing. Yet he took with him effective compensation for his premature death. He had missed that final period, when Domitian, no longer at intervals and with breathing-spaces, but in a continuous and as it were single onslaught drained the blood of the Commonwealth.   45. Agricola did not live to see the senate-house under siege, the senate hedged in by armed men, the killing of so many consulars in that same act of butchery, so many most noble women forced into exile or flight. A single victory was all that Carus Mettius as yet had to his credit, it was still only inside the Alban citadel that Messalinus was rasping out his vote, and Massa Baebius was still a defendant. But soon we ourselves led Helvidius to prison, the faces of Mauricus and Rusticus put us to shame, we were stained by Senecio's innocent blood. Nero at least averted his gaze: he ordered crimes to be committed but did not look on. A special torment under Domitian was to see him watching us, our very sighs being noted down against us, and all the while that savage gaze was able to mark down so many who had turned pale

with shock, that flushed face that saved him from blushing with shame.

You were indeed blessed, Agricola, not only in the brilliance of your life, but because of the moment of your death. Those who were present to hear your last words tell us that you met your fate with a cheerful courage. You seemed to be doing your best, as far as a man could, to acquit the emperor of guilt for your death. But for myself and for your daughter the pain of losing a father is increased by grief that we could not sit by your sick-bed, sustain your failing strength, sate our sorrow with a last look and last embrace. We should certainly have caught from your lips some instructions, some words to engrave for ever in our hearts. This is our special sorrow, this is what specially hurts us, that through the circumstance of our long absence he was lost to us four years earlier. Everything, there is no doubt, dearest of fathers, was done in abundance, by the devoted wife at your side, to honour you. Yet too few tears were shed as you were laid out; and there was something more that your eyes, in their final glimpse of light, had longed for.

46. If there is a place for the spirits of the just, if, as philosophers believe, great souls do not perish with the body, may you rest in peace. May you call us, your family, from feeble regrets and the weeping that belongs to women to contemplate your noble character, for which it is a sin either to mourn or to shed tears. May we rather honour you by our admiration and our undying praise and, if our powers permit, by following your example. That is the true respect, the true duty, of each of us closest to you. That is what I would enjoin on his daughter and his wife, that they revere the memory of a father and a husband by continually pondering his deeds and his words in their hearts, and by embracing the form and features of his soul rather than of his body.

Not that I would think of banning any statues in marble or bronze. But images of the human face, like that face itself, are weak and perishable. The beauty of the soul lives for ever, and you can preserve and express that beauty, not by the material and artistry of another, but only in your own character. All that we have loved in Agricola, all that we have admired in him, abides and is destined to

abide in human hearts through the endless procession of the ages, by the fame of his deeds. Many of the men of old will be buried in oblivion, inglorious and unknown. Agricola's story has been told for posterity and he will survive.

GERMANY

THE ORIGIN AND LAND OF THE GERMANS

I. GENERAL CHARACTERISTICS OF THE LAND AND ITS PEOPLE

The Boundaries of Germany

1. Germany as a whole is separated from the Gauls, Raetians, and Pannonians by the Rhine and Danube rivers, from the Sarmatians and Dacians by mutual fear or by mountains. The Ocean, embracing wide peninsulas and islands, measureless expanses, flows round the remainder. It is only recently that certain peoples and kings have become known: war has opened them up. The Rhine rises in a remote and precipitous peak of the Raetian Alps and then turns slightly westward to flow into the northern Ocean. The Danube, issuing from a gentle and gradually rising slope of Mount Abnoba [the Black Forest], passes more peoples in its course, until it breaks out into the Pontic [Black] Sea through six channels; a seventh is lost in the marshes.

The Origins and Name of the Germans

2. The Germans themselves are the original inhabitants of the country, so I incline to believe, and have very little foreign blood from admixture through invasions by other peoples or through friendly dealings with them. For in former times those who sought new homes travelled not by land but on ship, and the Ocean, which stretches beyond them without limit and so to speak lies on the other side, is seldom visited by ships from our world. In any case, apart from the danger of the wild and unknown sea, who would have left Asia, Africa, or Italy to make for Germany, with its unattractive landscape and raw climate, harsh to cultivate or even to look at—unless it were his home country?

In the ancient songs, which are their only form of record and are a kind of chronicle, they celebrate Tuisto, an earth-born god. To him they attribute a son, Mannus, the forefather and founder of their people, and to Mannus three sons, after whom were named the Ingvaeones, nearest to the Ocean, the Herminones in the interior, and the remainder Istvaeones. Remote antiquity gives free range to conjecture: some assert that the god had further offspring and that there are further peoples, called Marsi, Gambrivii, Suebi, and Vandili, and that these are the genuine and ancient names. Further, the name 'Germania' is said to be a new and recent application: it was because the ones who first crossed the Rhine and expelled the Gauls, and are now called Tungri, were called Germani at that time. Thus, it is said, what was the name of a people, not of the whole nation, gradually acquired a wider usage: the conqueror, through fear, applied it to them all, and in due course, once they had got to know the name, they all called themselves Germani.

3. It is said that Hercules visited them as well. In fact they sing of him as the foremost of all heroes when about to go into battle. Further, they too have those songs, which they call *baritus*, the recital of which stirs up their courage, and they forecast the outcome of the coming battle from the chanting alone. For they either terrify the enemy or become frightened themselves according to how it sounds in the ranks. What they listen to is not so much the words, but rather the sound of unison as an expression of fighting spirit. By putting their shields in front of their mouths so that their voices swell fuller and deeper as they echo back, they aim principally to achieve a harsh tone and a muffled roaring noise. At all events, some believe that Ulysses, in those long and legendary wanderings of his, also sailed to this part of the Ocean and visited the lands of Germany, and that Asciburgium, situated on the bank of the Rhine and inhabited to this day, was founded by him and named *Askipurgion*. At any rate, an altar dedicated by Ulysses, also inscribed with the name of his father Laertes, is supposed to have been found at this same place long ago; and monuments and funerary barrows with inscriptions in Greek lettering are said still to

exist on the borders of Germany and Raetia. It is not my intention either to argue in support of, or to refute, these assertions: according to their own inclination, each may either disbelieve or accept them.

4. I myself accept the view of those who judge that the peoples of Germany have never been contaminated by intermarriage with other nations and that the race remains unique, pure, and unlike any other. As a result, their physical appearance too, if one may generalize about so large a population, is always the same: fierce blue eyes, red hair, and large bodies. Their bodies, however, are strong only for a violent outburst. These same large frames cannot last out for work and effort, and can scarcely tolerate thirst or heat, although their climate has made them accustomed to cold and their poor soil to hunger.

The Country and its Natural Resources

5. The land may vary a certain amount in its appearance, but in general it either bristles with forests or festers with marshes. It is wetter on the side facing the Gauls, windier opposite Noricum and Pannonia. It is fertile for sown crops but will not grow fruit-trees. It is rich in livestock, but these are mostly undersized. Even on their foreheads the cattle lack their proper distinction and glory. The people take pride in their quantity, for cattle are their sole, greatly prized wealth.

Silver and gold have been denied them by the gods, whether as a sign of favour or of anger I cannot say. Yet I would not claim that no veins of silver and gold exist in Germany. After all, who has searched for them? They lack the necessary interest in their possession or use. One can see among them silver vessels given as presents to their envoys or chiefs which are put to the same use as earthenware ones. All the same, those who live nearest to us recognize the value of gold and silver for trade, and know and pick out particular types among our coinage. The peoples of the interior, being simpler and more old-fashioned, use barter. They approve of the old and long-familiar coins, the ones with notched

edges or stamped with two-horse chariots. They also prefer silver to gold, not because of any special liking for it, but because the value of silver money is more convenient for buying cheap everyday goods.

Arms and Military Tactics

6. Even iron is not plentiful, as is inferred from the way they are armed. Only a few use swords or large lances. They carry spears, or as they call them in their own language, *frameae*, with a short and narrow iron point, which are, however, so sharp and easy to handle that they fight with the same weapon at close quarters or long range, as required. Even their horsemen are content with just shield and spear. The infantry also hurl javelins, of which each man has several, and they throw them a vast distance. They are either naked or lightly clad in short cloaks. Their weapons have no ostentatious decoration—only the shields are marked out in very bright colours. A few have a breastplate, one or two at most a metal helmet or leather cap. Their horses are remarkable neither for beauty nor for speed and are not trained, as ours are, to execute various turns. They ride them straight ahead or with just a single wheel to the right, keeping their line together in such a way that no one falls behind.

Generally speaking, their strength lies more in their infantry. That is why they fight in mixed formations. The speed of the foot soldiers, picked out of the whole body of young men and placed in the front of the battle-line, is such that they can easily keep up with a cavalry encounter. The number of these picked men is also fixed: there are one hundred from each district, and that is exactly what they are called among their own people—thus what was originally just a number has now become a name of distinction as well. The battle-line is made up of wedges. To give ground, providing that you return to the attack, is considered prudent rather than cowardly. They recover the bodies of their own fallen even in unsuccessful battles. To leave one's shield behind is the supreme disgrace, and the dishonoured loses the right to attend religious ceremonies or to enter the assembly. Many such survivors

from the wars have put an end to their shame by hanging themselves.

7. Their kings they choose for their noble birth, their army commanders for their valour. Even the kings do not have absolute or unrestricted power, and their commanders lead by example rather than by issuing orders, gaining respect if they are energetic, if they stand out, if they are at the front of the line. Executions, imprisonment, even floggings, are allowed to no one other than the priests, and are not carried out as a punishment or on the orders of the commander, but as it were at the behest of the deity whom they believe to be present as they wage war. They actually bring with them into battle certain images and symbols taken from the sacred groves.

It is a particular incitement to valour that their squadrons and wedges are not formed at random or by chance mustering but are composed of families and kinship groups. They have their nearest and dearest close by, as well, so that they can hear the shrieks of their women and the crying of their children. For each man these are the most sacred witnesses, their praise is the most highly valued. It is to their mothers and their wives, who do not shrink from counting and examining their cuts, that they go with their wounds. They also bring food and words of encouragement to the men as they fight. 8. It is recorded that some armies that were already wavering and on the point of collapse have been rallied by women pleading steadfastly, blocking their path with bared breasts, and reminding their men how near they themselves are to being taken captive. This they fear by a long way more desperately for their women than for themselves. Indeed, peoples who are ordered to include girls of noble family among their hostages are thereby placed under a more effective restraint. They even believe that there is something holy and an element of the prophetic in women, hence they neither scorn their advice nor ignore their predictions. Under the Deified Vespasian we witnessed how Veleda was long regarded by many of them as a divine being; and in former times, too, they revered Albruna and a number of other women, not through servile flattery nor as if they had to make goddesses out of them.

9. Among the gods Mercury is the one they principally worship. They regard it as a religious duty to offer to him, on fixed days, human as well as other sacrificial victims. Hercules and Mars they appease by animal offerings of the permitted kind. Part of the Suebi sacrifice to Isis as well. I have little idea what the origin or explanation of this foreign cult is, except that the goddess's emblem, which resembles a light warship, indicates that the cult came in from abroad. In general, they judge it not to be in keeping with the majesty of heavenly beings to confine them within walls or to portray them in any human likeness. They consecrate woods and groves and they apply the names of gods to that mysterious presence which they see only with the eye of devotion.

10. They attach the highest importance to the taking of auspices and the casting of lots. Their usual procedure with the lot is simple. They cut off a branch from a nut-bearing tree and slice it into strips. These they mark with different signs and throw them at random onto a white cloth. Then the state's priest, if it is an official consultation, or the father of the family, in a private one, offers prayer to the gods and looking up towards heaven picks up three strips, one at a time, and, according to which sign they have previously been marked with, makes his interpretation. If the lots forbid an undertaking, there is no deliberation that day about the matter in question. If they allow it, further confirmation is required by taking the auspices. The widespread practice of seeking an answer from the call or flight of birds is, to be sure, known here too, but it is a speciality of this people to test horses as well for omens and warnings. The horses are maintained at public expense in the above-mentioned sacred woods and groves; they are pure white and undefiled by any kind of work for humans. They are yoked to a sacred chariot and the priest or king or chief of the state walks beside them, taking note of their whinnies and neighing. No kind of omen inspires greater confidence, not only among the common people but even among the nobles and priests, who regard themselves as but the servants of the gods, the horses as the gods' messengers. There is yet another kind of auspice-taking, used to

forecast the outcome of serious wars. They somehow take prisoner a man from the state with which they are at war and set him to fight a champion from their own side, each armed with his national weapons. The victory of one or the other is taken as determining the result in advance.

Form of Government

11. On minor matters only the chiefs decide, on major questions the whole community. But even cases where the decision lies with the commons are considered in advance by the chiefs. Except when there is some chance or sudden happening, they assemble on fixed days, either just before the new moon or just after the full moon. This they reckon to be the most auspicious starting-point for transacting business. Indeed, they do not reckon time by days, as we do, but by nights. All their decisions, all their agreements, are made in this way: night is seen as ushering in the day.

Their freedom of spirit involves a drawback, in that they do not assemble all at the same time or as if commanded, but take two or three days over it, hanging back. When the assembled crowd is ready, they take their seats, carrying arms. Silence is commanded by the priests, who have on these occasions the right to enforce obedience. Then the king or the chiefs are heard, in accordance with each one's age, nobility, military distinction, or eloquence. The power of persuasion counts for more than the right to give orders. If a proposal displeases them, they shout out their dissent. If they approve, they clash their spears. Showing approval with weapons is the most honourable way to express assent.

12. One may also bring in an accusation in the assembly, including a capital charge. The penalty varies according to the crime. Traitors and deserters are hanged on trees. Cowards, those who will not fight, and those who have defiled their bodies, are plunged into a boggy mire, with a wicker hurdle pressed on top of them. The difference in penalty is evidently according to the principle that, in general, crimes should be punished in public, to make an example of them, but that deeds of shame should be hidden away. There are also proportionate penalties for less serious offences.

Those convicted are fined a certain number of horses or cattle, of which part is paid to the king or the state, part to the victim of the crime or his relatives. In these assemblies they also elect the chiefs to administer justice in the districts and villages. Each is assisted by a hundred assessors chosen from the people, as an advisory body, and at the same time to increase his authority.

Admission to Citizenship and Enrolment in a Chief's Retinue

13. They transact no business, public or private, except under arms. But it is their practice that no one may bear arms until the community has recognized him as fit to use them. Then in the assembly itself either one of the chiefs or his own father or his kinsmen present the young man with shield and spear. These are their equivalent of our toga; this is the first distinction conferred in youth. Up to this time the young men are regarded as belonging to their family, from now on they are part of the commonwealth. Especially noble birth or great services rendered by their fathers can gain the approval of a chief even for boys in their teens. They are attached to others of maturer years and those who have been already approved, and there is no shame in being seen among the chief's companions. There are grades of rank, indeed, within the retinue, determined by the chief whom they follow. There is great competition between the followers to gain the highest place in the chief's estimation, and among the chiefs as to which one has the largest and bravest retinue. This is their form of prestige, this means power for them: to be continually surrounded by a large train of picked young warriors is in time of peace a distinction, in war a protection. And it is not only in their own states that the chiefs gain glory and renown if they excel others in the number and valour of their followers. They are courted by embassies and honoured with presents. Very often their reputation itself decides the outcome of wars.

14. When it comes to battle, it is a disgrace for a chief to be surpassed in bravery by his retinue, likewise for the retinue not to equal the bravery of their chief. And indeed it means lifelong infamy and shame to leave a battle alive when one's chief has fallen. To defend and protect him and to give him the credit for one's own deeds of

valour are the most solemn obligations of their oath of allegiance. The chiefs fight for victory, their followers for the chief.

If the country of their birth is stagnating in a long period of peace and inactivity, many noble youths deliberately seek out other states who are engaged in some war. For peace is unwelcome to this people and they can more easily win renown amid danger; and a large body of retainers cannot be kept together except by violence and war. They are always making demands on the generosity of their chief, asking for a coveted war-horse or a spear stained with the blood of victory. In fact, feasts, at which the fare is not elegant but at least plentiful, are counted as pay. The wherewithal for this open-handedness comes from war and booty. You cannot so easily persuade them to plough the soil or to wait for the harvest as to challenge an enemy and earn wounds as a reward. Indeed, they think it tame and spiritless to accumulate slowly by sweat what they can get quickly by losing some blood.

15. When they are not waging war they occupy a little of their time in hunting but a good deal more is spent without occupation: they devote themselves to sleeping and eating. The bravest and most warlike do nothing, as the care of the house, home, and fields is given over to the women and old men and to the weaklings in the family. They themselves merely lounge about, for, by a bizarre contradiction of character, the same people love idleness as much as they hate peace.

It is usual for the communities, man by man, to make voluntary gifts of cattle or crops to the chiefs. These are accepted as a token of honour but at the same time supply their needs. They particularly appreciate gifts from neighbouring peoples, which are sent not only by individuals but as official gestures: choice horses, massive weapons, embossed discs, and necklaces. They have now been taught to accept money as well—by us.

Housing and Settlement

16. It is well known that none of the German peoples live in cities and that they cannot even bear to live in adjoining houses. They dwell apart from one another, scattered about, wherever a spring, a plain, or a wood attracts them. They do not lay out their villages

in our style, with buildings joined and connected together. Each of them leaves an open space around his house, either as a protection against the risk of fire, or because they lack skill in building. They do not even use stones or bricks. They employ timber for all purposes, roughly cut, for they are not concerned to achieve a pleasant external appearance. Some parts, however, they smear quite carefully with clay that is so pure and shining that it resembles painting or coloured design. They also have the practice of digging underground caves and loading piles of manure on top of them, as a refuge in the winter and a storehouse for crops. Places like this mitigate the harshness of the cold weather—and, if an enemy comes, he ravages the open country, while the excavated hideouts are either not known about or escape detection because they have to be searched out.

Clothing

17. As clothing they all wear a cloak fastened with a brooch or failing that with a thorn. They spend whole days by the fireside wearing nothing else but this. The wealthiest are distinguished by a garment, which does not flow loosely, as with the Sarmatians and Parthians, but fits tightly and shows the shape of each limb. They also wear skins of wild animals—those nearest the river-bank with no regard to appearance, the more distant tribes in a more elaborate fashion, since they cannot acquire any finery through trade. They select the animals, strip off the hides, and decorate them with patches of fur from the beasts found in the outer Ocean and its unknown waters. The women's clothing is no different from the men's, except that they quite often wear linen garments, decorated with purple. They do not add sleeves to the upper part of the dress, so their arms are bare from shoulder to wrist—indeed, the adjoining parts of their breasts are also exposed.

Marriage and Social Customs

18. Nevertheless, the marriage code is strict there and there is no aspect of their morality that deserves higher praise. They are

almost the only barbarians who are content with a single wife, except for a very few, who are not motivated by sexual appetite—it is, rather, that they are courted with numerous offers of marriage on account of their noble rank. The dowry is not brought by the wife to the husband but by the husband to the wife. The parents and relatives are in attendance and approve the gifts—gifts which are not selected to please female fancy or to adorn the new bride, but oxen, a horse with bridle, and a shield with spear and sword. Such are the gifts with which a wife is gained, and she herself in turn brings her husband some weapons. This is what they regard as their most important bond of union, these are their mystic rites, their gods of wedlock. The woman must not think herself excluded from considerations of valour and from the hazards of war: hence she is reminded in these very rituals at the outset of her marriage that she is entering into toil and danger as a partner, to suffer and to dare with her man alike in peace and in war. This is the meaning of the yoked oxen, of the bridled horse, of the gift of arms. Thus she must live and thus she must die. She is receiving a trust that she must pass on with undiminished worth to her children, which her son's wives may receive and in turn pass on to her grandsons.

19. This means that they live a life of sheltered chastity, uncorrupted by the temptations of public shows or the excitements of banquets. Men and women alike know nothing of clandestine letters. Considering the great size of the population, adultery is very rare. The penalty for it is instant and left to the husband. He cuts off her hair, strips her naked in the presence of kinsmen, and flogs her all through the village. They have no mercy on a woman who prostitutes her chastity. Neither beauty, nor youth, nor wealth can find her another husband. In fact, no one there laughs about vice, nor is seducing and being seduced called 'modern'. Even better is the practice of those states where only virgins can marry: the hopes and aspirations of a wife are settled once and for all. They are content with a single husband, just as they are content with one body and one life. She has no thoughts beyond him, nor do her desires survive him. They must love not so much the husband himself as their marriage. To limit the number of their children or to kill one

of the later-born is regarded as a crime. Good morality is more effective there than good laws elsewhere.

20. In every household the children grow up, naked and dirty, to that size of limb and stature which we admire in them. Each mother breastfeeds her own child and does not hand them over to maids or nurses. You cannot distinguish between master and slave by the delicacy of their upbringing: they live together among the same flocks and on the same earth floor until maturity sets the free apart and valour claims them. The young men are slow to mate, and reach manhood with unimpaired vigour. Nor are the virgins hurried into marriage. Being as old and as tall as the men, they are equal to their mates in age and strength, and the children inherit the robustness of their parents. The sons of sisters receive the same honour from their uncles as from their fathers. Some even regard this a more sacred and a closer tie of blood and when demanding hostages insist on it for preference. It is as if they thereby have a tighter grip on the affections and a wider hold on the family. However, each man's own sons inherit, and they do not make a will. Where there are no children, the order of succession is first to brothers, then to the father's brothers, finally to the mother's brothers. The more kinsmen and relatives by marriage a man has, the more honoured he is in old age. There is no worth attached to childlessness.

21. It is an obligation to take over the father's or kinsman's feuds and friendships. But feuds do not go on with no reconciliation. In fact, even homicide can be atoned for with a fixed number of cattle or sheep. The whole family receives this compensation. This is an advantage for the community, since feuds are rather dangerous where freedom exists.

No other people indulges more lavishly in feasting and entertainment. It is regarded as a sin to turn away any person from their house. Each according to his means receives guests with an elaborate meal. When his supplies have run out, the man who has been the host accompanies the guest to show him another lodging. They enter the next house even without an invitation. It makes no difference: they are received with equal warmth. No one makes any distinction, as far as the right of hospitality is concerned, between

friend and stranger: food is shared between host and guest. As the guest leaves, it is the custom to grant him anything he asks for, and the host is likewise free to ask for a present in his turn. They take delight in gifts but expect no repayment in return and feel under no obligation in accepting them.

22. As soon as they wake up, which is often well after sunrise, they wash, generally with warm water, as is natural with people among whom winter lasts so long. After washing they take a meal, each one having a separate seat and table. Then they go out, with their weapons, to business, or often enough to a feast. No one thinks it disgraceful to carry on drinking all day and all night. As is natural among men who are drunk there are frequent quarrels, which are occasionally settled by violent words, more often by killing and wounding. All the same, they also frequently deliberate at feasts on reconciling feuds, forming marriage connections, and appointing chiefs, and even the question of peace or war. At no other time, they think, is the heart so open to frank thoughts or so warm towards noble sentiments. This people is neither cunning nor subtle: in the freedom of such surroundings their inmost feelings are still expressed. Hence every man's thoughts are open and laid bare. On the next day the subject is discussed again, and account is taken of both occasions. They debate while they are incapable of deceit and take the decision when they cannot make a mistake.

23. For drink they have a liquid made out of barley or other grain, fermented into a certain resemblance to wine. Those who live nearest to the river-bank buy wine as well. Their food is plain: wild fruit, fresh game, or curdled milk. They satisfy their hunger without elaborate preparation or seasonings. But as far as thirst is concerned they are less restrained: if you indulge their intemperance by supplying as much as they crave, they will be as easily defeated by their vices as by force of arms.

24. They have only one kind of public show and it is the same at every gathering. Naked youths whose sport this is fling themselves about in a dance between swords and spears levelled at them. Training has produced skill, and skill grace, but they do it not for gain or for any payment. However daring their abandon, their sole reward is the spectators' pleasure. They play at dice when sober,

surprisingly enough, as one of their serious pursuits, with such recklessness in winning and losing that, when they have lost everything, they stake their liberty and their own person on a last and decisive throw. The loser goes into voluntary servitude: even if a younger man, even if he is stronger, he submits to being bound and sold. Such is their persistence in a perverse practice, which they themselves call a matter of honour. They dispose of slaves of this category by way of trade, to escape the shame of winning in this way.

25. Their ordinary slaves are not employed, as ours are, for particular duties in the household. Each controls his own holding and home. The master exacts a certain measure of grain or livestock or cloth, as from a tenant; to this extent the slave obeys him. The other tasks in the household are carried out by the wife and children. They seldom flog a slave or punish him by imprisonment or hard labour. When they kill a slave it is usually not as a matter of harsh discipline but in a fit of rage, as they might kill an enemy, except that there is no punishment. Freedmen are not much superior to slaves. They rarely have any influence in a household and never in the state, except in monarchies, in which they rise not only higher than freemen but higher even than nobles. In other states the inferior status of freedmen is a demonstration of freedom.

26. The practice of lending out capital and stretching it out into interest is unknown: ignorance is a surer protection than any prohibition. Lands are occupied by the whole people to be cultivated, the quantity determined by the number of cultivators. They then divide the lands out among themselves according to rank. The great extent of the land makes the division easy. They plough different fields every year and there is still spare land available. In fact, however, for all that their land is fertile and extensive, they make no effort to work at planting orchards, fencing off pasturage, or irrigating gardens. Their only demand on the soil is for corn. Hence even the year itself is not divided up into as many seasons: winter, spring, and summer they understand and have names for, the name of autumn is completely unknown, as are its blessings.

27. There is no ostentation about their funerals. The only special observance is that the bodies of famous men are cremated with

particular kinds of wood. They do not load up the pyre with garments or spices. Only the dead man's weapons in each case, in some cases his horse too, are cast into the flames. The tomb is a turf mound. They disdain a lofty and elaborately constructed monument as being an honour that would weigh down the dead. They soon leave off weeping and lamenting but are slow to put aside their grief and sorrow. It is the honourable thing for women to mourn, for men to remember the dead.

Such is the information that has reached us about the origin and customs of the Germans as a whole.

II. THE INDIVIDUAL STATES

I shall now set out the institutions and practices of the individual states, the extent to which they differ from one another, and which peoples have migrated from Germany into the Gallic provinces.

Frontier Peoples in the West and South

28. That the Gauls were once more powerful is recorded by the highest authority, the Deified Julius. It is therefore probable that there were also migrations of Gauls into Germany. There was only a river as an obstacle, hardly sufficient to keep any people that grew in strength from seizing lands and exchanging them for others that were as yet unappropriated and not yet divided among powerful kingdoms. Thus the Helvetii occupied the land between the Hercynian forest and the rivers Rhine and Main, and beyond them the Boii, both of them Gallic. The name Boihaemum still survives, attesting the old traditions of the area even though the inhabitants have changed.

Whether the Aravisci migrated into Pannonia from the Osi, a people that lives among the Germans, or the Osi moved into Germany from the Aravisci, is uncertain: both peoples still have the same language, institutions, and customs, and in former times the same poverty and the same freedom existed on both banks of

the Danube, so that the advantages and disadvantages were identical.

The Treveri and the Nervii boast openly of their claims to German origin, as if the glory of their descent sets them apart from any resemblance to the unwarlike Gauls. The actual bank of the Rhine is inhabited by peoples of undoubted German origin, the Vangiones, Triboci, and Nemetes. Even the Ubii are not ashamed of their origin, although they have earned the rank of a Roman *colonia* and prefer to call themselves Agrippinenses after the name of their founder. They crossed the river long ago and, as they had given proof of their loyalty, were settled on the actual bank of the Rhine not so that they could be watched, but to guard it.

29. Of all these states the Batavians are the most notable for their bravery: they do not possess much of the river-bank but occupy the Rhine island. They were once a section of the Chatti but because of internal dissension migrated to their present territory, where they were to become part of the Roman empire. Their honoured status remains, and the distinction of the old alliance: they are not humiliated by tribute, nor does the tax-farmer grind them down. Exempt from burdens and special contributions, and set apart exclusively for use in battle, they are reserved like spears and other weapons as instruments of war.

The same allegiance is found in the people of the Mattiaci: for the greatness of the Roman People has pushed forward fearful respect for its empire out beyond the Rhine and beyond the old frontiers. By their location and boundaries they are on their own bank of the river, but in their hearts and spirit they follow us. In other respects they resemble the Batavians, except that the soil and climate of their country to this day give their spirit a keener edge.

I should not reckon among the peoples of Germany, although they have settled on the far side of the Rhine and Danube, those who cultivate the 'Ten-Lands'. All the least reliable sort among the Gauls, emboldened by their poverty, occupied a country of which the ownership was uncertain. Now that the frontier line has been drawn and the garrisons moved forward, they are treated as a projection of the empire and part of a province.

The Chatti

30. Beyond them, from the Hercynian forest onwards, the territory of the Chatti begins. It is less open and marshy than the lands of the other peoples in the open plains of Germany, since the hills run on and only gradually thin out. The Hercynian forest escorts its Chatti all the way to their borders and takes its leave of them there. This people has a tougher physique, with well-knit limbs and fierce countenances, and a greater mental vigour. For Germans they have a great deal of judgement and shrewdness. They elect their leaders and obey their orders; they can keep their ranks together and recognize an opportunity or postpone their attack. They plan their daytime routine and construct defences for the night; they reckon fortune to be fickle but they depend on courage; and, what is rarest of all, and is owed to their judgement and discipline, they put more trust in their general than in their army. All their strength lies in their infantry, which, as well as carrying arms, is burdened by tools and provisions as well. You may see other peoples going out to battle, the Chatti to wage war. They rarely engage in sudden forays or chance encounters. It is, of course, characteristic of mounted men to win a quick victory and make a quick retreat. Speed and timidity go together; deliberate action is a quality that goes rather with steadfastness.

31. There is a practice sometimes, though rarely, found among other German peoples—and with them as a sign of individual daring—which has become the universal custom among the Chatti. As soon as they reach manhood they let their hair and beard grow long and do not cut them until they have killed an enemy. It is a vow and a pledge to valour to cover their face. When they are standing over the bloody corpse and the spoils they lay bare their faces and say that they have at last brought back booty deserving of recognition and have shown themselves worthy of their parents and their fatherland. The cowards and the unwarlike retain their unkempt hair. The bravest also wear an iron ring like a manacle, a mark of dishonour among that people, until they have released themselves from it by killing an enemy. Many of the Chatti like this

fashion and even when their hair is now grey are still conspicuous for it, pointed out by both the enemy and their own side alike. It rests with them to begin every battle, they are always in the front rank, a startling sight. In fact, even in peacetime they are not any gentler and do not assume a milder appearance. None of them has his own home or land or any occupation. To whichever man they go they get their keep from him, wasting the goods of others and despising their own, until their blood grows thin with old age, rendering them incapable of such harsh valour.

Further Western Peoples

32. Next to the Chatti, where the channel of the Rhine is well defined and forms a boundary line, live the Usipi and Tencteri. The Tencteri, over and above the general military distinction, excel in the art of horsemanship. Indeed, the fame of the Chatti as infantrymen is no greater than that of the Tencteri as cavalry. This began with their ancestors and their descendants follow suit. The small children ride for sport, the young men compete with one another, even the old men keep at it. Horses are handed down along with the household, the homestead, and the rights of succession. A son inherits them, not necessarily the eldest, as with the rest of the property, but the one who shows himself the fiercest and the best in battle.

33. The Bructeri used to come next to the Tencteri in former times. Now the Chamavi and Angrivarii are said to have migrated there. The Bructeri were driven out and utterly cut to pieces by a coalition of neighbouring peoples, who either hated their arrogance or were attracted by the prospect of booty—unless it was through some special favour of the gods towards us, for they did not even begrudge us being spectators of the battle. Over sixty thousand were killed, not by Roman swords or spears, but, what was far more splendid, to gladden Roman eyes. Long may the barbarians continue, I pray, if not to love us, at least to hate one another, seeing that, as fate bears remorselessly on the empire, fortune can offer no greater boon now than discord among our enemies.

34. The Angrivarii and Chamavi are bordered on the far side by

the Dulgubnii and Chasuarii and other peoples of no special note, on the nearer side they are followed by the Frisii. These are labelled 'Greater' and 'Lesser' Frisii in accordance with their strength. Both peoples have the Rhine as their boundary right down to the Ocean and they also dwell around vast lakes, which have been navigated by Roman fleets. We have indeed even made trial of the Ocean itself in that quarter, and rumour had it that Pillars of Hercules still remained to be explored. This is either because Hercules did go there or perhaps only because we have agreed to ascribe all marvels anywhere to his credit. Drusus Germanicus was not lacking in daring either, but the Ocean resisted research either into itself or into Hercules. Subsequently no one has made the attempt and it has been judged more religious and reverent to believe in the deeds of the gods than to know the facts about them.

The Peoples of the North

35. Thus far we have learnt about Germany towards the west. Towards the north it falls back with a huge bend, and here first of all is the people of the Chauci. Although they start next to the Frisii and occupy part of the coast, they also stretch out along the flanks of all the states that I have described, and finally curve back towards the Chatti. This vast tract of land is not merely held by the Chauci but filled by them too. They are the noblest people among the Germans and one that prefers to maintain its greatness by righteous dealing. Free from greed and from ungovernable passion, they live in peaceful seclusion; they provoke no wars and do not engage in raids for plunder or brigandage. The principal proof of their excellence and their strength is that they do not rely on damaging others to maintain their superior position. Yet every man has weapons ready to hand and, if the occasion demands, they have an army, with men and horses in great abundance. So, even when they are at peace, their reputation remains just as high.

36. On the flank of the Chauci and Chatti, the Cherusci, not having been subject to attack, have long cultivated peace, which has been excessive and enervating. This situation has indeed been pleasant rather than bringing security, since when you live among

violent and powerful peoples a pacific posture is a mistake. Where force is decisive, restraint and uprightness are labels applied only to the stronger side. Hence the Cherusci, once known for being just and honourable, are now called lazy and stupid, whereas the good luck enjoyed by the conquering Chatti was counted as wisdom. The fall of the Cherusci dragged down the neighbouring state of the Fosi too, who are in adversity their equal partners, although they had a lesser share in their successes.

37. This same peninsula of Germany is occupied, nearest to the Ocean, by the Cimbri, now a small state, although their renown is enormous. Widespread traces of their ancient fame survive, vast encampments on both sides of the river-boundary [of the Rhine], by the size of which one can still gauge the strength and numbers of the people and the truth of that great exodus.

Our city was in her 640th year when the alarm of the Cimbrian arms was first heard, the consuls being Caecilius Metellus and Papirius Carbo [113 BC]. If we reckon from that year to the second consulship of the emperor Trajan [AD 98], the total is about two hundred and ten years. For all this time have we been conquering Germany. During this long period there have been great losses on each side. Neither the Samnites nor the Carthaginians nor Spain nor Gaul nor even the Parthians have taught us more frequent lessons. The freedom of the Germans does indeed show more aggression than the despotism of the Arsacids. After all, what else can the East taunt us with except the slaughter of Crassus, the East which itself lost Pacorus and was cast down beneath the feet of Ventidius? But the Germans routed or captured Carbo and Cassius and Scaurus Aurelius and Servilius Caepio and Maximus Mallius and robbed the Roman people at a stroke of five consular armies— and Caesar [Augustus] himself of Varus and three legions with him. Nor was it without loss that Gaius Marius smote them in Italy, the Deified Julius in Gaul, Drusus and Nero [Tiberius] and Germanicus in their own country. Later, the grandiloquent threats of Gaius Caesar [Caligula] made him a laughing-stock. Peace then prevailed until, taking advantage of our dissensions and the Civil Wars, they stormed the legions' winter quarters and even aspired to win over the Gallic provinces before being once more driven back.

In recent times, certainly, they have been the objects of triumphs rather than victories.

The Suebian Peoples of the East and North

38. Now something must be said about the Suebi, who do not, like the Chatti or Tencteri, constitute a single nation. Indeed, they occupy the greater part of Germany, divided as yet into separate states, each with its own name, although they share the common designation Suebi. The special characteristic of this people is that they comb their hair back over the side of the head and tie it in a knot behind. This marks off the Suebi from the other Germans and the free-born Suebi from their slaves. The practice does exist among other peoples, either because of some kinship with the Suebi or through imitation, as often happens, but it is rare and confined to the period of youth. Among the Suebi, the hair is twisted back so that it bristles, even when it has turned grey, and is often knotted behind on the very crown of the head. The chiefs have an even more elaborate hair-style, such is the attention they pay to their personal appearance, yet in all innocence. It is not for lovemaking or to inspire passion that they adorn themselves, but for the eyes of their enemies, dressing their hair when about to go to war so as to add considerably to their height and appear more terrifying.

39. The Semnones claim that they are the oldest and the noblest of the Suebi. Their antiquity is confirmed by a religious rite. At a fixed time deputations from all the peoples who share the same origin meet in a wood sanctified by their forefathers' auguries and by ancient dread. A human victim is slaughtered on behalf of all present to celebrate the gruesome opening of the barbarous ritual. Another form of reverence marks the grove as well: no one enters it unless bound with a chain, as an inferior being, outwardly acknowledging the power of the divinity. If they happen to fall down, they are not permitted to get up on their feet again: they roll out along the ground. This whole superstition is based on the belief that from this wood the people derives its origin and that the god who reigns over all dwells there, the rest of the world being his obedient

subjects. The good fortune of the Semnones gives them prestige as well: they dwell in a hundred cantons and by virtue of their numbers consider themselves the chief people of the Suebi.

40. By contrast, the Langobardi are distinguished by being few in number. Surrounded by many mighty peoples they have protected themselves not by submissiveness but by battle and boldness. Next to them come the Reudigni, Aviones, Anglii, Varini, Eudoses, Suarines, and Huitones, protected by rivers and forests. There is nothing especially noteworthy about these states individually, but they are distinguished by a common worship of Nerthus, that is, Mother Earth, and believe that she intervenes in human affairs and rides through their peoples. There is a sacred grove on an island in the Ocean, in which there is a consecrated chariot, draped with a cloth, which the priest alone may touch. He perceives the presence of the goddess in the innermost shrine and with great reverence escorts her in her chariot, which is drawn by female cattle. There are days of rejoicing then and the countryside celebrates the festival, wherever she deigns to visit and to accept hospitality. No one goes to war, no one takes up arms, all objects of iron are locked away, then and only then do they experience peace and quiet, only then do they prize them, until the goddess has had her fill of human society and the priest brings her back to her temple. Afterwards the chariot, the cloth, and, if one may believe it, the deity herself are washed in a hidden lake. The slaves who perform this office are immediately afterwards swallowed up in the same lake. Hence arises dread of the mysterious, and piety, which keeps them ignorant of what only those about to perish may see.

41. This part of the Suebi stretches into the inner recesses of Germany. Nearer to us, if I now follow the Danube, just as a little earlier I followed the line of the Rhine, comes the state of the Hermunduri, which is loyal to the Romans. For this reason they are the only Germans who trade not only on the river-bank but deep inside the frontier and in the province of Raetia's splendid *colonia*. They cross over at all points and without a guard. To other peoples we only show our arms and our forts, to them we open our town houses and country mansions—and they do not covet them. In the land o'

the Hermunduri rises the Elbe, a river that was famous and well known once. Now it is known only from hearsay.

42. Next to the Hermunduri live the Naristi and then the Marcomani and Quadi. The Marcomani are especially famous and powerful and in former times they won their very territory by driving out the Boii. Nor do the Naristi and Quadi fall below this standard. These peoples form as it were the front presented by Germany along the line marked by the Danube. The Marcomani and Quadi down to our own memory retained kings from their own nation, the noble house of Maroboduus and Tudrus, but now they submit to ones from outside too. The material resources and power of the kings depend on our support. They are occasionally backed up by our armed forces, more often by money, which is equally effective.

43. The Marsigni, Cotini, Osi, and Buri, behind the Marcomani and Quadi, shut them in at the back. Of these peoples the Marsigni and Buri resemble the Suebi in language and way of life. The Cotini speak Gallic and the Osi speak Pannonian, which proves that they are not Germans, as does the fact that they pay tribute, as being foreigners, levied on the one by the Sarmatians, on the other by the Quadi. The Cotini, more to their shame, have iron-mines. All these peoples occupy a country with little plain but plenty of uplands and mountain peaks.

In fact, an unbroken chain of mountains runs through Suebia and divides it. Beyond live many peoples, among which the name of the Lugii is the most widespread, covering several states. It will suffice to name the strongest, the Harii, Helvecones, Manimi, Helisii, and Naharvali. Among the Naharvali a grove of ancient sanctity is pointed out. The presiding priest is dressed in women's clothes, but they say that their deities, according to the Roman interpretation, are Castor and Pollux: that is the character of their godhead, of which the name is 'the Alci'. There are no images and no trace of the rite being imported, although they are worshipped as brothers and as young men. Further, besides their strength, in which they surpass the peoples listed just previously, they are fierce-spirited and enhance their inborn savagery by artificial

means and by their choice of time. They blacken their shields and dye their bodies black and choose pitch dark nights for their battles. Their terrible shadowy appearance, like an army of ghosts, creates panic, as no enemy can endure so strange and almost hellish a sight. Defeat in battle always begins with the eyes.

44. Beyond the Lugii are the Gotones, under the rule of kings, exercised here more strictly than among the other German peoples, yet still not inconsistent with freedom. Then, immediately bordering the Ocean, come the Rugii and Lemovii. All these peoples are distinguished by round shields, short swords, and submission to kings.

The peoples of the Sviones that follow, in the midst of the Ocean itself, are strong not only in arms but in their fleets. Their ships differ from normal ones in having prows at both ends, so that they are always ready to put in to shore. They do not use sails or regular banks of oars fixed to the sides, but their oars are loose, as is sometimes the case with river-boats, and can be moved, as needed, from one side to the other. These peoples even respect wealth, which is why a single ruler is in power whose authority is now unrestricted, with an absolute right to obedience. Weapons are not in general use here, as in the rest of Germany, but are kept locked up and under the guard of a slave. This is because the Ocean makes any sudden invasion impossible and in peacetime armed men can easily become indisciplined. And indeed, it is in the king's interest that no noble or freeman, or even a freedman, should have charge of the weapons.

45. Beyond the Sviones is another sea, sluggish and almost motionless, which is believed to be the girdle and boundary of the earth. For the last rays of the setting sun continue to shine until sunrise, bright enough to dim the stars. Popular belief adds further that the sound of the sun's emergence from the sea can be heard and the shape of his horses and the rays on his head can be seen. Thus far and no further—and the report is true—does the world extend.

Passing then to the right-hand shore of the Suebian Sea, here it washes the peoples of the Aestii, whose customs and appearanc are those of the Suebi, while their language is closer to Britis

They worship the Mother of the Gods and as a symbol of that cult they wear the figure of a wild boar. They all carry this instead of weapons: it is a protection for the worshipper of the goddess even in the midst of his enemies. They seldom use iron weapons, clubs frequently. Grain and other crops they cultivate with a perseverance unusual among the generally lethargic Germans. They also scour the sea and are the only ones out of all the Germans who gather amber, which they themselves call *glesum*, in the shallows and on the shore itself. Being barbarians, they have never enquired or discovered what substance or process produces it. In fact, for a long time it just lay among the other jetsam of the sea, until our luxury gave it a reputation. They have no use for it themselves: it is gathered crude and passed on unworked, and they are astonished at the price they get for it. You can, however, tell that it is gum from trees, for creeping and sometimes even winged creatures are often imbedded in it. They have been trapped when the substance is liquid, and it has subsequently hardened. Hence, I imagine, that in the islands and lands of the west there are also woods and groves more than usually productive, just as there are in the remote regions of the east, where trees exude frankincense and balsam. For there these are drawn out by the rays of the sun, which is close by, ooze out into the nearest part of the sea in liquid state, and are cast up by the force of storms onto the shores opposite. If you test the amber by applying fire to it, it kindles like a torch and feeds an oily and pungent flame, and then dissolves into a sort of pitch or resin.

Bordering on the Sviones are the peoples of the Sithones, who resemble them in other respects, with the single difference that they are ruled by a woman. To this extent they have fallen lower not merely than free men but than slaves.   **46.** Here Suebia ends.

Frontier Peoples in the East

As for the Peucini, Venethi, and Fenni, I am uncertain whether to classify them among the Germans or the Sarmatians. The Peucini, whom some call the Bastarnae, are certainly like the Germans in their language, way of life, and in their type of houses—and all of them are characterized by squalor. But, as a result of mixed

marriages, their lofty physique is to some extent taking on the mis-shapen appearance of the Sarmatians. The Venethi have taken over a good many customs from the Sarmatians, for they go to and fro on plundering raids all over the wooded ridge that rises between the Peucini and Fenni. All the same, they are on the whole to be classified as Germans, because they build houses, carry shields, and pride themselves on using their fleetness of foot—in all these respects differing from the Sarmatians, who live in wagons and on horseback.

The Fenni are remarkably savage and wretchedly poor. They have no weapons, no horses, and no homes. They feed on wild plants, wear skins, and sleep on the ground. Their only hope is their arrows, which for lack of iron they tip with bone. Men and women alike live by hunting. The women accompany the men everywhere and insist on taking a share in the spoils. Their only way of protecting infants against wild beasts or rain is a shelter made from inter-woven branches. This is what the young men come back to and where the old men take refuge. Yet they think this is a happier lot than to groan over the tillage of the fields, toiling over house-building, or speculating between hope and fear with their own and other people's money. Having nothing to fear at the hands of men or gods, they have reached a state that is very difficult to attain: they do not even need to pray for anything.

Everything after this point is in the realm of fable. The Hellusii and Oxiones are said to have human faces and features, the bodies and limbs of animals. As this has not been confirmed, I shall leave the matter open.

EXPLANATORY NOTES

Tacitus' writings are abbreviated as *Agr.*, *Ger.*, *Dial.*, *Hist.*, and *Ann*. The following abbreviations are also used:

AE	*L'Année épigraphique*
Anderson	J. G. C. Anderson (ed.), *Cornelii Taciti De origine et situ Germanorum* (Oxford, 1938)
ANRW	*Aufstieg und Niedergang der römischen Welt*, ed. H. Temporini and W. Haase (Berlin and New York, 1972–)
CIL	*Corpus Inscriptionum Latinarum* (Berlin, 1862–)
FRB	A. R. Birley, *The Fasti of Roman Britain* (Oxford, 1981)
Hanson	W. S. Hanson, *Agricola and the Conquest of the North* (London, 1987)
ILS	H. Dessau, *Inscriptiones Latinae Selectae* (Berlin, 1892–1916)
Jones– Mattingly	B. Jones and D. Mattingly, *An Atlas of Roman Britain* (Oxford, 1990)
Lund	A. A. Lund (ed.), *P. Cornelius Tacitus: Germania* (Heidelberg, 1988)
Ogilvie– Richmond	R. M. Ogilvie and I. A. Richmond (eds.), *Cornelii Taciti De vita Agricolae* (Oxford, 1967)
R.-Charlier	M.-T. Raepsaet-Charlier, 'Cn. Iulius Agricola: Mise au point prosopographique', in W. Haase (ed.), *Aufstieg und Niedergang der römischen Welt*, II. 33. 3 (Berlin and New York, 1991), 1808–57
RIB	R. G. Collingwood, R. P. Wright, *et al.*, *The Roman Inscriptions of Britain*, i: *Inscriptions on Stone* (Oxford, 1965; repr. Stroud, 1995); ii: *Instrumentum Domesticum* (Stroud, 1990–5)
Rivet–Smith	A. L. F. Rivet and C. Smith, *The Place-Names of Roman Britain* (London, 1979)
RP	R. Syme, *Roman Papers*, i–vii (Oxford, 1979–91)
Syme	R. Syme, *Tacitus*, 2 vols. (Oxford, 1958)
Timpe	D. Timpe, *Romano-Germanica: Gesammelte Studien zur Germania des Tacitus* (Stuttgart and Leipzig, 1995)
TV ii	A. K. Bowman and J. D. Thomas, *The Vindolanda Writing Tablets* (*Tabulae Vindolandenses*, ii) (London, 1994)
Wells	C. M. Wells, *The German Policy of Augustus* (Oxford, 1972)

ANCIENT AUTHORS

The citation of ancient authors and their works is, it is hoped, in most cases straightforward. There are a few cases where ambiguity might arise, e.g. when only the author's name is given, or where works have been cited in abbreviated form:

Ammianus	Ammianus Marcellinus, *History of Rome*
Caesar, *BG*	Caesar, *De bello Gallico*, i.e. *The Gallic War*
Columella	Columella, *De re rustica*, i.e. *On Agriculture*
Dio	Cassius Dio, *Roman History*
Herodotus	Herodotus, *Histories*
Juvenal	Juvenal, *Satires*
Livy	Livy, *History of Rome*
Martial	Martial, *Epigrams*
Mela	Pomponius Mela, *Geography*
Orosius	Orosius, *History of Rome*
Pliny, *Ep.*	the Younger Pliny, *Epistulae*, i.e. *Letters*
Pliny, *NH*	the Elder Pliny, *Natural History*
Pliny, *Pan.*	the Younger Pliny, *Panegyric*
Ptolemy	Ptolemy, *Geography*
Strabo	Strabo, *Geography*
Valerius Maximus	Valerius Maximus, *Memorable Deeds and Sayings*
Velleius	Velleius Paterculus, *History of Rome*

THE LIFE OF AGRICOLA

1 *Rutilius*: Publius Rutilius Rufus, born *c.*160 BC, consul 105 BC and a distinguished military commander, was an adherent of Stoic philosophy. He was unjustly convicted of corruption in 92 BC by a jury sympathetic to the tax-collectors, whom Rutilius had strictly controlled in the province of Asia. He went into exile at Smyrna and there wrote an autobiographical history of his time.

Scaurus: Marcus Aemilius Scaurus, consul 115 BC, and from then until his death *c.*89 BC one of the most influential men in Rome, 'whose nod almost ruled the world', according to Cicero, was perhaps the first Roman to write an autobiography.

I needed permission: this suggests that Tacitus had originally planned to write a biography of Agricola soon after the latter's death and had been discouraged or deterred by Domitian or his advisers.

2 *Arulenus Rusticus . . . Paetus Thrasea . . . Priscus Helvidius . . . Herennius Senecio*: respectively, Quintus Junius Arulenus Rusticus, consul AD 92, Publius Clodius Thrasea Paetus, consul 56, Gaius Helvidius Priscus, and Herennius Senecio (first name unknown); as often, Tacitus inverts the order of names in the case of Thrasea and Helvidius, an archaizing trick of style. All four were Stoic senators, opposed to despotic rule. Thrasea was forced to suicide under Nero (AD 66), his son-in-law Helvidius Priscus was executed under Vespasian (*c.*74). Thereafter the leadership of this group was assumed by the younger Helvidius, consul *c.*87; he, Rusticus, and Senecio were executed under Domitian late in 93, as Tacitus recounts below, in ch. 45.

Board of Three, *Comitium*, *Forum*: see Glossary.

liberty of the senate: *libertas*, 'liberty' or 'freedom', is a recurrent theme in all Tacitus' writings. Cf. below on *monarchy and freedom* in ch. 3.

teachers of philosophy: An expulsion of intellectuals, mainly Greeks, took place at the time of Rusticus' execution (Suetonius, *Domitian* 10, cf. Pliny, *Ep.* 3. 11).

the former age: the last years of the Republic.

espionage: under Domitian, as previously under Tiberius and Nero, there were numerous 'informers', *delatores*, active in Rome.

3 *Nerva Caesar*: Marcus Cocceius Nerva became emperor on 18 September AD 96, the same day that Domitian was assassinated, and at once acquired the names Caesar and Augustus.

monarchy and freedom: one of Tacitus' best-known phrases. The admirers of Disraeli chose his misquotation of 'principatus ac libertas', 'Empire and Liberty', as the motto of the Primrose League (cf. Introduction, p. xxxix).

Nerva Trajan: Trajan was adopted by Nerva in the autumn of AD 97, perhaps on 27 or 28 October, and added the latter's last name to his own. Nerva died three months later, on 27 January 98, and shortly afterwards was deified. As he is not here called 'the Deified Nerva', that ought strictly to mean that Tacitus was writing between October 97 and January 98. However, in ch. 44 he appears to refer to Trajan as already emperor, so was perhaps still at work on *Agr.* in late January 98.

fifteen years: i.e. AD 81–96, the reign of Domitian.

a record of our former servitude . . . present blessings: Tacitus here announces his intention to write a major work, presumably covering the years 81–98. In the event, his *Histories* began earlier, with AD 69, and ended with the death of Domitian in 96; the account of 'the principate and Nerva and the reign of Trajan' was there reserved for his old age, if he survived (*Hist.* 1. 1. 4). However, he actually turned to the Julio-Claudian period for his last work, the *Annals*.

4 *came from the . . . colonia of Forum Julii*: Agricola's date of birth, 13 June AD 40, is not given until near the end of the work, ch. 44. 'ortus', normally translated as 'was born at', probably means 'came from' here: Forum Julii was Agricola's home town. But his parents, as members of the senatorial order, would have lived mainly in Rome, where his father was buried (*AE* 1946. 94). So Agricola was probably born there. For *colonia*, procurator, equestrian, see Glossary.

Julius Graecinus: Lucius Julius Graecinus must have died at earliest in September AD 39, at latest a few months after Agricola's birth in June 40, since Caligula, who caused his death, was himself murdered on 24 January 41. Graecinus was praised for moral excellence by Seneca (*De beneficiis* 2. 21. 5), who also quotes a sarcastic remark of his about the philosopher Aristo (*Letters* 29. 6). Graecinus wrote two volumes on viticulture, referred to by Columella and the Elder Pliny.

4 *Marcus Silanus*: there were two men of the name Marcus Junius Silanus, consuls in AD 15 and 19, from a family related to the Julio-Claudians; the former was already dead in 37 or early in 38, forced to suicide by Caligula, the latter's fate is unknown.

Julia Procilla: assumed also to be from southern Gaul because of her names; her tragic death nearly thirty years later is described in ch. 7.

liberal studies: defined by Tacitus in *Dial*. 30, summing up Cicero's education, as geometry, music, grammar, dialectic, ethics, natural science.

Massilia: founded by Greek settlers from Asia Minor *c.*600 BC, technically a 'free state' in alliance with Rome.

he used to tell: one of a small number of such direct reminiscences, cf. also ch. 24, 'I have often heard him say', and 44, 'Trajan's principate, which he used to predict . . . in our hearing'.

from philosophy . . . a sense of proportion: the epigram indicates Tacitus' attitude to philosophy, and also introduces the theme of 'moderation', a recurrent quality of Agricola, cf. chs. 6, 7, 39, 40, and especially 42.

5 *His first lessons in army life . . . Paulinus' staff*: this means that Agricola was appointed by Paulinus as the senatorial tribune (the other five being equestrian) of one of the four legions stationed in Britain (there is no means of deciding which one). It does not necessarily mean that he had a special 'staff appointment'. Gaius Suetonius Paullinus (so spelt in inscriptions) had gained a military reputation two decades earlier when he led an army across the Atlas mountains during the war that led to the annexation of Mauretania. He was appointed governor of Britain in AD 58, after the sudden death of Quintus Veranius (ch. 14). He again held command during the Civil War of 69, on the side of Otho. Details in *FRB* 54 ff.

Britain has certainly never . . . : this refers to the rebellion of Boudicca in AD 60, described at greater length here in chs. 15–16 and more fully still in *Ann*. 14. 29–39.

coloniae *burned down*: rhetorical plural. Only Camulodunum (Colchester) was a *colonia* (see Glossary) at that date. The other two towns destroyed by the rebels, Verulamium (St Albans) and Londinium (London), are said by Tacitus in the *Ann*. (14. 33) to have had a lesser status.

glory: one of the key themes of the *Agr*. Cf. ch. 8.

6 *Domitia Decidiana*: presumed to be daughter of Domitius Decidius, who had become a senator in AD 44 (*ILS* 966) and was probably also from Gallia Narbonensis. She was still alive at the time Tacitus was writing (ch. 46).

material support: marriage and fatherhood had been made more attractive for senators through privileges granted by Augustus (to increase the birth rate among the upper orders).

quaestorship . . . Asia . . . Salvius Titianus: this term of office under the pro-consul Lucius Salvius Otho Titianus, elder brother of the future short-lived emperor Otho, was evidently for the twelve months beginning in spring or

early summer 63: *FRB* 75. The province of Asia (roughly equivalent to western Turkey) was extremely wealthy, hence opportunities for enrichment.

daughter: Tacitus' future wife, not named here or elsewhere but presumably called Julia and probably having a *cognomen* too, was thus born in AD 63 or 64 and aged only 13 or 14 when she married (ch. 9). The birth of this daughter and that of the son who died in infancy, would each have reduced by a year the minimum age for Agricola to hold office.

tribunate of the plebs . . . indolence was then a kind of philosophy: the tribunate was now a largely empty office, although in the year that Agricola probably served one of the other nine tribunes, Arulenus Rusticus (chs. 2 and 45), offered to use the by then virtually obsolete veto to block the condemnation of Thrasea (*Ann.* 16. 26). Thrasea stopped him, calling it an empty gesture. Tacitus would thus be making an indirect allusion to and contrast with Rusticus, a practitioner of Stoic philosophy ('sapientia' in the Latin).

praetorship . . . Galba: Galba's reign officially ran from *c.*8 June AD 68 to his death on 15 January 69: Dio 63. 6. 5; *Hist.* 1. 27 ff. Agricola's praetorship is thus dated to 68, confirmed by ch. 7 below, 'The following year', referring to AD 69: he was in his twenty-eighth year when elected, two years earlier than the regular minimum because of his two children.

7 *Otho's fleet . . . Intimilian district*: in March AD 69, as Vitellius' forces approached northern Italy over the Alps, Otho sent the fleet to create a diversion by attacking southern Gaul, but it only engaged in looting. The chief town of the Intimilii, Albintimilium (Ventimiglia) in Liguria, was sacked, as Tacitus relates, *Hist.* 2. 13, where he does not mention Procilla's death, but describes the heroic behaviour of another woman, killed for refusing to reveal her son's whereabouts.

Vespasian's bid . . . at once went over: Vespasian was proclaimed emperor at Alexandria on 1 July AD 69, and in Judaea, where he then was, on 3 July, *Hist.* 2. 79. For letters canvassing support for him in the Gallic provinces soon afterwards, see *Hist.* 2. 86. If 'at once' is taken seriously, Agricola must have joined the Flavians well before their victory at the second battle of Bedriacum, 24–5 October 69, *Hist.* 3. 15 ff.

Mucianus: Gaius Licinius Mucianus, governor of Syria AD 67–9, urged Vespasian to bid for the throne and commanded the Flavian expeditionary force which captured Rome on 20 December 69, *Hist.* 2. 76, 4. 11, etc.

Domitian: born on 24 October AD 51, nearly twelve years younger than his brother Titus, and only 18 when his father's forces seized Rome. He was at once hailed as Caesar and appointed praetor. Vespasian and Titus were both still in the east. Domitian's sudden change of fortune went to his head. His conduct in late 69 and 70 is depicted by Tacitus in very negative terms in *Hist.* (it had been glorified when Domitian was emperor).

Mucianus appointed: the Latin has 'is', 'the former', which must mean Mucianus, rather than Domitian, as the person who gave Agricola the

legionary command. It is not clear who had ordered him to carry out the levy, presumably in autumn AD 69: *FRB* 76.

7 *Twentieth legion . . . treasonably*: the mutiny is referred to again briefly in ch. 16 below, and Tacitus gives more detail in *Hist.* 1. 60.

praetorian legate: the praetorian legate of the Twentieth, who took the lead in booting the hated consular legate Trebellius out of Britain, is named in *Hist.* 1. 60: Marcus Roscius Coelius.

8 *Vettius Bolanus*: Marcus Vettius Bolanus was hastily chosen by Vitellius to replace Trebellius in April AD 69, and was retained in office by Vespasian until 71. His governorship is briefly referred to again in ch. 17, in the same negative terms. Yet the poet Statius credited Bolanus with 'capturing the breastplate of a British king' (*Silvae* 5. 2, 54 ff., 140 ff., esp. 149). This must mean Venutius, the anti-Roman ex-husband of Queen Cartimandua of the Brigantes. The pro-Roman queen was rescued by Roman forces in AD 69, *Hist.* 3. 45, not naming Bolanus, who must have given the order. Agricola, arriving in 70, did not experience what was perhaps Bolanus' only piece of action. The army in Britain was in any case weakened in 69, as Vitellius had withdrawn 8,000 men early in 69, *Hist.* 2. 57. Bolanus tried to delay sending more troops 'as Britain was never peaceful enough', ibid. 2. 97.

Petilius Cerialis: Quintus Petilius Cerialis Caesius Rufus was governor from AD 71 to 73 or 74 (spelt Peti*ll*ius in inscriptions), *FRB* 66 ff. He had served in Britain before, as legate of the legion IX Hispana at the time of the Boudiccan revolt: he failed to rescue Camulodunum (Colchester), a 'disaster', caused by Cerialis' 'rashness', *Ann.* 14. 32–3. But Cerialis, closely related to Vespasian (*Hist.* 3. 59. 2), was chosen to suppress the Batavian revolt in the Rhineland, described by Tacitus fully (with much criticism) in *Hist.* His governorship of Britain recurs in ch. 17, below.

9 *As he was returning . . . the Deified Vespasian enrolled him among the patricians*: Vespasian, with his elder son Titus, not here mentioned, as colleague, held office as censor from March AD 73 to October 74, in this capacity revising the senate's membership and creating new patricians (cf. Glossary). Agricola's enrolment probably occurred early in the censorship. He clearly did not serve in Britain under Cerialis' successor, Frontinus (ch. 17), who would otherwise have been mentioned in ch. 8.

Aquitania. . . . particularly splendid . . . consulship: not many other governors of this province, modern south-west France, are known; one was the future emperor Galba (Suetonius, *Galba* 6). Agricola can hardly have been formally designated to the consulship over two years in advance (cf. below), but Tacitus doubtless knew that most legates of Aquitania and of comparable provinces, e.g. Belgica, Lugdunensis, and Lusitania, became consul immediately after their term of office ended.

the military temperament: Agricola is here regarded as having been a 'military man' (cf. ch. 41 below for the explicit use of this term) on the strength of his

service with the army for, up to this point, a total of some six years at most, more, perhaps, than the average senator during the Principate.

Sullenness . . . he had cast aside: a surprising statement, which some commentators wish to delete or emend on the grounds that it implies that Agricola *had* once displayed these negative qualities. Tacitus perhaps meant that sullenness etc. were assumed by provincials to be normal characteristics or 'public front', *persona*, of a governor and that Agricola, unlike others, when he 'came to assume the *persona* of office had already removed from it these three traditional . . . features': Ogilvie–Richmond, 161.

disputes with procurators: these equestrian officials, responsible for financial matters (cf. Glossary), were directly accountable to the emperor and not clearly subordinate to the governor. Even if e.g. the future emperor Hadrian as legate of Lower Pannonia 'restrained procurators who were overstepping their powers' (*Historia Augusta, Hadrian* 3. 9), conflict of authority could easily develop, as indicated in ch. 15, below: 'Whether our masters [i.e. legate and procurator] quarrel or agree'. The dispute between the governor Paulinus and the new procurator Classicianus after the rebellion of Boudicca led to the former's dismissal (*Ann.* 14. 38).

less than three years: although tenure of office in such provinces was entirely at the emperor's discretion and subject to no rules, by implication three years had become the 'standard term'. In *Ann.* 14. 29 Tacitus reports the claim made in his testament by the governor Veranius, who died after only a year in Britain, that he would have 'conquered the rest' if he had survived for the next two years, which again implies a three-year 'norm'.

immediate prospect of a consulship: Agricola had presumably been designated, in January, to be suffect consul (cf. Glossary) later in the year, which was probably AD 76: D. B. Campbell, *Zeitschrift für Papyrologie und Epigraphik*, 63 (1986), 197 ff.; R.-Charlier, 1842 ff.

As consul he betrothed his daughter . . . gave her in marriage: the term of office of suffect consuls was variable but scarcely ever less than two months. In AD 76 Vespasian (for the seventh time) and Titus (for the fifth time) were the ordinary consuls, probably remaining in office no later than the end of April; two suffect consuls (cf. Glossary) were in office on 2 December, who must have entered office at latest on 1 November. Agricola and his unknown colleague were thus probably consuls for between two and six months in the period May–October. The period of betrothal was thus fairly short. Agricola's daughter was at most 13 when married (cf. ch. 6 above), while Tacitus may only have been 18 (cf. Introduction, p. xx).

pontifex: cf. Glossary.

10–17 Tacitus now leaves the chronological account of his subject's life to provide appropriate background: the ethnography (10–12) and history of Britain (13–17).

10 *many writers*: the best known pre-Tacitean writers on Britain are Caesar, Strabo, whom Tacitus had probably not read, and the Elder Pliny. Their

British references are discussed in Rivet–Smith, 58f., 87ff., and 79f. Note also Pomponius Mela, ibid. 75f., and generally on literary sources for British geography 49ff. For *Livy* and *Fabius Rusticus* cf. the notes to this ch. further below.

10 *for the first time completely conquered*: Agricola's achievement as the man who completed the conquest begun decades before is reiterated e.g. in ch. 33, his speech before the battle of the Graupian Mountain, and in *Hist.* 1. 2, the summary of the events covered in that work, including 'Britain completely conquered and at once let go'. 'for the first time' is repeated here below in connection with the circumnavigation.

faces Germany on the east and Spain on the west: that Britain was 'opposite' Spain on the west was a common ancient misconception, cf. e.g. Caesar, *BG* 5. 13, Pliny, *NH* 4. 102.

Livy: Titus Livius (59 BC–AD 17), author of a history of Rome from its origins to AD 9, in 142 books, of which books 1–10 and 21–45 survive. This is the only place in his work where Tacitus cites Livy, presumably referring here to the lost book 105 in which Caesar's expeditions were covered.

Fabius Rusticus: a friend of Seneca, *Ann.* 13. 20, who wrote on the time of Nero.

an elongated shoulder-blade or . . . an axe: Ogilvie–Richmond, followed here (168ff.), read 'scapulae' rather than the MSS 'scutulae', 'rhombus', and understand *oblongae* as 'longer than normal'. They show that 'bipenni' means just an axe, not a double axe, and that both shapes were basically triangles.

Caledonia: perhaps more correctly spelt *Calidonia*: Rivet–Smith (289f.), who take 'the regional name as doubtless a Roman creation . . . a sort of abstraction from the ethnic name *Calidonii* . . . "hard men, tough men" . . . generally applied to Scotland north of the Forth–Clyde isthmus and occasionally to the whole of northern Britain'. However, it might be that it was the other way round, i.e. that the ethnic name derived from the name of the land.

Those who have gone past this point: in other words, Agricola and his army were the first to get beyond the Forth–Clyde line. If, as suggested in the Introduction (p. xxii), Tacitus was in fact a young military tribune in that army until the summer of AD 79, he would himself have had the chance to see Scotland up to the Tay estuary (cf. ch. 22).

a Roman fleet for the first time circumnavigated: Dio, writing in the third century, notes in his account of Caesar's invasion that it had been disputed whether Britain was a continent or an island, adding that 'In the course of time, however, it has been clearly proved to be an island, first under the governor Agricola and now under the emperor Severus', 39. 50. 4. Cf. below on chs. 28 and 38.

hitherto unknown . . . Orcades: Tacitus here exaggerates slightly, as the Orkneys were in fact already known to Roman writers (Mela 3. 6. 54; Pliny,

NH 4. 103), and perhaps before that to Greek ones: Rivet–Smith (433 f.), who discuss various possible meanings of the name in Celtic, e.g. 'whale islands'. Cf. Juvenal 2. 159 ff. (tr. N. Rudd): 'Granted, our armies | have pushed beyond the Irish coast and the recently captured | Orkneys, and also Britain with its paltry ration of darkness.'

Thule: a Greek name, first mentioned by Pytheas in the late fourth century BC, quoted by Strabo 1. 63, as six days' sailing distance north of Britain, probably referring to Iceland, *c.* 600 miles (970 km) beyond northern Scotland: Ogilvie–Richmond, 172. 'The name is obviously very ancient . . . both a geographical term . . . and a semi-mythical and literary commonplace', a proverbial expression (cf. Virgil, *Georgics* 1. 30) for the remotest North, 'not, properly speaking, a British island'. Tacitus here and Ptolemy 2. 3. 14 apply the name to Shetland, presumably because Agricola chose to do so: Rivet–Smith 473, cf. id. 42 f.

the sea there is sluggish: in *Ger.* 45 the sea beyond the Sviones (Swedes) of Scandinavia is similarly described as 'sluggish and almost motionless'. 'The idea of the immovable and windless character' of the northernmost Ocean 'dates back to Pytheas', who, however, 'was certainly alluding to the freezing sea round Iceland': Ogilvie–Richmond (172 f.), who explain the phenomenon described here by Tacitus as what Roman ships coming from the North Sea would have experienced, long periods of being immobilized by the North Atlantic Drift Current.

Ocean and the tides . . . dealt with by many writers: it is not clear which ones Tacitus means; not all that many ancient specialist writings on tidal seas are now known. A pioneering work was that of Posidonius, *On the Ocean*, based on personal observations, e.g. at Gades (Cadiz), of which only excerpts survive, principally in Strabo's *Geography*.

They flow far inland: clearly based on eyewitness accounts of the western sea lochs.

11 *native-born or immigrants*: Tacitus continues this excursus with the standard enquiry about the origins of the inhabitants, indigenous or immigrant. Cf. Caesar, *BG* 5. 12. 1, who gives his view that the inland peoples of Britain were indigenous and those of the coastal regions immigrant, and *Ger.* 2, where Tacitus pronounces the Germans to be indigenous.

as is usually the case with barbarians: one of the few places in *Agr.*—there are rather more in *Ger.*—where Tacitus uses the word 'barbari' of the Britons or Germans. Here it is neutral, meaning something like 'underdeveloped' (and, in this case, lacking historical records); cf. ch. 33, 'the barbarian fashion'. In *Ger.* 18, barbarians are referred to as mainly polygamous, cf. n. on *almost the only barbarians*, and in 45 as ignorant about amber. But cf. 'the savagery common to barbarians' in *Agr.* 16, and 'the barbarous ritual' in *Ger.* 39, where the sense 'barbaric' is clear. (In *Ger.* 33, 'Long may the barbarians continue' translates 'maneat . . . duretque gentibus', where the word 'barbaris' has to be understood; cf. accompanying note in *Ger.* 33.)

11 *the inhabitants of Caledonia, their red-gold hair and massive limbs proclaim German origin*: Celts and Germans were described in similar terms by Greeks and Romans, as large-framed and with red or blond hair and blue eyes. Strabo 7. 1. 2 says that the Germans were only slightly different from the Celts, being 'wilder, taller, and having yellower hair'. Cf. *Ger.* 4, where Tacitus writes of the Germans having 'fierce blue eyes, red hair, and large bodies'. No doubt Agricola passed on his view that the Britons north of the Forth–Clyde line were larger and with redder hair than those to the south, hence more like Germans. There is no evidence for Germanic origin for the Caledonians: immigrant Celtic elements were mixed with a pre-existing population, whose language developed into Pictish, cf. F. T. Wainwright (ed.), *The Problem of the Picts* (Edinburgh, 1956).

Silures, their swarthy features and . . . curly hair . . . Spain: Tacitus is influenced by the mistaken idea that Spain lay opposite Britain, cf. on ch. 10 above, *faces . . . Spain on the west*. But the appearance of the Silures clearly reflected a strong pre-Celtic element in this people, which occupied Glamorgan, Monmouthshire, and southern Brecknockshire. There may have been contact between Wales and Spain in the later Iron Age. Ostorius Scapula (ch. 14) campaigned against the Silures led by Caratacus, *Ann.* 12. 32–3, and they were only subdued by Frontinus in the AD 70s (ch. 17). Their chief town was later Venta Silurum (Caerwent) and a legion was based first at Burrium (Usk) and then at Isca (Caerleon) in their territory.

Those nearest the Gauls: Caesar had already commented on the similarity between the Britons of Kent and the Gauls, *BG* 5. 14. 1.

their rites and their religious beliefs: archaeological evidence confirms the basic identity of religious cult of insular and continental Celts. The Druids, not mentioned here by Tacitus, were strong in both Gaul and Britain, cf. Caesar, *BG* 6. 13; for the importance of Mona (Anglesey) as a Druid centre, *Ann.* 14. 30. Tacitus uses the word 'superstitiones', here translated 'religious beliefs', as often of foreign religions, e.g. of the Germans (*Ger.* 39, 43), Jews (*Hist.* 5. 8), or Christians (*Ann.* 15. 44), rather than *religiones*.

The language: British and Gaulish Celtic were very close to one another, Irish Celtic was markedly different.

We are told . . . their courage has been lost along with their liberty: Tacitus is referring to Caesar, *BG* 6. 24. 1, 'There was once a time when the Gauls were superior in courage to the Germans', as in *Ger.* 28, where he names Caesar as his source. Liberty for subject peoples is as much a major theme for Tacitus as liberty for the Roman élite, but he clearly sees it as in Rome's interest to deprive the 'barbarians' of this freedom, cf. e.g. 24, on Ireland.

12 *infantry*: the Britons did have cavalry, cf. Caesar, *BG* 4. 24. 1 and 32. 5, but most of the regiments of Britons in the Roman army were to be infantry: twelve cohorts against only one *ala*. A Vindolanda writing-tablet, *TV* ii. 164 (*c.* AD 100), refers to the 'Brittones' having 'too many' or 'very many' cavalry; the writer, presumably a Roman officer, adds derogatory comments about their poor skills—and calls them 'Brittunculi', 'nasty little Brits'.

chariots: probably obsolete in Gaul by Caesar's day, but he met them in Britain in 55 BC, *BG* 4. 33.

In former times the Britons owed obedience to kings: Caesar refers to Cassivellaunus ruling over several states, *BG* 5. 11. 9, to the father of Mandubracius having had the kingship of the Trinovantes, 5. 20. 1, and to four separate kings in Kent, 5. 22. 1. Suetonius, *Caligula* 44. 2, calls Cunobellinus (Shakespeare's 'radiant Cymbeline') 'king of the Britons', and Claudius claimed to have conquered 'eleven kings of the Britons' (*ILS* 216). Rome continued some in office and established others, cf. below on chs. 14 (Cogidumnus), 16 (Prasutagus), and 17 (Queen Cartimandua).

Now they are formed into factional groupings: i.e. at the time Tacitus was writing no more kings remained on the island.

nothing . . . helps us more . . . than their lack of unanimity: cf. a similar thought in *Ger.* 33. In *Agr.* 29, the Britons 'had at last learned the lesson' by AD 83. Tacitus makes the Caledonian leader Calgacus aware that Rome has profited 'by our quarrels and disunion', ch. 32.

The climate is miserable: this passage on Britain's climate and natural products at first sight seems to interrupt the discussion of the character of the people, resumed at the beginning of ch. 13. Still, there Tacitus is beginning a new section, 13–17, the history of the island from Caesar's first attempt to conquer it until the arrival as governor of Agricola, the man who finally completed the conquest.

The days last longer: Tacitus is thinking only of the summer, like Juvenal 2. 161, quoted above, n. on ch. 10, *hitherto unknown . . . Orcades*. Pliny, *NH* 2. 186, reported the longest day in Britain as lasting 17 hours, but did not have the latest information about the far north, where it is markedly longer.

apart from the olive and the vine: the Romans were to introduce viticulture, at least as far north as Herefordshire and Lincolnshire.

gold and silver and other metals: gold was mined by the Romans only at Dolaucothi in Wales, whereas silver was extracted from argentiferous lead on a large scale in various parts of the province, the Mendips, Flintshire, the Peak District, and the Pennines. Copper (mainly in North Wales), Cornish tin, and iron were also exploited: Jones–Mattingly, 179 ff.

pearls . . . Red Sea: as elsewhere, it is not clear whether Tacitus refers by this term to the Indian Ocean as a whole; 'rubrum mare' was also used of the Persian Gulf and what we now call the Red Sea.

lacking in quality . . . lacking in greed: as often, Tacitus ends this passage with an epigram, a dry moralizing comment. The nine Latin words are far pithier than translation allows (twenty-three words here).

13 *conscription and taxes*: for conscription, cf. on *infantry* in ch. 12 above; complaints about it, and about taxation, in chs. 15 and 31. In ch. 19 Agricola is said to have made the levying of corn and taxes fairer in his first winter.

13 *the Deified Julius*: i.e. Julius Caesar, declared a god after his murder in 44 BC. There was no need for Tacitus to spell out the fact that Caesar invaded twice. His 'control of the coast' was of course transitory.

The Civil Wars: i.e. between Caesar and the Pompeians, 49–45 BC, and the renewed conflict after his murder, ending with Augustus defeat of Antony and Cleopatra and capture of Alexandria on 1 August 30 BC.

The Deified Augustus . . . 'injunction': on several occasions Augustus is supposed to have planned an invasion of Britain, but nothing came of it. He exercised considerable influence there through diplomacy; and cf. his *Res Gestae* 32. 1, the granting of sanctuary to the 'kings of the Britons Dumnovellaunus and Tincommius' listed among foreign policy successes. Augustus advised Tiberius to 'keep the empire within its existing limits', *Ann*. 1. 11. 4, and he treated 'all [Augustus'] actions and words as having the force of law', ibid. 4. 37. 3.

Gaius Caesar: Caligula's northern expedition, AD 39–40, is also referred to in *Ger*. 37. The sources are all hostile, but, whether or not Caligula planned an invasion, he left the Channel coast without attempting one: A. A. Barrett, *Caligula: The Corruption of Power* (London, 1989), 125 ff.

The Deified Claudius: Claudius' invasion was launched in summer AD 43, with a force of four or five legions and numerous auxiliary regiments under Aulus Plautius. The emperor came later for a token sixteen days to accept the surrender of Camulodunum (Colchester) and the peoples of south-east England, and renamed his new born son Britannicus and celebrated a triumph the next year: G. Webster, *The Roman Invasion of Britain* (London, 1980).

Vespasian: commanded the legion II Augusta in the invasion army with considerable success, including 'the subjugation of two very strong native states and the capture of the Isle of Wight and of twenty settlements ('oppida')', gaining an honorary triumph, Suetonius, *Vespasian* 4. This was still remembered in AD 66 when Nero needed a good general to suppress the Jewish revolt: *FRB* 225 ff.

14 *the consulars*: cf. Glossary.

Aulus Plautius: lacked a *cognomen*, as did Quintus Veranius (below); this style was by this date very old-fashioned. Plautius led the invasion force and remained as first governor until AD 47. On his return he was actually allowed an *ovatio*, a 'minor triumph', usually reserved, like the full triumph, for emperors and their close relatives. Discussed in *FRB* 37 ff.

Ostorius Scapula: Publius Ostorius Scapula, governor from AD 47 until his death in office, evidently in 52. Tacitus is much fuller on him in *Ann*. 12. 31–40. His successes included suppressing an Icenian revolt, founding the *colonia* at Camulodunum (Colchester), and capturing Caratacus, who had escaped to Wales after failing to stop the invasion in 43. Scapula was rewarded with an honorary triumph in 51: *FRB* 41 ff.

colonia: Camulodunum (Colchester) founded in AD 49 or 50, *Ann.* 12. 32.

Cogidumnus: perhaps really *T*ogidumnus, cf. Caratacus' brother Togodumnus, Dio 60. 20–1 (C. E. Murgia, *Classical Philology*, 72 (1977), 339). He is presumably the king on an inscription at Chichester, *RIB* i. 91: the name (in the genitive) is partly restored, '[Ti(beri)] Claud(ii) [Co]gidubni' (or [To]gidubni'). He had become a Roman citizen, taking the emperor's family names. (There is no difficulty about *-dubnus*, rather than Tacitus' *-dumnus*: variation between *b* and *m* is common in Latin versions of Celtic names.) On the stone he is called 're[g(is) m]agni Brit(anniae)', 'Great King of Britain' (as read by J. E. Bogaers, *Britannia*, 10 (1979), 243 ff.) He had this overblown title because by Roman convention client rulers over more than one state were called 'Great King', cf. Herod Agrippa I or II (*ILS* 8957). Cogidumnus (or whatever his exact name was) ruled—at the very least—the area, centred on Sussex and Hampshire, subsequently called the *civitas* of the 'Regni' or 'Regnenses', perhaps 'the people of the kingdom': Rivet–Smith, 445 f. The great Roman house at Fishbourne may have been his palace.

even kings as instruments of enslavement: a characteristic sardonic epigram.

Didius Gallus: Aulus Didius Gallus, consul in AD 39; probably took part in the invasion of 43 with a special cavalry command; gained an honorary triumph after restoring Rome's client king of the Crimea. But in Britain, which he governed from 52 to 57, he was disinclined to do much, although he had to support the client queen of the Brigantes, Cartimandua (*Ann.* 12. 40 and 14. 29, a fuller account than here): *FRB* 44 ff.

Veranius: Quintus Veranius succeeded Gallus in AD 57 but died after only a year, claiming in his will that he would have 'conquered the rest' if he could have had two more years, *Ann.* 14. 29. An inscription from Rome (*AE* 1953. 251) shows that he had a good military record, five years as the first governor of Lycia, 43–8, involving mountain warfare; Onasander dedicated a work on generalship to Veranius: *FRB* 50 ff.

Paulinus: see above, n. on ch. 5, *His first lessons in army life* . . . , where the uprising was mentioned in the context of Agricola's military tribunate.

Mona [Anglesey], which, he thought, was a source of support to the rebels: in *Ann.* 14. 29–30, Tacitus explains the role of Mona, here only hinted at—it was the 'Holy Island' of the Druids. The term 'rebels' is here used from the Roman point of view: natives who 'fought back', instead of submitting, not necessarily those who had already been subjected and made an uprising, as was the case with most of Boudicca's followers. On the revolt and its background, G. Webster, *Boudica* (London, 1978).

15 *the Britons began to discuss*: this is followed by a long section in indirect speech, reporting the grievances of the Britons, turned into direct speech here. It is naturally freely invented by Tacitus, but the grievances were genuine, cf. what Agricola tried to alleviate (ch. 19). In Dio 62. 3–5 Boudicca

herself highlights the contrast between freedom and slavery. Dio also accuses Seneca of provoking the rebellion by suddenly calling in his loans. Tacitus has a fuller version in *Ann.* 14. 29–39: specific causes are named, exactions among Boudicca's people, the Iceni, outrages on Boudicca herself and her daughters, the greed of the veteran colonists at Camulodunum (Colchester), and the introduction of emperor-worship. Some are at least hinted at here.

15 *In former times . . . a single king*: cf. n. above on ch. 12, *In former times the Britons . . .*

the legate . . . the procurator: the oppressive and unjust conduct of the procurator Decianus Catus is stressed both by Tacitus, *Ann.* 14. 32, cf. 38, and Dio 62. 2. 1. He fled the province in panic after the rebels sacked Camulodunum (Colchester), to be replaced by the milder Julius Classicianus, who later complained about Paulinus' harsh treatment of the defeated rebels (cf. n. above on ch. 9, *disputes with procurators*, and text of ch. 16, 'their personal fear of the legate . . . undue severity'): *FRB* 288 f.

the Germanies: Tacitus uses the plural in the Roman fashion, referring to the two military districts, later provinces, of Upper and Lower Germany.

another island: i.e. Mona (Anglesey), cf. ch. 14 above.

16 *Boudicca*: the widow of Prasutagus, client king of the Iceni of East Anglia, *Ann.* 14. 31 ff. The queen's name was earlier misread in both Tacitus' accounts and various other forms were current, 'Boadicea' eventually entering the national consciousness as a national heroine, with a statue on the Thames Embankment. What Tacitus actually wrote was close to what Celtic specialists regard as the probably correct spelling, *Boudica* with one *c*, a name meaning, in effect, 'Victoria'. Further detail in G. Webster, *Boudica* (London, 1978).

they do not distinguish between the sexes: hardly correct. Although the Brigantes had a queen regnant, Cartimandua, Tacitus' statement is not borne out by any other evidence from Celtic peoples. For the German Sithones, ruled by women, at which Tacitus expressed horror, cf. *Ger.* 45, below.

colonia: Camulodunum (Colchester). Its sack is described in detail in *Ann.* 14. 31–2.

seat of their enslavement: in *Ann.* 14. 31 Tacitus improves this phrase: the temple of Claudius there seemed the 'citadel of eternal domination'. For Paulinus' return and victory, somewhere in the Midlands, and the aftermath, *Ann.* 14. 33–9.

the savagery common to barbarians: cf. *Ger.* 39, 'A human victim is slaughtered . . . barbarous ritual', with accompanying note, for another use of *barbarus* in this very negative sense.

Petronius Turpilianus: Publius Petronius Turpilianus, consul at the beginning of AD 61, one of the indications that the date of the rebellion was 60 rather than 61, the year under which Tacitus places his account in

Ann. 14. 29 ff., see further Syme, ii. 765 f. Evidently governor for less than two whole years, since he became curator of aqueducts at Rome in 63: *FRB* 57 f.

Trebellius Maximus: Marcus Trebellius Maximus, consul *c.* AD 56, governor 63–9: *FRB* 59 ff.

never inspected the camps: the phrase ('nullis castrorum experimentis') is generally rendered 'with no military experience', although A. J. Church and W. J. Brodribb (tr.), *Tacitus: Agricola* (London, 1877), 16, offered 'never ventured on a campaign'. This, like the translation given here, matches what is said about the soldiers' idleness shortly afterwards. This governor is almost certainly the same man as the Trebellius who had conducted a successful campaign in the Taurus mountains thirty years earlier, *Ann.* 6. 41, and thus did have military experience: *FRB* 60 f.

seductive vices: this must refer to the Britons adopting Roman practices. Agricola was to encourage this himself, cf. ch. 21 (and accompanying notes), where the process is portrayed more positively.

the Civil Wars: cf. chs. 7 and 8 and accompanying notes. Trebellius' downfall is described in more detail in *Hist.* 1. 60, where it emerges that the mutiny was orchestrated by the commander of the Twentieth legion, Marcus Roscius Coelius, cf. ch. 7 and n. on *praetorian legate*. Trebellius joined Vitellius at Lugdunum (Lyons). Vettius Bolanus, who happened to be there, was made his successor, *Hist.* 2. 65.

Bolanus: cf. ch. 8 and n. on *Vettius Bolanus* for Agricola's service under this governor.

17 *when . . . Vespasian recovered Britain as well*: Vespasian had not exactly 'recovered Britain', but clearly Bolanus, an appointee of Vitellius, recognized him, probably well before the end of AD 69, and was retained in office.

great generals . . . Petilius Cerialis: Frontinus, below, and Agricola himself, ch. 18, are described as great men—not, however, Cerialis, see above on *Petilius Cerialis* in ch. 8, whom Tacitus regarded as lucky but rash.

the Brigantes: the 'high people' (Rivet–Smith, 278 ff.), whose territory spanned the Pennines and perhaps extended into south-west Scotland, were initially pro-Roman. On their queen, Cartimandua, cf. ch. 8 above on *Vettius Bolanus*.

victory or war: the phrase suggests less than total success. Still, the new dating (based on dendrochronology) of the foundation of Carlisle (Luguvalium) to AD 72–3 (*Britannia*, 21 (1990), 320) rather than to Agricola's governorship, shows that Cerialis got further north than is generally assumed in modern accounts, probably into southern Scotland (as argued long ago by E. Birley, *Roman Britain and the Roman Army* (Kendal, 1953), esp. 13 f., 39 ff.). Cf. also n. on ch. 20, *had operated on equal terms*. Cerialis probably left Britain after the campaigning season of 73, to be succeeded by Frontinus (see next note).

17 *Julius Frontinus, a great man, in so far as it was then possible*: Sextus Julius Frontinus was one of the new emperor Trajan's most important allies, consul for the second time when Tacitus was finishing this work; in AD 100 he was to be consul again, as Trajan's colleague: details in *FRB* 69 ff. Tacitus is irritatingly brief here: presumably it would have been inappropriate to say more about a man then so prominent.

took up and sustained the burden: may be taken to mean that Frontinus continued Cerialis' operations in the north, as well as launching a new campaign in South Wales.

the Silures: see on ch. 11, above. On Frontinus in Wales (clearly active not just in the south): Hanson, 51 ff.; Jones–Mattingly, 72 f. and full bibliography; M. G. Jarrett, *Early Roman Campaigns in Wales* (7th Caerleon Lecture; Cardiff, 1994).

18–40 Agricola's governorship, which lasted seven years, is allotted almost half the biography, from Agricola's arrival (ch. 18) up till the handover to his unnamed successor (ch. 40). Within this more than half the space is devoted to the final battle of the Graupian Mountain (chs. 29–38)—and the lion's share within this battle narrative goes to the speeches by the opposing leaders (chs. 30–34).

18 *already midsummer*: i.e. late June or early July of AD 77, rather than 78 (as Ogilvie–Richmond and others): see Introduction, on Tacitus' career (pp. xx ff.), and R.-Charlier, 1842 ff. *aestas*, 'summer', in a military context refers to the campaigning season, from spring to autumn equinox, 22 March to 22 September, as elsewhere here, e.g. chs. 20, 23, 25, 29.

Ordovices: occupied much of North Wales, including Snowdonia. Their name evidently means 'hammer-fighters': Rivet–Smith, 434. For this campaign: Hanson 46 ff.; id., *ANRW* II. 33. 3 (1991), 1757 ff.

The summer was over: i.e. it was late September by the time that the new governor had arrived at the nearest major military base, Viroconium (Wroxeter), where his old legion, XX Valeria Victrix, was stationed, or Deva (Chester), under construction for II Adiutrix (three lead pipes from this fortress have been found, dated AD 79, with Agricola's name: *ILS* 8704a, etc. = *RIB* ii. 2434. 1–3).

Mona . . . Paulinus: see above, on ch. 14.

who knew the fords: thus Ogilvie–Richmond (211), inferring that the phrase refers to men who had served in Paulinus' aborted invasion of Mona in AD 60. It might, however, just mean 'who had experience of shallow waters', meaning the Batavian auxiliaries.

whose national practice was to swim while carrying their weapons: on the Batavians' skills, cf. *Hist.* 4. 12, *Ann.* 2. 8, and on the people, below, n. on ch. 36, *four Batavian . . . cohorts*, and *Ger.* ch. 29.

laurel-wreathed dispatches: Pliny, *NH* 15. 33, mentions this custom when a victory was reported. Agricola, no doubt properly, treated the undertaking as minor.

19 *force achieves little if followed by undue harshness*: this surely refers to Paulinus' suppression of the Boudiccan revolt and his measures after it, ch. 17. Agricola 'had learned from' Paulinus' experience.

his own household: 'household', 'domus', probably refers not to the governor's official staff establishment, as Ogilvie–Richmond (213 f.), but to Agricola's personal slaves and freedmen, a fair number of whom must have accompanied him. Cf. the next sentence, '. . . no use of freedmen or slaves for official business'.

staff appointments: selected soldiers and centurions served on the headquarters staff, *officium*, of the governor. Cf. text below, 'staff and administrative posts', 'officiis et administrationibus'.

levying of corn and taxes: J. C. Mann (*Britannia*, 16 (1985), 21 ff.) stresses that taxes, *tributa*, were paid in money; the corn-levy was not a tax, but a compulsory purchase at a fixed price, much as in Sicily in the 70s BC, Cicero, 2 *Verrines* 3. 188 ff. Mann also argues that this passage is nothing but rhetoric, 'the stock description of the "Good Governor"'. It is true that if these abuses really were going on when Agricola arrived, they must by implication have been tolerated or overlooked by his predecessor, the excellent Frontinus. Still, it is not impossible that they had just resumed, after an interval, i.e. that soldiers or civilian officials had taken the chance to line their pockets precisely while Agricola was campaigning in North Wales.

20 *the negligence or arrogance of previous governors*: cf. above, on the corn-levy abuses. If Tacitus meant to exempt Frontinus and Bolanus (cf. ch. 16, 'an upright man and not hated for any misdeeds') from this criticism, 'previous governors' must refer principally to the long-serving Trebellius (ch. 16) and to Cerialis. (This sentence is placed at the start of ch. 20 in the traditional arrangement, but obviously belongs to the previous paragraph.)

when summer came: i.e. the campaigning season, late March, of his second year, AD 78.

estuaries and forests: the former term must refer principally to the coast of north-west England up to the Solway, but perhaps to south-west Scotland also, e.g. the mouth of the river Nith (Wigtown Bay was no doubt outside the area reached at this stage). But if Carlisle had been established as a base some five years earlier, cf. above on ch. 17, the Solway should have been reconnoitred already, if not necessarily the estuaries to its south, e.g. Morecambe Bay or the Ribble.

many states: this should refer to more than just the Brigantes, even if they had subdivisions. Tacitus uses the same word here, in the plural, 'civitates', 'states', as in ch. 17 for the Brigantes, there specifically a single *civitas*, 'the most populous in the whole province'. The only known names south of the Forth–Clyde are, from west to east, the Novantae, Selgovae, and Votadini: Rivet–Smith, 425, 455, 508 f. Perhaps there were also some smaller *civitates*, the names of which have disappeared from the record.

had operated on equal terms: Ogilvie–Richmond (219) render this as 'had lived on a footing of equality with others (i.e. independent)', which is

unsatisfactory. The natural sense is that peoples that had previously held their own against Rome—initially when Cerialis was governor, probably under Frontinus too—were now prepared to make peace.

20 *no new part of Britain . . . so little damage*: i.e. a new part added onto the Roman province of Britannia. The area between the Tyne–Solway and Forth–Clyde lines must be meant, but it is impossible to be sure how much of it was involved.

21 This chapter is unique in the literary sources for Roman history as a record of officially sponsored 'Romanization'.

the following winter: i.e. that of AD 78–9. An inscription from Verulamium (St Albans), *AE* 1957. 169, very fragmentary, records the erection of some public building under Agricola. This might reflect the measures here mentioned—although if it recorded the completion of the work, the building was no doubt begun under Frontinus or Cerialis.

widely dispersed and primitive settlements: cf. *Ger.* 16, on the Germans' dislike of living in towns.

temples, market-places, and town houses: three characteristic features of a Roman town. Tacitus might have added e.g. basilicas, theatres, and water-supply and drainage. He does mention baths later, but negatively. 'Town houses' is perhaps too restrictive for 'domos'. The country house or farm was generally called a *villa*, but Tacitus may here just mean 'Roman-style houses', whether in the towns or the countryside, to replace the round wooden buildings normal among the native population.

the liberal arts: cf. n. on *liberal studies*, ch. 4 above.

the Roman tongue . . . desire for eloquence: Juvenal 15. 110 f., reflects the fruits of this policy: 'Today the entire world has its Graeco-Roman culture; smooth-tongued Gaul has been coaching British barristers.' It was not just the '*sons* of the leading men' that took to liberal studies. Martial, 11. 53, writing about the same time as *Agr.*, praises the culture, Greek as well as Latin, of a young British woman, Claudia Rufina.

the toga was everywhere to be seen: this ought to mean more than just a fashion for Roman dress: wearing the toga was prohibited for non-citizens, cf. e.g. Suetonius, *Claudius* 15. 2. Agricola may have secured citizenship for substantial numbers of the southern British élite.

allurements of evil ways: cf. on *seductive vices*, in ch. 16 above. The 'evil ways' do not strike us as being particularly undesirable. Indeed, baths are deservedly regarded as a major Roman contribution to health and civilization. Tacitus is here thinking as a moralist: the Britons (those who could afford it) were led astray, abandoning the simple life in favour of decadent idleness and luxury.

The Britons . . . called it 'civilization', although it was part of their enslavement: the cynical epigram comes oddly at the end of a passage praising Agricola's measures. Tacitus could not resist making comments of this kind;

cf. *Ger*. 23, and *Hist*. 4. 64, where the Tencteri, who had joined the Batavian Revolt, urge the citizens of Cologne—formerly the German Ubii, now the Romanized Agrippinenses—to renounce the 'pleasures that help the Romans, more than force of arms does, to control their subjects'.

Either here or in ch. 19 Tacitus could have mentioned a change, perhaps on Agricola's recommendation: the appointment of a *iuridicus*, or assistant governor for civilian affairs. But this might have detracted too much from the focus on his hero. With northern campaigns taking him further and further from the 'civilian' zone of the province each year, Agricola presumably found it difficult to carry out judicial duties without assistance. See *FRB* 211 ff. for the known *iuridici*, the earliest perhaps appointed in AD 79.

22 *The third year . . . opened up new peoples*: the campaign of AD 79: such successes against 'new peoples' accords well with Dio's statement, 66. 20. 3, that Titus, emperor since June of this year, 'received the title of *imperator* for the fifteenth time' because of Agricola's successes in Britain. (This is preceded, in the abbreviated version of Dio, by an account of Agricola's campaigns which summarizes his whole governorship, 20. 1–2.) The peoples in question may have included the Dumnonii and Venicones: Rivet–Smith, 343 f., 490 f. (who, however, place the latter north of the Tay).

the Taus [Tay]: Rivet–Smith, 470.

Experts commented: Ogilvie–Richmond (230) take 'adnotabant', imperfect in Latin, as 'analogous to an epistolary imperfect', implying that Tacitus had consulted written sources. It is hard to see what these could have been. It is far likelier that Tacitus had spoken to 'experts' or old hands—for example experienced centurions and equestrian officers—who had served under Agricola. Besides, it has been argued in the Introduction (p. xxii) that Tacitus is likely to have been there himself, as a young military tribune, conceivably until the end of this campaigning season. Whether Agricola selected a site for a new legionary fortress at Inchtuthil on the Tay as early as this season must be doubted. Many would argue that Tacitus here exaggerates Agricola's special skills: praise of good generals for this quality was standard, cf. Livy 35. 14. 9 on Hannibal, or Statius, *Silvae* 5. 2. 41 ff. on Vettius Bolanus in Armenia.

No fort established by Agricola was ever taken . . . by storm or abandoned by capitulation or flight: at the time Tacitus was writing, many, if not most, Agricolan forts in Scotland had been given up, in fact since *c*. AD 87 or soon after, cf. Hanson, 143 ff. Tacitus does not actually say here that any had been given up, stressing here only that none had been overrun. The change of policy about which he complained in *Hist*. 1. 2, 'Britain completely conquered—and let go', had caused the planned Roman withdrawal, which he chooses not to mention here.

The enemy . . . had been used to making good the summer's losses: these opponents, although 'new peoples', had, to judge from this sentence, already been in regular conflict with Rome, albeit only in the campaigning season. What

Agricola's 'opening up' of these peoples, as far as the Tay, involved for the first time was the establishment of forts which kept the natives under control throughout the winter as well.

22 *he was rather harsh*: one of the few really personal touches, which, combined with the brief remark in ch. 44, 'he was good-looking, if not particularly tall', produces the picture of a peppery little general. But see next note.

his anger left no hidden traces . . . you did not need to fear his silence: the unspoken contrast is with the despotic Domitian, who 'brooded over his resentment in silence', ch. 39.

23 *The fourth summer was spent in securing what he had overrun*: i.e. the campaigning season of AD 80 was spent mainly building the forts for which he had chosen such excellent sites in the previous year. Cf. Hanson (107 ff.) for discussion of where Agricola's forts were.

if the . . . glory of the Roman name had permitted it, a frontier had been found within Britain itself: the Forth–Clyde line, on which the Antonine Wall was later built, would certainly have made a suitable frontier. What really lay behind this may have been rather different: Titus, perhaps on Agricola's advice, ordered a halt; the limit of the province had been reached. Hence in the next season, AD 81, Agricola turned to the area south-west of the Clyde, ch. 24; then in 82, after Titus' death, Domitian ordered total conquest, ch. 25. Tacitus would not, however, wish to write: 'if Domitian had permitted it', or 'if Domitian had not countermanded it'.

the enemy had been pushed back, as if into a different island: this phrase is echoed in the *Historia Augusta*, *Antoninus Pius* 5. 4: that emperor 'conquered the Britons through his legate Lollius Urbicus, another wall, of turf [i.e. the Antonine Wall], being erected when the barbarians had been pushed back'.

24 *In the fifth year . . . he crossed in the leading ship*: there have been various proposals to amend 'nave prima', 'in the first ship', e.g. by adding or substituting 'Anavam' (the river Annan) or 'Itunam' (the Solway Firth); neither necessary nor plausible: Ogilvie–Richmond, 235.

defeated peoples up to that time unknown: that they were previously unknown makes it hard to believe, as often argued, that they were in south-west Scotland, i.e. Galloway. The people of that area, the Novantae (Rivet–Smith, 425) must have been known since at latest the early 70s AD, when Carlisle was occupied, a good eight years. One may suggest the Epidii of Kintyre (ibid. 360) and e.g. the inhabitants of the Isle of Arran and the land between Loch Long and Loch Fyne. No names have been transmitted.

that part of Britain that faces Ireland: Ogilvie–Richmond, 236: 'the Rhinns of Galloway'. More plausible is the Mull of Kintyre, anyway considerably closer to Ireland than Portpatrick is.

midway between Britain and Spain: cf. above, n. on ch. 10, *faces . . . Spain on the west*, for the misconception about the position of Britain in relation to Spain.

I have often heard him say: 'often', i.e. in the years between Agricola's return in AD 84 and Tacitus' departure from Rome in 90. At the very time when Agricola was close to Tacitus the forces supposedly adequate to conquer Ireland had been withdrawn from Britain: one legion and some *auxilia*, Hanson, 151. Agricola's thought was perhaps that not only could his conquests in northern Britain have been held on to—Ireland could have been conquered as well, if Domitian had not taken troops away. (J. C. Mann (*Britannia*, 16 (1985), 23 f., defends Agricola's estimate as realistic in the light of the figures on each side at the Graupian Mountain, cf. ch. 33.)

advantageous against Britain as well, if . . . freedom were . . . removed from sight: Agricola thought freedom for subjects of Rome or 'barbarians' outside the empire who might threaten it a bad thing—from Rome's point of view. Yet Tacitus is capable of putting into eloquent language these peoples' yearning for freedom, e.g. chs. 15 and 30–2.

25 *in . . . his sixth year in post he enveloped the states . . . beyond the Bodotria*: in AD 82 Agricola returned to the area he had reached three years before (ch. 22) and began fortifying it. 'enveloped' is thus not metaphorical: Ogilvie–Richmond (239) refer to the line of posts blocking the glens. See on these Hanson, 115 ff. Shortly before the end of the previous campaigning season, Titus had died; the new emperor Domitian retained Agricola in post and clearly authorized a final drive to conquer the whole island, reversing the decision of AD 80 to make the Forth–Clyde line the frontier, cf. on ch. 23 above, *if the . . . glory of the Roman name*.

the fleet: the *classis Britannica*, of which the main base was normally across the Channel, at Boulogne (Gesoriacum, later Bononia), in Gallia Belgica; its British headquarters, later at Dover, was at this time probably at Richborough (Rutupiae): H. Cleere, in V. A. Maxfield (ed.), *The Saxon Shore* (Exeter, 1989), 18 ff. Cf. below, n. on ch. 38, *the Trucculensian harbour*.

The peoples who inhabit Caledonia: evidently the whole of 'Scotland north of the Forth–Clyde Isthmus', as Rivet–Smith (289 f.), already implied by 'all the peoples on the further side' earlier in this ch. At least ten peoples may be involved, cf. the names in Ptolemy 2. 3. 8–9, from the Creones to the Vacomagi, among them 'the Caledonii'; but it is not clear whether there was really a people or state of this name. Full discussion of Ptolemy, including the problem of the 'turning' of Scotland, by Rivet–Smith (103 ff., text and translation of 2. 3. 8–9, 140 f.). Tacitus here and elsewhere (chs. 10, 11, 27, 31) only uses the term 'Caledonia', for the land north of the isthmus, never 'Caledonii'.

he himself divided his army into three divisions: traces of Agricola's army are no doubt revealed by marching-camps, but it is difficult to relate them precisely to this or other seasons: Hanson, 121 ff. Division into three was a sensible measure, not merely 'to avoid encirclement' but to simplify logistics: a three-pronged, parallel advance would allow the army to move faster and to live off the land.

26 *the Ninth Legion, as being by far the weakest*: as its fortress was at York (Eburacum), the most northerly of the legionary bases, it may have left a greater proportion of its men behind than the other three legions, to guard the Pennines: Syme, *RP* vi (1991), 21 n. 17.

Had not marshes or forest covered the retreating enemy, that victory would have ended the war: it is difficult not to infer that this sentence quotes Agricola's dispatch to the emperor, which resulted in him being allowed one more season. He had by this time had twice the normal tenure, cf. above on ch. 9, *less than three years*, and must have expected to be replaced at any time.

27 *the opportune actions and skills of the general*: Tacitus neatly imagines the Britons paying tribute to Agricola's generalship.

28 *That same summer a cohort of Usipi*: this brief digression marks a pause before the climax of the biography, the great victory of AD 83. It may also suggest that Tacitus was thinking of his next work. In any case, these mutineers had already gained publicity, cf. Martial 6. 60: 'the fickle people of the blond Usipi and whoever does not love Ausonian [i.e. Italian] rule'. They are mentioned again in *Agr.* in the speech of Calgacus, ch. 32.

conscripted in the Germanies: by the Flavian period the Usipi, previously in the Lippe valley, had settled on both sides of the river Lahn, opposite the dividing line between Upper and Lower Germany, hence 'Germanies' here, plural (cf. *Ger.* 32, where the Usipi are briefly mentioned as neighbours of the Chatti). The Usipian territory may only have been formally annexed by Domitian in the following year, AD 83; as often the case with border peoples, they had clearly been compelled to supply recruits for the Roman army before then, cf. n. on *Ger.* 34, *Frisii*.

they sailed round Britain: also reported by Dio 66. 20. 1–2. His account, drastically condensed by Xiphilinus, suggests that it was only through the mutineers' voyage that Agricola proved Britain to be an island. This is misleading—their fate and where they had sailed was not to be known for some time; see chs. 10 and 38 with accompanying notes.

the Suebi: cf. *Ger.* chs. 2 and 38 ff. Most of the Suebian Germans, a designation which covered 'the greater part of Germany', were east of the river Elbe. It is not clear where the ones who captured the shipwrecked mutineers were, but presumably not far from the Frisii.

the Frisii: they occupied the northern coast of the Netherlands, cf. n. on *Frisii* in *Ger.* 34.

29–38 These chapters are devoted to the battle of the Graupian Mountain.

29 *losing a son that had been born the previous year*: Agricola's wife Domitia Decidiana, who had borne her first child in AD 62 (cf. n. on *daughter*, ch. 6 above), was thus with Agricola in Britain. She was probably still in her mid-thirties.

show of endurance: cf. on *ostentatious deaths*, ch. 42 below. The same word, 'ambitiose', is used as here translated by 'show of', hence it is hard to avoid

the conclusion that Tacitus is contrasting the naturalness of Agricola with the Stoics' demeanour. For work providing relief from sorrow, cf. *Ann.* 4. 13. 1, Tiberius consoling himself for the loss of his son Drusus by dealing with 'negotia' ('business').

loud expressions . . . that belong to women: naturally avoided by the manly Agricola; but cf. below on *weeping that belongs to women*, ch. 46, where Tacitus seems to disapprove of it even for women, namely Agricola's widow and daughter.

reinforced by the bravest of the Britons: this must refer to troops from southern Britain. No units of Britons are as yet attested serving in Britain itself. A few examples are known of Britons recruited in the 80s AD, from the Dobunni and Belgae and from Ratae (Leicester): A. R. Birley, *The People of Roman Britain* (London, 1979), 102, cf. 188 ff. for a list of units. Conscription of Britons is also referred to in chs. 13, 15, 31, and 32.

loyalty . . . tested in a long period of peace: cf. ch. 11, the Britons 'not yet . . . made soft by prolonged peace'.

the Graupian Mountain: the name was mistakenly printed as 'ad montem Grampium' in the first edition by Francisco dal Pozzo (Puteolanus), *c.*1475–80, which led to the renaming of part of the Scottish Highlands as the Grampians, in what was thought to be the place of the battle: Ogilvie–Richmond, 84, 251 f. Some argue that the correct form should be Craupius, comparing Welsh *crwb*, 'hump', others regard the name as pre-Indo-European or Pictish: Rivet–Smith (370 f.), who prefer to leave the matter open after full discussion. G. Maxwell, *A Battle Lost: Romans and Caledonians at Mons Graupius* (Edinburgh, 1990), is the most detailed and most recent study, reviewing all the proposed locations of the battlefield from Perthshire to near John o' Groats (cf. Map 2). Jones–Mattingly (76 f.) have an excellent map with a brief review of seven different sites, and (77 ff.) discuss, with further maps, the numerous Roman marching-camps so far identified in northern Britain, the northernmost being at Fochabers (also called Bellie), close to where the river Spey flows into the Moray Firth. In favour of the most northerly location speak Calgacus' claim that 'there is no people beyond us, nothing but tides and rocks', ch. 30, and Agricola calling the battlefield 'the furthest point of Britain', and referring to 'such a long march', ch. 33. Both are in rhetorical passages, to be sure, but cf. A. A. R. Henderson, *Classical Views*, 29, NS 4 (1985), 318 ff.

a common danger could only be warded off by a united front: cf. ch. 12 above, 'their lack of unanimity', and ch. 32, Calgacus on 'our quarrels and disunion'.

'old age was still fresh and green': this is a quotation from Virgil, *Aeneid* 6. 304, slightly adapted.

decorations: this may be an eyewitness item, from Agricola, referring to Celtic torques.

29 *Calgacus*: otherwise unknown; the name evidently means 'swordsman', see K. H. Jackson, in F. T. Wainwright (ed.), *The Problem of the Picts* (Edinburgh, 1956), 135, citing the Irish *calgach*.

words like these: whether or not the Caledonian army was inspired by a speech, the one here, chs. 30–2, is a free composition by Tacitus. It has much in common with other speeches put in the mouths of Rome's enemies, e.g. Sallust, *Jugurtha* 10 and 14; Caesar, *BG* 7. 77; and cf. Tacitus' own *Hist.* 4. 17 and 32, and *Ann.* 12. 34 and 37. Here Tacitus is most of all influenced by the letter of King Mithridates denouncing Roman imperialism in Sallust's *Histories* 4. 69. Cf. Syme, ii. 528 f.; Ogilvie–Richmond, 253 ff.

30 *freedom for the whole of Britain*: cf. the words attributed to the Briton Caratacus before his final battle, *Ann.* 12. 34. The whole of the present speech is dominated by the contrast between freedom and servitude.

the last people on earth: cf. ch. 10 above, 'this coast of the remotest sea'.

the last to be free: but cf. ch. 25, on Ireland, clearly able to retain its freedom, which Agricola would have liked to end. Calgacus is understandably allowed to overlook this last home of the free.

everything unknown is given an inflated worth: one of the best known of Tacitus' epigrams ('omne ignotum pro magnifico'), although the thought is naturally not new, cf. Caesar, *Civil War* 3. 36. 1; and, indeed, above, ch. 25, 'exaggerated, as the unknown usually is, by rumour'. The general denunciation of Roman imperialism at the end of this ch., where e.g. 'they have pillaged the world' echoes Sallust, *Histories* 4. 69. 22 (cf. Ogilvie–Richmond, 256 ff.), is often cited, especially the climax: see next note.

They make a desert and call it 'peace': again, the thought was not new, cf. Pliny, *NH* 6. 182, 'Roman arms have not yet made a desert there [in Ethiopia]'; Tacitus has a variant in *Hist.* 4. 17. 2, where the rebel leader Civilis is made to say that the Romans 'call wretched servitude by the false name of peace'. (Cf. also Introduction, p. xxxix.)

31 *torn away by conscription to be slaves in another land*: service of Britons in other parts of the empire is better attested than in Britain itself, cf. n. on ch. 29 above, *reinforced by the bravest of the Britons*.

Wives and sisters . . . raped: cf. *Ann.* 12. 34, where Caratacus urges the Britons to resist, and keep the bodies of their wives and children inviolate, and 14. 31. 1, the rape of Boudicca's daughters.

taxation . . . grain-requisition . . . building roads: cf. n. on ch. 19 above, *levying of corn and taxes*.

those born to be slaves: a typical Roman viewpoint, cf. Livy 36. 17. 5 on the Greeks of Asia, 'the most worthless sort of men and born to be slaves'. The contrast with Britons, born to be free, remains implicit; instead 'logic is sacrificed to rhetorical point' (Ogilvie–Richmond, 259), and a different cause for resentment is named.

the latest newcomer . . . is the object of derision even to his fellow slaves . . . in this slave-houshold . . . we are the new ones . . . who are picked out to be

destroyed: the comparison of the provinces to the members of a slave-houshold may be rhetorical. Yet the Vindolanda writing-tablets, very close in date to *Agr*., confirm that the northern Britons, Rome's newest subjects in the west, were looked down on and maltreated by men from the continent. British conscripts, whose qualities as cavalrymen were disparaged, were referred to contemptuously as 'Brittunculi', '(nasty) little Brits', *TV* ii. 164 (cf. also n. on ch. 12 above, *infantry*). In a draft letter, ibid. 344, the writer complained bitterly that he, 'a man from overseas', *homo tra*(n)*smarinus*, probably from Gaul or Germany, as well as 'innocent', should not have been flogged: he clearly implies that the natives *could* be chastised with no redress.

the Brigantes, with a woman as their leader: Tacitus might have deliberately made Calgacus confuse the larger and more northerly Brigantes, about which a Caledonian might be supposed to have heard, with the smaller and remoter Iceni of East Anglia. But he has probably made a slip (unless the error was created by a copyist who remembered the Brigantes from ch. 17). It was the Iceni, with support from others, including the Trinovantes—neither named in *Agr*.—who rebelled, with the widowed queen consort (not a queen regnant) Boudicca, as their leader, cf. above, chs. 5 and 15–16, and *Ann*. 14. 31 ff. The Brigantes, ruled by Cartimandua, were by contrast largely pro-Roman until she was expelled in AD 69, *Hist*. 3. 45; *Ann*. 12. 36 and 40.

set a colonia *in flames*: cf. chs. 5 and 16 above.

and stormed a fortress: Petillius Cerialis, legate of the Ninth legion, after failing to rescue Camulodunum (Colchester) and losing a lot of his men, escaped into his *castra* ('camp'), probably not Lindum (Lincoln) but a 'half-legionary' base, at Longthorpe near Peterborough (Jones–Mattingly, 88 ff.), where he was protected by its defences, *Ann*. 14. 32. One need not call 'stormed' a mistake by Tacitus; here one may reasonably suppose that 'the speaker is made to exaggerate': Ogilvie–Richmond, 260.

32 *Gauls and Germans and . . . many Britons*: Gallic and German units were strongly represented in the army of Britain, although Spain, the Danubian provinces, Thrace, and other areas were also represented: details in M. G. Jarrett, *Britannia*, 25 (1994), 35 ff. On Britons, cf. n. on ch. 29 above, *reinforced by the bravest of the Britons*.

gold and silver: a reference to the gold leaf on the legionary eagles and the silver decoration of the other standards, cf. *Ann*. 15. 29. 1.

coloniae of old men: probably a rhetorical plural, as only Camulodunum (Colchester) is known to have been a *colonia*. But Lindum (Lincoln) could also have become one by this time. It was a Flavian foundation (inferred from *CIL* xiii. 6679), and the empty fortress which was used for the new town had been vacated by the legion II Adiutrix *c*. AD 77, cf. above on ch. 18, *The summer was over*. The third *colonia*, Glevum (Gloucester), was founded under Nerva, AD 96–8, *ILS* 2365.

towns sick and disunited: the word here rendered 'towns', 'municipia', was a technical term for chartered towns. Only Verulamium (St Albans) is known

to have had this status in Britain, if the term is used in the strict sense in *Ann.* 14. 33. 2; there may have been one or two others by now, or the word may be used imprecisely here—or it may be a rhetorical plural.

33 *the barbarian fashion*: 'barbarian' is here used neutrally, cf. n. on ch. 11 above, *as is usually the case with barbarians*; cf. also *Ger.* ch. 3 on the *baritus*.

Agricola . . . addressed them as follows: Tacitus may have heard about Agricola's speech from his father-in-law, but this is doubtless largely his own composition. In any case, while Roman generals did harangue their troops before battles, it is a question how many of the men would have been able to hear the speech. (J. C. Mann (*Britannia*, 16 (1985), 23 f.) estimates that Agricola had some 17,000 in his army on this occasion. The same applies, even more strongly, to Calgacus' 30,000 Caledonians.)

under the auspices of the Roman empire: Agricola would, it may be supposed, actually have referred to the three successive emperors, Vespasian, Titus, and Domitian, under whose auspices he and his army had been campaigning during these years. Apart from Tacitus' wish not to name Domitian here— so Ogilvie–Richmond, 266—one may assume that his wish for concision influenced his phrasing.

To have accomplished such a long march: only through this remark and similar items earlier in Agricola's speech does Tacitus give an idea of what happened during the six months or so of the campaigning season of AD 83. It was not until late September that the battle took place, cf. on *summer was already over*, ch. 38 below. The march involved 'passing through forests and crossing estuaries'—could this mean not just the Firths of Forth and Tay, no longer novelties, but also the Moray and Dornoch Firths? Cf. on *the Graupian Mountain*, ch. 29 above.

their abundant supplies: the contrast is with Agricola's army 'marching light', ch. 29. Of course, the Romans could be and no doubt were to some extent supplied by sea, while Calgacus is made to say that 'we have [no] fertile lands', ch. 31. North-east Scotland—Angus, Moray, Nairn, and the Buchan plateau—has some excellent agricultural land, cf. Hanson, 128. But perhaps Agricola's men were beyond the Moray Firth.

34 *new peoples*: cf. on this expression n. in ch. 22, *The third year . . . opened up new peoples*, and in ch. 24, *defeated peoples up to that time unknown*.

last year: i.e. in the sixth season, AD 82, the attack on the Ninth legion, ch. 26.

crown forty years: this translation assumes a textual corruption, 'L' for 'XL'; this was only the forty-first year since the invasion under Claudius.

35 *the auxiliaries . . . the infantry, which numbered eight thousand*: the 8,000 would include the 'four Batavian and two Tungrian cohorts' mentioned below (ch. 36), totalling at least 3,000 if the cohorts were still all 'quingenary'. Cf. Glossary on *auxilia* and cohort, and n. on ch. 36, *four Batavian and two Tungrian cohorts*.

three thousand cavalry: not necessarily made up just of six 500-strong cavalry *alae*. The cavalry elements in mixed cohorts could have been detached and brigaded together for the battle. Cf. Glossary on *ala* and cohort.

no Roman blood: the thought is not far different from that in *Ger*. 33, where Tacitus rejoices at sixty thousand Germans being killed by one another, while the Romans watched.

the charioteers: cf. on *chariots* in ch. 12 above.

the colours: the 'vexilla' were the flags of the auxiliary regiments, as here (also of legionary detachments, as in ch. 18, where 'legionum vexillis' is translated 'the legionary detachments').

36 *four Batavian and two Tungrian cohorts*: cf. notes on *Ger*. chs. 29 (*Batavians*) and 2 (*the ones who first crossed the Rhine . . . Tungri*) for these two German peoples. These Batavian cohorts (reorganized after the eight original cohorts had rebelled under Civilis in the Rhineland, AD 69–70) were the First, Second, Third, and Ninth, the Tungrians the First and Second. The Batavians were probably all *equitata*, i.e. with a cavalry detachment. It is not known whether any were yet *milliaria*, '1,000 strong'. The Ninth Batavians, and for a time all or part of the Third Batavians, were stationed at Vindolanda *c*.90–105, when they left for the Danube region, where they were certainly *milliaria*; they left numerous records on writing-tablets at Vindolanda, cf. *TV* ii, *passim*, and Introduction, pp. xvi, xxxii. The two Tungrian cohorts, the second being part-mounted, remained in Britain throughout their history, apart from being temporarily in the Rhineland when they also joined the rebellion. By the early second century both had become *milliaria*. Cf. also Glossary on *ala*, *auxilia*, cohort, decurion, etc.

The other cohorts: how many are meant depends on the size of the Batavian and Tungrian units, which could have accounted for between *c*.3,000 and 4,500 of the 8,000 auxiliary infantry mentioned in ch. 35. Thus there could have been between seven and ten 'other cohorts', if these were all normal size, to supply the remaining 3,500–5,000 men. (But all the regiments concerned would have left some men at winter quarters.)

the cavalry squadrons: these could well be squadrons, 'turmae', detached from the cavalry section of the part-mounted cohorts, rather than from the *four regiments of cavalry* mentioned in ch. 37 (cf. n. below) or other cavalry *alae*.

37 *four regiments of cavalry*: these 'alae', kept in reserve, were more highly trained than the troopers in the part-mounted cohorts.

a vast and grim spectacle: this opening and the description that follows are influenced by Sallust on Marius' victory near Cirta in Numidia, 106/5 BC, *Jugurtha* 101. 11.

strong light-armed cohorts: 'light-armed' probably refers just to auxiliary, as opposed to legionary cohorts.

37 *the cavalry*: here probably from the mounted sections of the Batavian or
other *cohortes equitatae*, cf. above on *four Batavian and two Tungrian cohorts*
in ch. 36, rather than from *alae*.

some ten thousand of the enemy: perhaps merely 'a guess' as (Ogilvie–
Richmond, 280), and no doubt at best an estimate made by Agricola's men.
In the Republic only generals who 'had killed at least five thousand enemy in
a single battle' were permitted to hold a triumph, Valerius Maximus 2. 8. 1.
Agricola's figure is exactly twice the minimum. This underlines his standing
as the true heir of the great Republican commanders, rather than the
emperor with *his recent sham triumph*, cf. on ch. 39 below, where the 'many
thousand dead' in Agricola's battle are again stressed.

three hundred and sixty: this figure is presumably authentic. Tacitus is said by
Orosius 7. 10. 4 to have declined to register Roman casualties in *Hist.*—but
that probably referred only to the Danubian disasters, cf. on *so many armies
had been lost* in ch. 41 below. In *Ann.* 14. 37. 2 he gives Roman losses in the
final battle against Boudicca's Britons as 'about four hundred', compared
with 'a little more than eight thousand' of the enemy. When Roman losses
were small, it was a matter of pride to register them.

Aulus Atticus, prefect of a cohort: this is the sole name of any of Agricola's
subordinates that Tacitus chooses to supply. He only gives *praenomen* and
cognomen, not the family name, which was probably Julius. This young man
could, for instance, have been son of the Julius Atticus who wrote on viticulture, 'more or less as a pupil' of Agricola's father Graecinus: Columella 1. 1.
4. The prefecture of a cohort was the first grade in the equestrian officer's
career. Such prefects were often very young: E. Birley, *Roman Britain and the
Roman Army* (Kendal, 1953), 133 ff.

38 *summer was already over*: i.e. it was after the equinox, 23 September, cf. R.-
Charlier, 1843, and notes on *already midsummer* and *The summer was over* in
ch. 18 above, and on *his recent sham triumph* in ch. 39 below. (The incorrect
translation, 'the summer was almost over', in H. Mattingly's Penguin translation, 1948, p. 89, has been retained in the revised version of 1970, p. 90.
Other versions somewhat blur the meaning: 'iam exacta' can surely only
mean 'already completed'.)

the Boresti: otherwise unknown, cf. Rivet–Smith, 272 f. Their location, evidently beyond *the Graupian Mountain*, cf. on ch. 29, above depends of
course on where that was. Might the 'Cornovii' of Ptolemy 2. 3. 8, located in
Caithness (Rivet–Smith, 325) be a MSS misreading of 'Boresti', misled by
the Cornovii of England, 2. 3. 11 (and in Greek the name begins KOR-, easy
to confuse with BOR-)?

sail round Britain: cf. above on *a Roman fleet for the first time circumnavigated*
in ch. 10, *they sailed round Britain* in ch. 28, and 'fleet' in ch. 29.

new peoples . . . winter quarters: who and where these peoples were depends
on the location of the battle and, to some extent, on the position of the
winter quarters. The term 'hiberna', is found in a draft letter by Flavius

Cerialis, prefect of the Ninth Batavians at Vindolanda, written *c.* AD 100, *TV* ii. 225. Some forts at least (all of turf and timber) had probably been built by Agricola north of the Forth before the end of his last season, cf. Hanson, 143 ff. A note of hand by Quintus Cassius Secundus, soldier of the Twentieth legion, promising to repay his comrade 100 *denarii*, written on 7 November AD 83, has been found at Carlisle (Luguvalium): R. S. O. Tomlin, *Britannia*, 23 (1992), 146 ff. Tomlin (150 ff.) shows that some at least of the legion was probably stationed there in 83 and that it may have been Agricola's base (ibid. 152 n. 57, referring to unpublished texts). The Twentieth is the likeliest legion to have occupied the fortress of Inchtuthil in Perthshire; but this base was probably not begun until soon after Agricola had left Britain, only to be abandoned before completion, *c.* 87: L. Pitts and J. K. S. St Joseph, *Inchtuthil: The Roman Legionary Fortress* (London, 1985); Hanson, 146 ff., 150 f.

the Trucculensian harbour: a much discussed name, often emended to 'Rutupensem', i.e. Richborough, but Rivet–Smith (478 ff.) argue in favour of retaining 'Trucculensem' (even if the exact name has been distorted in transmission), to be interpreted as a harbour in northern Scotland.

39 *Agricola's dispatches*: the Latin 'epistulis', plural, can often refer to a single letter or dispatch. The time taken for a letter to reach Rome from the south coast of Britain is estimated at twenty-five days in summer: Ogilvie–Richmond, 318. In autumn it would be longer; and as the news first had to come from the north of Britain, the letter is unlikely to have reached Rome before mid-November at earliest.

his recent sham triumph over Germany: this refers to the expedition against the Chatti, following which Domitian took the title 'Germanicus', 'conqueror of the Germans', as well as holding a triumph. (Suetonius, *Caligula* 47, has a similar story about fake German prisoners, extra large Gauls with hair died blond, who were even made to learn some German to be more convincing. Cf. n. on *the grandiloquent threats of Gaius Caesar* in *Ger.* 37.) Cf. further the notes on *Ger.* 29, *'Ten-Lands'*, and *Ger.* 37, *In recent times . . . the objects of triumphs rather than victories*. Tacitus' friend the Younger Pliny likewise called Domitian's triumphs (he held another in AD 89) 'imitations, for victory that had been faked', *Pan.* 16. 3; and Dio, 67. 3. 5–4. 1, although giving no detail on the triumph, is derogatory about the Chattan campaign. Frontinus, by contrast, writing under Domitian, *Strategemeta*. 2. 11. 7, cf. 2. 3. 23, is understandably positive, if not flattering, and the poets, particularly Martial and Statius, praised the emperor to the skies. Whether or not the triumph was deserved, its date has been controversial, affecting the chronology of Agricola's governorship: see n. on *immediate prospect of a consulship* in ch. 9 above. For autumn 83, before the news of Agricola's victory reached Rome: *FRB* 77 ff. and R.-Charlier, 1844 ff., with further references.

public eloquence . . . brought to silence: cf. n. on *fifteen years* in ch. 3 above.

he brooded over his resentment in silence: cf. Pliny, *Pan.* 48. 3, describing Domitian as 'that fearful monster lurking in his den'. By contrast Agricola

would sometimes show hot temper but never harbour hidden resentment, cf. n. on ch. 22 above, *his anger left no hidden traces* . . .

39 *Agricola still held Britain*: i.e. Domitian perhaps thought that Agricola, commanding a very large and battle-trained army, with which he was undoubtedly very popular, might have mounted a *coup d'état*. This was indeed to be attempted in AD 89 by the commander of the Upper German army, Lucius Antonius Saturninus. But Agricola was not this sort of man, cf. on ch. 42 below, *there can be great men under even under bad emperors*.

40 *an honorary triumph*: the last non-member of the imperial family to hold a triumph was Lucius Cornelius Balbus in 19 BC. The substitute devised by Augustus was the 'honorary triumph', with various honours of which the statue in triumphal dress was the most prominent: D. E. Eichholz, *Britannia*, 3 (1972), 149 ff. Dio, 66. 20. 3, apparently says that Agricola was given the honour 'by Titus', but this may be a textual error.

the province of Syria . . . reserved for senior men: Syria had at this time some four legions, like Britain. Titus Atilius Rufus, whose death created the vacancy, had previously been governor of Pannonia, *CIL* xvi. 26, a province with several legions. Cf. *FRB* 28 f. It is not known who actually replaced Rufus in AD 84.

a freedman from one of the senior palace departments: the last three words render 'secretioribus ministeriis', literally 'the more secret ministries' or 'ministers', the latter retaining the sense 'servants' as well (cf. 'civil servant'). Ogilvie–Richmond (289) take the expression to refer 'to a personal freedman of Domitian's and not an official from one of the civil service departments'. They compare the sending of Polyclitus to Britain by Nero in AD 61, to inspect the conduct of Suetonius Paulinus (*Ann.* 14. 39), evidently overlooking this freedman's prominence, cf. e.g. Tacitus, *Hist.* 2. 95; Pliny, *Ep.* 6. 31. 9.

an imperial letter of appointment: 'codicillos', the word reserved for letters in the emperor's own hand, cf. *ILS* 8826; *AE* 1962. 183.

may be true, or it may be a fiction: a characteristic Tacitean alternative. The story can hardly have come from Agricola himself.

Agricola handed over to his successor a province peaceful and secure: Agricola's successor is unknown. The only other governor of Britain under Domitian so far on record is Sallustius Lucullus, put to death allegedly for naming a lance that he had invented after himself, Suetonius, *Domitian* 10. 2–3. That 'untamed' Britain (ch. 8) was now pacified was a special achievement. Whether newly conquered Caledonia was a 'desert', as Calgacus is made to claim (ch. 30), is another matter.

His style of life was modest: 'cultu modicus' might just mean 'he dressed simply', i.e. that he never wore the triumphal dress, cf. on *an honorary triumph*, above. But holders hardly ever did wear the regalia. Moderation and self-restraint are among Agricola's hall-marks, cf. n. on *from philosophy* . . . *a sense of proportion* in ch. 4 above, and on *self-restraint*, ch. 42 below.

41 *He was often accused in his absence before Domitian*: as the next sentence, 'not any actual charge or a complaint', shows, Agricola was not actually prosecuted and acquitted. Informers presumably tried without success to induce Domitian to take action against Agricola, knowing that the emperor was jealous of him. Cf. Dio 67. 64. 4: 'he [Domitian] hated those who were successful.'

so many armies had been lost, in Moesia and Dacia, in Germany and Pannonia: the principal disasters were those to the governor of Moesia, Oppius Sabinus, in AD 85, and the Prefect of the Guard, Cornelius Fuscus, in 86 or 87. Both were defeated and killed by the Dacians, 'in Moesia' and 'in Dacia' respectively, both with heavy losses, for which Tacitus in his *Hist*. declined to give figures, according to Orosius 7. 10. 4. In a later defeat, AD 92, by the Sarmatian Jazyges (cf. on *Ger*. 1, *Sarmatians* and *Dacians*), the legion XXI Rapax was wiped out and its commander killed. This was part of a campaign against Suebian Germans (Marcomanni and Quadi, cf. on them in *Ger*. ch. 42) and Sarmatians (cf. on them in *Ger*. ch. 1), hence presumably 'in Pannonia'. 'Whether "in Germany" refers to this "Suebo-Sarmatian" war or to the second campaign against the Chatti, following the revolt of Saturninus, in 89 is not clear. The sources are meagre, cf. esp. Suetonius, *Domitian* 6. 1; Dio 67. 7 ff. P. Southern, *Domitian: Tragic Tyrant* (London, 1997), 92 ff., has a concise and clear discussion.

so many military men: the expression 'militares viri' here probably refers to officers, as distinct from *milites*, 'soldiers'. This might include a few of senatorial rank, as well as equestrians and centurions, who lost their lives 'with so many cohorts', through the 'folly or cowardice of their generals'.

the frontier of the empire and the river-bank: the terms 'limes' and 'ripa' refer respectively to the land frontiers, e.g. in Upper Germany and Raetia beyond the Rhine and Danube (cf. n. on *frontier line* in *Ger*. 29), and to the river lines, of Rhine and Danube. *Limes* was just coming into vogue as a term for frontier line when Tacitus wrote. Tacitus declines to mention here that a result of these defeats and losses was the withdrawal of the legion II Adiutrix and some *auxilia* from Britain to reinforce the Danube army and the consequent abandonment of Agricola's Caledonian conquests. Cf. Hanson, 151 ff.; P. Southern, *Domitian: Tragic Tyrant* (London, 1997), 75 ff.

42 *to ballot for the proconsulship of Africa or Asia. The recent murder of Civica*: the two provinces, approximately equivalent to modern Tunisia with Tripolitania and part of western Turkey, were the most prestigious of the ten governed by annual proconsuls in the Republican fashion, cf. Introduction (p. xx). The year in question for Agricola was probably at earliest AD 88, some twelve years after his consulship, depending on how long after the 'murder of Civica' is meant by 'recent'. In any case, the exact date at which Gaius Vettulenus Civica Cerialis was put to death while serving as proconsul of Asia, for—allegedly—planning a coup (Suetonius, *Domitian* 10. 2), is not known. Civica was replaced in the first instance by an equestrian procurator, *ILS* 1322.

42 *plea to be excused*: for another man who won the proconsulship of Asia in the ballot but withdrew, cf. *ILS* 1011, Salvius Liberalis, a slightly younger contemporary of Agricola who was *iuridicus* of Britain and may have been in Britain with him, *FRB* 211 ff.

the proconsular salary: all provincial governors received a salary from Augustus onwards, Dio 53. 15. 4. The figure for the two consular proconsuls, who probably received the highest salary of all governors, was 1,000,000 sesterces in AD 217, Dio 78. 22. 5. Agricola was well off, cf. 'handsome fortune' in ch. 44 below, but would no doubt have appreciated this money, more than eight hundred times the annual pay of a legionary (just increased to three instalments of 400 sesterces each, Dio 67. 3. 5).

self-restraint: 'moderatio', and in ch. 7 above, where it was translated 'moderation', 'modestia', 'discretion', further on in this chapter, and 'modus', 'a sense of proportion' (ch. 4), related expressions, describe a quality which Tacitus especially valued (cf. also e.g. Agricola's 'middle course' when praetor (ch. 6), his restraint as legionary legate (ch. 8), his refusal to quarrel with procurators (ch. 9), his modesty about his capture of Anglesey (ch. 18)). Tacitus would later praise Marcus Lepidus for having similarly trodden the 'middle way', *Ann*. 4. 20. 2–3, and Lucius Calpurnius Piso the *pontifex* for his wise moderation, ibid. 6. 10. 3. This chapter in particular is what makes *Agr*. something of a political manifesto as well as a biography. *Agr*. 'offers a temperate defence of political opportunism', as Syme (ii. 540), put it, 'interrrupted by a violent and personal outburst'.

court renown and ruin by defiance and an empty parade of freedom: the reference is to the 'Stoic opposition', cf. above on *Arulenus Rusticus* and others in ch. 2, and below on *Helvidius* and others in ch. 45. But rather than being disgusted by the Stoic 'martyrs' themselves, for whom Tacitus obviously had some respect, and about whose deaths he confesses in ch. 45 to a feeling of guilt, he was clearly sickened by their admirers.

Those whose habit is to admire what is forbidden: these people are the main object of Tacitus' scorn, 'the noisy advocates of the heroes and martyrs' (Syme, i. 25). After Domitian's murder, when it was safe to speak out, these unnamed persons 'had not confined their reprobation to evil men, the willing agents of despotism' but had, by implication, 'arraigned Agricola's conduct, or his own, for cowardice and subservience', Syme, ibid. Cf. Dio 68. 1. 2–3 and Pliny, *Ep*. 9. 13, for the situation after Domitian's murder.

there can be great men even under bad emperors: Tacitus was determined to reinstate this principle, cf. n. on *Julius Frontinus* in ch. 17 above; for Agricola as a 'famous and great man' after his first victory, cf. ch. 18; and for the summing up cf. ch. 44, 'You would . . . be glad to think him a great [man]'.

ostentatious deaths that do not benefit the Commonwealth: Martial 1. 8 had expressed this view about twelve years before. On 'great Thrasea', Nero's victim, and the younger Cato, he remarked that he does not regard as laud-

able the man who 'buys his fame by easy shedding of his blood'. Whether Tacitus was here thinking just of the 'martyrs of AD 93' (see ch. 45) or, more generally, of the tradition going back to Cato (46 BC), and including Thrasea and the elder Helvidius (Priscus), is not clear. His account of Helvidius Priscus' death is not extant, but when he introduces him in *Hist.* 4. 5 f., the presentation is positive, except for 6. 1: 'some thought him too eager for fame—for even with philosophers desire for glory is the last failing to be shed.' Further, ibid. 4. 8. 3, a reply to Helvidius by a 'time-server' in AD 70, may reflect Tacitus' feelings: 'we all hope for good emperors, we have to put up with whatever we get . . . let Helvidius be put on a par with Cato and Brutus—I am just an ordinary senator.'

43 *the persistent rumour that he had been poisoned*: it is not clear whether Tacitus, who was not in Rome at the time (cf. n. on *he was lost to us four years earlier* in ch. 45 below), believed the rumour, although *his premature death* in ch. 44 below (cf. n.), suggests that he may have. When describing the death of Agricola again, in his *Hist.*, Tacitus may have stated his firm belief in the truth of the rumour: that would explain why Dio, 66. 20. 3, who probably used the *Hist.* as a source, says that Agricola 'was murdered by Domitian'. Dio also reports an alleged outbreak of wholescale posioning under Domitian, 67. 11. 6: probably in fact 'pestilence', cf. R. Syme, *Some Arval Brethren* (Oxford, 1980), 21 ff.; id., *RP* vii (1991), 564, registering a string of premature deaths in the years *c.*89–93. The odds are that Agricola succumbed to some epidemic—late August (ch. 44 below) is often an unhealthy season in Rome.

relays of messengers: if, as often, Domitian was not in the Palace but at his summer retreat, 'the Alban citadel' (cf. n. on *Carus Mettius . . .* in ch. 45 below), which would have been much pleasanter than the city at this time of year, it would have been worth using relays of messengers to cover the fifteen miles or so (25 km.) from there to wherever Agricola's house was in Rome.

Agricola's will: it had become common to make the emperor a joint heir in the hope that the rest of the will would be respected, cf. Suetonius, *Caligula* 38 and *Ann.* 14. 31. 1, Boudicca's husband Prasutagus. Domitian had at first declined to accept such bequests, Suetonius, *Domitian 9.* 2, but this changed, 10. 1, 12. 1–2.

44 *Agricola was born . . . when Gaius Caesar was consul for the third time*: there is no need to emend this year-date, AD 40: R.-Charlier, 1827 ff. The year was so described, rather than as usual by the names of a pair of consuls, because Caligula's intended colleague died just before 1 January, Suetonius, *Caligula* 17; Dio 59. 13. 2.

good-looking, if not particularly tall: 'decentior quam sublimior' can be translated in various slightly different ways, e.g. 'well-proportioned if not particularly imposing'. I prefer to take *sublimior* rather literally—admittedly it is hard to find an exact parallel for such usage, for the word is poetic, not normal prose language. Tacitus was perhaps thinking of Corbulo, the arche-ypal great general who was cheated of the rewards of fame: he was 'corpore ¬gens', 'huge in stature', *Ann.* 13. 8. 3. Agricola could not match that.

44 *to have escaped what was to come*: this is more than the conventional thought, as in Seneca, *Consolatio ad Marciam* 20. 4, etc. Domitian's 'purge', ch. 45 below, began within weeks of Agricola's death.

Trajan's principate, which he used to predict . . . in our hearing: this prophecy and prayer, evidently repeated, could surely only have been made during the period when Agricola was back at Rome, from AD 84, until Tacitus' departure, probably in 90, cf. *he was lost to us four years earlier*, ch. 45 below. A plausible moment might theoretically have been early in 89, when Trajan came into prominence as legate of the legion VII Gemina. He brought it rapidly from Spain to the Rhine to help suppress the revolt of Saturninus, Pliny, *Pan.* 14. 2–5, perhaps also at the beginning of 90, when he would have been designated to be consul *ordinarius* for 91. But the prediction may well have been invented by Tacitus, 'a happy artifice' (Syme, i. 29) to associate Agricola (and himself) in people's minds with the new emperor.

his premature death: this suggests Tacitus was inclined to believe *the persistent rumour . . .* of poisoning, cf. on ch. 43 above. 'premature' is on the face of it contradicted in ch. 45 by 'felix . . . opportunitate mortis', often rendered 'happy in his timely death'.

He had missed that final period: Syme, *RP* vii (1991), 561 ff., discusses the timing.

45 *the senate-house under siege*: cf. *Ann.* 16. 27. 1, the meeting of the senate in the temple of Venus Genetrix surrounded by the Praetorian Guard at the time when Thrasea was facing death.

so many consulars in that same act of butchery: only two ex-consuls, Rusticus and Helvidius, are known to have been executed at this time. But perhaps some of the other consular victims of Domitian, listed as well as these two and Civica (cf. n. on *to ballot for the proconsulship . . .* ch. 42 above) by Suetonius, *Domitian* 10. 2 ff., 11. 1, met their death late in AD 93. Syme, *RP* vii (1991), 568 ff., discusses the Stoic 'political group' in detail.

so many most noble women: apparently only three, namely Arria, widow of Thrasea, Fannia, daughter of Thrasea and widow of the elder Helvidius (Priscus), and Gratilla, presumed wife of Rusticus: Pliny, *Ep.* 3. 11. 3; 5. 1. 8, discussed by Syme, *RP* vii (1991), 575 ff. But it is likely enough that Anteia, wife of the younger Helvidius, was also exiled for a time, and the wives of Mauricus and Senecio (identity unknown), Syme, op. cit. 579, 582.

Carus Mettius . . . inside the Alban citadel: Carus was a notorious informer and prosecutor, *delator*, normally referred to as Mettius Carus (names inverted here in archaizing fashion). He had defended Baebius Massa (below) at his trial for corruption and then hit back by prosecuting Senecio and Fannia, Pliny, *Ep.* 1. 5. 3, 7. 19. 5. His 'single victory' up till then is not identifiable, unless it was the condemnation of the Vestal Virgin Corneli* which took place at the 'Alban citadel', cf. Pliny, *Ep.* 4. 11. 6. This * Domitian's country retreat, close to the Papal residence at Castel Gand*

south of Rome. The word 'citadel', 'arx', recalls the ancient city of Alba Longa, incorporated within the imperial villa.

Messalinus: Lucius Valerius Catullus Messalinus, the much feared blind senator, who had been colleague of the young Domitian as consul *ordinarius* in AD 73, was consul again in 85, and served Domitian as an adviser, cf. e.g. Juvenal 4. 113ff., Pliny, *Ep.* 4. 22. 5f.

Massa Baebius was still a defendant: normally referred to as Baebius Massa. He was still an equestrian procurator in AD 70; *Hist.* 4. 50. 2; he had been made a senator and was prosecuted by the Younger Pliny and Senecio in 93 for corruption as proconsul of Baetica. Massa was duly found guilty and then turned on his accusers with a countercharge of treason against Senecio. Pliny, *Ep.* 7. 33, supplied Tacitus with his own account for him to use in the *Hist.*

we ourselves: Tacitus, evidently back at Rome by the time the vote came in the senate, had to give his verdict against the defendants. This is a confession of his guilt—but guilt in which all those in the senate at the time obviously should have shared.

Helvidius: son of Helvidius Priscus (ch. 2 above), cf. Syme, *RP* vii (1991), 574ff., 585f. His offence was to have mocked Domitian in a play with an ostensibly mythological theme, Suetonius, *Domitian* 10. 4.

Mauricus and Rusticus: Quintus Junius Mauricus and Quintus Junius Arulenus Rusticus, brothers, cf. n. on *Arulenus Rusticus . . .* in ch. 2 above, and Syme, *RP* vii (1991), esp. 571 ff. Both were friends of the Younger Pliny. The son of Rusticus became a mentor of Marcus Aurelius, cf. his *Meditations* 1. 7; Syme, *RP* vii. 584. Mauricus returned from exile after Domitian's murder, Pliny, *Ep.* 1. 5, etc.

Senecio's . . . blood: Herennius Senecio was the most junior member of the group; he had refused to seek office higher than the quaestorship, which was treated as suspicious; he was the colleague of the Younger Pliny in prosecuting Massa, then himself accused and convicted of treason. Pliny, *Ep.* 7. 33; Dio 67. 13. 2, etc.

A special torment under Domitian: unlike Nero, who stayed away from the trials of Thrasea and others, *Ann.* 16. 27. 1, Domitian took pleasure in attending.

that flushed face: his complexion was apparently naturally flushed, Suetonius, *Domitian* 18. 1, taken as a sign of modesty when he was young, *Hist.* 4. 40. 1, and later regarded as a screen to hide the shame he should have felt, but did not, Pliny, *Pan.* 48. 4.

he was lost to us four years earlier: as often with Roman numbers, this figure is probably rounded up and may well mean 'more than three years earlier'. If so, Tacitus may not have left to take up an appointment abroad, probably as commander of a legion, until spring AD 90, to serve for about three years, returning to Rome late in 93, after Agricola's death.

46 *If there is a place for the spirits of the just*: that the soul may survive is a conventional sentiment found, e.g. in Sulpicius Rufus' letter consoling Cicero, *Ad familiares* 4. 5. 6, on the loss of his daughter, in the poets, such as Ovid, *Amores* 3. 9. 59, and on tombstones. Hence it need not reflect personal belief by Tacitus in an afterlife.

weeping that belongs to women: cf. ch. 29 above, Agricola's loss of a son, borne without 'the loud expressions of grief that belong to women', and *Ger*. 27, where German men are more restrained than their women. Unrestrained grief was regarded as unmanly, cf. Seneca, *Letters* 99. 24 and other passages cited by Ogilvie–Richmond, 312 f. Tacitus is here urging that 'we', Agricola's family, and thus, albeit female, his daughter and wife as well, as made explicit a few sentences later, should all refrain from 'feeble regrets and the weeping that belongs to women'.

Many of the men of old will be buried in oblivion: this is not just Horace's thought, *Odes* 4. 9. 25 ff.: there were many heroes before Agamemnon but no one knows about them because they had no Homer to sing their praises. Tacitus proclaims that many of those who are still heroes when he is writing will eventually be forgotten about, but this is not the case with Agricola.

Agricola's story has been told for posterity and he will survive: Tacitus is confident about the likely survival of this, his first work. If we did not have *Agr.*, then the three lead pipes from Chester (*RIB* ii. 2434. 1–3), the fragmentary stone inscription from St Albans (*AE* 1957. 169), and the two short passages in Dio, 39. 50. 4 and 66. 20, would have ensured that Agricola's existence, his governorship of Britain in AD 79, and his honorary triumph were none the less registered. It would presumably also have been accepted that 'he was murdered by Domitian', as the second Dio passage claims, cf. above on ch. 43, *the persistent rumour* . . . But nothing else about the man would have been known—and far less about the first four decades of Roman rule in Britain.

ON THE ORIGIN AND LAND OF THE GERMANS

The above was apparently the proper title of the work, *Germania* or *Germany* simply being a convenient short form: Anderson, 33; Lund, 17.

1 *Germany as a whole*: the phrase, 'Germania omnis' inevitably recalls the opening of Caesar's *Gallic War*, 'Gallia omnis', also used by Pliny, *NH* 4. 105, but it was a stock formula in ethnographic writings, cf. Herodotus 4. 17. 1, 'Scythia as a whole'.

the Gauls, Raetians, and Pannonians: as Germany's neighbours, peoples rather than Roman provinces are named. Tacitus' list omits the Celtic peoples of Noricum, mentioned in ch. 5 below, where two provinces are named. The Latin *Gallus*, *Gallicus*, etc., being equivalent to 'Celt, Celtic'

etc., 'Gallis' here was perhaps intended to cover the Celtic inhabitants of Noricum. A small province, Raetia, mentioned in ch. 3, occupying much of present Bavaria, took its name from the Raeti, but this people, who evidently spoke a pre-Indo-European language (Livy (5. 33) thought that they were of Etruscan origin), extended as far as Lake Como and South Tirol, while the province of Raetia (cf. on this in ch. 41 below) included several Celtic peoples. The Pannonians were Illyrian-speaking, but the Roman province Pannonia (chs. 5 and 28), like Raetia, also included several Celtic peoples. In ch. 29, cf. n. on *frontier line* there, it is clear that Tacitus was aware that the boundary between Rome and Germany was no longer formed along their entire course 'by the Rhine and Danube rivers', but he preferred to avoid complicating the picture at the outset. 'Germany' as so defined excludes the two Roman provinces constituted by Domitian in the 80s, formerly military districts, Germania Superior and Germania Inferior. Part of the population of both provinces is none the less treated in part II: the Upper German Vangiones, Triboci, Nemetes (ch. 28), and Mattiaci (ch. 29); the Lower German Ubii (ch. 28) are the exception that proves the rule, having been moved from the right to the left bank of the Rhine by Rome, while the Batavians lived on the Rhine island (ch. 29). Some other Germanic or supposedly Germanic peoples well to the west of the Rhine are mentioned but not treated in any detail: the Treveri and Nervii of Gallia Belgica (ch. 28); and the Tungri, supposedly the original 'Germani', who belonged either to Belgica or to Germania Inferior, crop up in ch. 4.

Sarmatians: a general name for peoples of Iranian descent who had begun moving from central Asia to the lands north of the Black Sea in the second century BC. The Romans were principally concerned with the westernmost group, the Jazyges, who occupied the Hungarian plain between the rivers Theiss and Danube *c.* AD 50, and the Roxolani, whose territory stretched from the river Dnieper to the Danube, cf. below on the Bastarnae and Sarmatians in ch. 46, with accompanying notes. The Roxolani and Jazyges were divided from one another by the Dacians.

Dacians: this large and powerful people, related to the Thracians of the Balkans, occupied the Transylvanian plateau and territory to the west and south of it. They had inflicted heavy losses on Rome a few years before Tacitus wrote, cf. n. on *so many armies . . . in . . . Dacia* in *Agr.* ch. 41, above, and were to be defeated twice by Trajan, AD 101–2 and 105–6, the second war being followed by the annexation of Dacia as a Roman province.

mutual fear or by mountains: a typically Tacitean phrase, combining the abstract with the material, with even more alliteration in the Latin. The mountains are the Carpathians.

The Ocean: the great river that flowed round the inhabited world. What is here referred to is both the North Sea and the Baltic, the latter called 'the Suebian Sea' in ch. 45 but nowhere else—just 'Ocean' in ch. 44.

1 *wide peninsulas*: Jutland is the obvious example.

and islands: especially Scandinavia, thought to be an island (cf. n. on *The peoples of the Sviones* in ch. 44) until the eleventh century: Anderson, 35.

Mount Abnoba: the Black Forest, from the east side of which the Danube rises. The name also occurs in Pliny (*NH* 4.79), on dedications to the goddess Diana Abnoba (*ILS* 3914–15, 9269, from the Black Forest), and in Ptolemy (2. 11. 5, 6, and 11).

2–4 As the 'origin of the Germans' is part of the title of the work, a detailed discussion was to be expected. This was standard in ancient ethnography, cf. e.g. Herodotus 4. 5 ff. on the Scythians, or Tacitus himself, *Hist.* 5. 2 ff., on the Jews. In *Agr.* whether the Britons were 'native-born or immigrants' is the subject of ch. 11.

2 *the original inhabitants . . . very little foreign blood*: the view that the Germans were autochthonous is first explained on negative grounds: their remote position and unfavourable climate must have deterred immigrants.

who would have left . . . ?: Anderson (39) renders 'peteret' 'would have left?', which suits what has gone before. Lund (112) argues that 'nisi si patria sit', 'unless it were his home country', requires a present sense for 'peteret'. This then becomes an expression of personal feeling by Tacitus, which is not very convincing. More probable is the suggestion that 'unless it were his home country' is an addition to the text, e.g. by a German monastic scribe.

raw climate: Seneca, *De providentia* 4. 14, is even more extreme, writing of Germany's 'perpetual winter, harsh climate, and infertile soil.' Cf. the slightly less critical view of the British climate and soil, *Agr.* 12.

In the ancient songs: the second proof that the Germans are the original inhabitants of their country is taken from their own traditions. These songs are not mentioned in any other sources, but cf. *Ann.* 2. 88. 4, German songs about Arminius. How Tacitus acquired this information is a matter of guesswork—from a predecessor, whose work is lost, from Roman or Gallo-Roman traders, or from Germans, e.g. those serving in the *auxilia*? Tacitus himself is only prepared to accept Tuisto and Mannus and is sceptical about the sons of Mannus.

Tuisto: the name means 'hermaphrodite', cf. the German word *Zwitter*: Lund, 113. Being descended from an 'earth-born' deity, the Germans were thus truly autochthonous or indigenous, not of immigrant origin.

Mannus: i.e. 'man', the first human being, manifestly an authentic Germanic name. The latest discussion is by Timpe, 1 ff.: the descendants of the three sons covered German territory on the coast, in the interior, and on the Rhine respectively, a concept from a period before the eastern Germans were known. Tacitus reports the genealogy here, but elsewhere ignores the three groupings.

Ingvaeones: Timpe (1 ff., cf. 51 f.) argues that this name originally belonge to a single people, not a group, and goes back to the Greek explorer Pyth late fourth century BC. The next two names probably became known in

first century BC, having been combined with the first one into a genealogy by Posidonius, a version ignored or tacitly rejected by Caesar: Timpe, 25 ff. He argues further (33 ff., cf. 53 ff.) that Posidonius' Germans (the 'descendants of the sons of Mannus') were a relatively small ethnic group, occupying the flat land bounded by the Rhine and Weser, North Sea, and Central German Uplands (*Mittelgebirge*). The spelling 'Ingvaeones' is that found in some MSS of Pliny, *NH* 4. 96, 'the people of the Ingvaeones, which is the first in Germany'. This north-west group is located by Pliny in Jutland and Scandinavia.

Herminones: the name may mean 'the people of the Almighty', referring to the war-god (cf. n. on Mars, ch. 9 below).

Istvaeones: again, the spelling is that in some MSS of Pliny, *NH* 4. 99, who puts them 'next to the Rhine', more specific than Tacitus' 'the rest'.

some assert that the god had further offspring and that there are further peoples: 'some assert' no doubt refers among others to Livy, book 104, and the Elder Pliny's *German Wars*, both lost. The latter's *NH* 4. 99 ff. contains some of this material: he lists five major groupings of Germans, of which the Vandals are the first, followed by Tacitus' first three, with the Peucini or Bastarnae (here in ch. 46) as the fifth.

Marsi: is elsewhere simply the name of a single state or people rather than of a group of peoples. But a sanctuary of a deity called Tanfana on their territory, probably between the upper reaches of the rivers Ruhr and Lippe, was evidently revered by all the peoples of the region: *Ann.* 1. 50, describing its destruction by Germanicus' troops in AD 14 and the German reaction. The Marsi are not mentioned after AD 41, when Gabinius recovered from them the last of the three eagles lost with Varus, Dio 60. 8. 7.

Gambrivii: otherwise mentioned only by Strabo 7. 1. 3. They are assumed to be connected with the *Sugambri* (who are not included in *Ger.*).

Suebi: unlike the other three peoples here said to have descended from 'alternative' sons of Mannus, the Suebi are treated again later, at great length, beginning in ch. 38, where they are said to 'occupy the greater part of Germany'.

Vandili: i.e. the Vandals, normally spelt Vandali. Pliny's Vandals, *NH* 4. 99, included the 'Burgodiones (Burgundians), Varinnae (the *Varini* of ch. 40 here, cf. n.), Charini (unknown, unless the same as *Harii* in ch. 43 here, cf. n.), and Gutones' (Goths, here *the Gotones* in ch. 44, cf. n.). Tacitus does not name the 'Vandili' again, but it is assumed that the *Lugii* in ch. 43 (cf. n.) are in fact the Vandals: 'the latter an extended ethnic name', 'Lugii' being 'probably a cult-title': Anderson, 198, cf. id. 42, 200.

Further, the name 'Germania' is said to be a new and recent application: 'one of the most disputed sentences in Latin literature', as Anderson (42) put it in 1938. Six decades have brought agreement no nearer. Tacitus' view is that 'Germani' was originally the name of one individual people or state, the Tungri.

2 *the ones who first crossed the Rhine . . . and are now called Tungri*: Timpe (61
ff.) insists that this is what Tacitus reports, not his own view. He presumably
means 'the Germani who live on this side of the Rhine' in Caesar, *BG* 2. 3 f.,
cf. 6. 2 and 32. The 'Tungri' are not mentioned by Caesar, who instead names
the 'Condrusi, Eburones, Caerosi, and Caemani, who are all called by the
one name of "Germani"' (2. 4). (In 6. 32 the 'Segni' are added.) The remnants of the five peoples Caesar knew (and, in the case of the Eburones, did
his best to wipe out, *BG* 6. 29 ff., 8. 24 f.) were no doubt regrouped into a new
civitas under Augustus. Its centre was at the modern Tongres or Tongeren;
the *civitas* in due course became a *municipium*, M.-T. Raepsaet-
Charlier, *Latomus*, 54 (1995), 361 ff. They supplied *auxilia*, notably to
Britain, cf. n. on *four Batavian and two Tungrian cohorts* in *Agr.* 36. Men from
the Second Tungrians serving in Britain specified their origin as from the
'pagus Condrustis', 'the Condrustis district', *RIB* i. 2108, i.e. Caesar's
'Condrusi'. The Tungri themselves could have claimed that they were Caesar's 'left-bank Germans' and the first to have borne the name. Timpe (78 ff.)
argues that the equation was made in or shortly after the Batavian Revolt of
AD 69–70, during which the Tungri threw off their allegiance to Rome and
joined the German side, but not by the Tungri themselves. Timpe suggests
that the Ubii, who had become Roman, as the 'Agrippinenses' of the *colonia*
(Cologne: cf. n. on ch. 28 below, *Even the Ubii . . .*), and had been under
appalling duress at the hands of the anti-Roman party, will have labelled
their hostile neighbours 'Germans'.

the conqueror, through fear, applied it to them all: 'ob metum' is often translated
as 'to inspire fear', although this is contrary to Tacitus' usage, and 'a victore',
'by the conqueror', is often rendered 'after the conqueror', which is abnor-
mal Latin. Both ideas or a combination of the two are based on the premise
that 'the conqueror' means the original Germani who were later called
Tungri. But Timpe (61 ff.) makes a good case for it referring to Rome, who,
after all, did indeed conquer these Germani but, with good reason, was
afraid of their kinsmen across the Rhine, to whom they applied the name.
Tacitus is here in effect giving a condensed version of Caesar's explanation,
although its accuracy is of course highly dubious.

they all called themselves Germani: this statement is certainly mistaken:
Anderson, 46. It was the Romans who applied the name to them. The
Germans had no national name until *diutisc* (later *Deutsch*) emerges in the
Middle Ages as the word for the 'people's' language as opposed to the Latin
used by the Church.

3 *It is said*: 'memorant', lit. 'they recall', cannot refer to the Germans, who are
'eos', 'them', in this sentence; and in any case, the Germans would not have
known about the Graeco-Roman hero. *Hercules visited them as well*: (like
Ulysses, below) Hercules/Heracles was the legendary ancestor of several
ancient peoples, but not of the Germans, even if he had 'visited them': cf.
Seneca, *Apocolocyntosis* 5. 3, 'Hercules, who had wandered round the whole
world and seems to have known every nation'. Cf. also Timpe, 46 ff. The

German songs must have been about a hero whom the Romans identified with Hercules, cf. also ch. 34, n. on *Pillars of Hercules* . . . For such songs, cf. *Ann.* 2. 88. 3, 'Arminius is still sung about among the barbarian peoples'. The German god identified as *Hercules* (on whom cf. n. in ch. 9 below) is presumably different from the hero here: Anderson, 47.

they too have those songs: as interpreted by Lund (117f.), 'they too' refers by implication to Roman battle-songs, called *classica*.

some believe that Ulysses: 'some' probably included Livy and certainly the Elder Pliny, who served as an equestrian officer close to Asciburgium.

Asciburgium: a Roman fort between Vetera (Xanten) and Novaesium (Neuss), *Hist.* 4. 33, near the modern village of Asberg. On Pliny's service in Germany, Syme, *RP* vii (1991), 496ff.

dedicated by Ulysses: rather than 'to Ulysses': Anderson, 51 (the Latin dative could give either meaning). Strabo 3. 5. 6 refers to travellers and conquerors marking the limits they had reached by erecting altars, towers, or pillars, cf. ch. 34 below, on *Pillars of Hercules*. Asciburgium would then be, supposedly, the most north-westerly point reached by Ulysses. Before long a remoter one was produced: Solinus, *Collection of Memorable Facts* 22.1, claims that 'an altar inscribed with Greek letters proves that Ulysses was driven to Calidonia [Caledonia]'. Cf. Rivet–Smith, 85 f., 289 f.

monuments and funerary barrows with inscriptions in Greek: Anderson (51) discusses (sceptically) the suggestion that someone had seen a Celtic inscription in the Greek alphabet in those parts.

4 *never been contaminated by intermarriage . . . the race remains unique, pure, and unlike any other*: taking further the thought in ch. 2, Tacitus insists that the Germans are not only autochthonous and one people, but because of the uniformity of their physical type must have always remained unmixed with other ethnic groups. This section of *Ger.* was misused more than any during the Third Reich, cf. Introduction (p. xxxvii).

fierce blue eyes, red hair, and large bodies: cf. n. on *the inhabitants of Caledonia, their red-gold hair* . . . in *Agr.* 11. An exception is the Bastarnae, whose physique is deteriorating because of intermarriage with the Sarmatians, cf. n. on *and all of them are characterized* . . . in ch. 46; cf. also ch. 20, 'that size of limb and stature which we admire in them'.

5 *The land*: the reference to 'soil', 'solo', at the end of the previous section makes a smooth transition to 'terra'.

forests or . . . marshes: the primeval forest, the *Urwald*, made a deep impression on the Romans, particularly the Hercynian (ch. 28), which stretched unbroken from the middle Rhine to the Vistula. The 'marshes' were principally in the coastal area. Cf. *Ann.* 1. 63 ff. for a description of Germanicus' army contending with them in AD 15.

Noricum: formally a client kingdom with a Celtic population, occupying much of what is now Austria, became a province at latest under Claudius, probably earlier: G. Alföldy, *Noricum* (London, 1974).

5 *will not grow fruit-trees*: exaggerated, unless Tacitus meant vines and olives. But 'with the exception of the apple . . . German names for fruits . . . are all derived from Latin': Anderson, 57.

cattle are their sole . . . wealth: similarly Caesar, *BG* 6. 35. 6, 'they are very covetous of cattle'. The same had applied to Rome, hence the word for money, *pecunia*, from *pecus*, 'cattle'.

Silver and gold . . . who has searched for them?: Tacitus had either forgotten or overlooked the silver-mines in the lands of the Mattiaci (cf. ch. 29), which he refers to in *Ann.* 11. 20. 4; but they did not produce very much or for very long. The famous Rhine gold of the Nibelungen saga 'is not heard of till the fifth century': Anderson, 58.

their envoys or chiefs: Tacitus uses Roman terminology here: the envoys are presumably those sent to deal with Rome; the 'chiefs' may just be 'the leading men' rather than elected magistrates as in ch. 12, 'they also elect the chiefs'.

with notched edges or stamped with two-horse chariots: Republican *denarii* issued before 55 BC. Nero reduced the silver content of the *denarius*, which contributed to the enduring popularity of these early issues; they continued to circulate inside and outside the empire until withdrawn by Trajan about ten years after Tacitus wrote: Anderson, 59 f.

6 *Even iron is not plentiful*: mention of precious metals in the previous section provides the transition to a discussion of iron and thus of weapons, which develops into a review of German manners and customs occupying the remainder of the first part.

as is inferred: translating 'sicut . . . colligitur'. Tacitus is quoting a source (probably the Elder Pliny), which exaggerated the lack of iron: Anderson, 61. But it suited Tacitus, concerned to portray the Germans as primitive, cf. ch. 45, the Aestii 'seldom use iron weapons', and ch. 46, the Fenni tip their arrows with bone 'for lack of iron'. Exceptionally, cf. n. on ch. 43, *The Cotini . . . have iron-mines*, but seem incapable of making use of them.

swords or large lances: only the large cutting sword was rare in the first century AD. Short swords were in common use by this time, as is implied by Tacitus himself in ch. 18, the bride's regular gift from the groom, 'shield with spear and sword'. 'Huge' German lances are referred to by Tacitus in *Hist.* 5. 18. 1 and *Ann.* 1. 64. 3, 2. 14. 3, etc., but were apparently not common: Anderson, 61.

in their own language, frameae: thought to come from *fram*, 'forwards'. The word is also found in Juvenal 13. 79, not referring to Germans, and elsewhere. Anderson (63 fig. 5) illustrates some specimens.

being either naked or lightly clad: i.e. they were able to throw their missiles extra far because they were not encumbered by clothing or armour. For stark-naked Germans fighting for the Gauls in Etruria, cf. Polybius, *History* 2. 28. But 'naked' might mean wearing just trousers, cf. n. on *fits tightly . . . each limb* in ch. 17.

breastplate . . . metal helmet or a leather cap: confirmed by other evidence: Anderson, 64f.

Their horses: likewise Caesar, *BG* 7. 65. 5, comments on the poor horses of his German *auxilia*.

a single wheel to the right: the right wheel was preferred, as it avoided exposing the side not protected by the shield. No doubt they could do a left wheel as well.

their strength lies more in their infantry: the same is said about the Britons, *Agr.* 12. For skilled German horsemen cf. ch. 32 below, on the *Tencteri*.

that is exactly what they are called among their own people: Tacitus' source evidently included the Germanic word *huntari*, 'hundred', which he has translated. He refers to 'a hundred' again in chs. 12 and 39, and some have argued that this passage misunderstands German subdivisions into the 'hundreds' known in later Germany and in Anglo-Saxon England as units within the shire. This is implausible, cf. Anderson, pp. lviii ff., a thorough discussion. Tacitus was probably comparing the German 'hundred' (*huntari*, Anderson, 66) with the Roman *centuria*, Lund, 133.

wedges: cf. *Hist.* 4. 20. 3, the rebel Batavians forming wedges at the battle of Bonn. Some German units in the Roman army were called 'wedge', *cuneus*, e.g. the 'cuneus Frisiorum' at Housesteads on Hadrian's Wall, *RIB* i. 1594.

7 *Their kings*: kingship was far from universal among the Germans, cf. Caesar, *BG* 6. 23, and several places here, e.g. chs. 10, 11, 'king or chief(s)'. A number of states evidently had an aristocratic or oligarchic government by *principes*, 'leading men'. Arminius was killed for trying to make himself king of the Cherusci, *Ann.* 2. 88. 2, although they later accepted a king, ibid. 11. 16. In AD 58 the Frisii had two kings, 'who reigned over that people, to the extent that Germans are ruled at all', *Ann.* 13. 54. The Batavians in AD 69 had a royal family, to which the rebel Julius Civilis belonged, *Hist.* 4. 13. 1. Cf. Anderson, pp. lii ff. on German kingship, clearly restricted in its powers, as this ch. shows; cf. further chs. 11, 42, 44.

their army commanders: here 'duces'; the later Roman title *dux*, 'duke', is the same as the German *Herzog*, lit. 'army leader'.

no one other than the priests: by apparent contrast, Caesar, *BG* 6. 23. 4, writes that the elected army commander had powers of life and death. The authority of the German generals might have been cut back in the 150 years since Caesar wrote. But Anderson (69) prefers to distinguish the sentence—pronounced by the commander—from the execution itself, the duty of the priests.

certain images and symbols: i.e. of animals sacred to particular deities, the German equivalent of the Roman army standards, which also of course were 'effigies', e.g. the legionary eagles. Cf. *Hist.* 4. 22. 2: at Vetera (Xanten) the Romans are confronted by 'the standards of the veteran cohorts' carried by the rebel Batavians, alongside their German allies from across the Rhine with 'the images of wild beasts taken down from their woods and groves'.

7 *families and kinship groups*: one might render the second part of this expression 'clans.'

the shrieks of their women: Civilis, the Batavian leader brought his own mother and sisters, with the wives and small children of his men bringing up the rear, 'to give encouragement for victory and to shame them if they were driven back', as the rebels marched on Vetera, *Hist.* 4. 18. 2.

8 *girls . . . among their hostages*: Suetonius, *Augustus* 21. 2, says that Augustus first demanded females, 'a new kind of hostages', after noticing that certain barbarian chiefs did not bother about male ones. For the wife and a sister of Civilis as hostages in AD 70, cf. *Hist.* 4. 79. 1.

Veleda: a prophetess from the Bructeri (cf. n. on this people in ch. 33 below), prominent in the Batavian Revolt: a captured legionary commander was sent to her, along with booty, *Hist.* 4. 61, later the captured Roman flagship, up the river Lippe, ibid. 5. 22. Delegates from Cologne bearing gifts were barred from direct access to Veleda in her 'high tower', ibid. 4. 65. She was eventually captured *c*. AD 77 by the general Rutilius Gallicus (Statius, *Silvae* 1. 4. 89 f.); as an inscription in Greek, *AE* 1953. 25 (fragmentary), revealed, Vespasian asked an oracle what should be done 'with the tall virgin whom the Rhine-drinkers worship', and apparently made her a temple servant at Ardea, near Rome.

Albruna: otherwise unknown; the spelling of the name, emended from the MSS 'Aurinia' or 'Albrinia', is not certain. 'Albruna' is Germanic, cf. the name of the river Elbe, 'Albis' (ch. 41). For German 'prophetesses' cf. also Dio 67. 5. 3 for the Semnonian, Ganna, said to be 'Veleda's successor', and Strabo 7. 2. 3 for the Cimbrian 'priestesses who were also seers'. These terrifying women, who accompanied the Cimbrian expeditions made 'an unearthly noise' during the battles by beating on the hides stretched over the wagons and sacrificed prisoners after cutting their throats and collecting the blood in a vast cauldron.

not . . . to make goddesses out of them: this is taken as an intended contrast to the Roman deification of various female members of the imperial family, Drusilla, Poppaea, etc. However, in *Hist.* 4. 61, Tacitus wrote of Veleda that 'this virgin of the Bructeran people ruled over a wide area, in accordance with an old German custom whereby they regard many women as prophetesses and, with increasing superstition, as goddesses.' The reference to Veleda and Albruna provides a suitable link to the next subject, religion.

9 *Among the gods Mercury is the one they principally worship*: this sentence is an exact quotation from Caesar, *BG* 6. 17. 1, who, however, is referring to the Gauls. On the Germans, ibid. 6. 21. 1, he asserts that, unlike the Gauls, 'they consider as gods only the ones they can see, the Sun, Fire and the Moon'. This was certainly mistaken, even if there was something behind it, cf. *Ann.* 13. 55. 6, on an aged German who evidently worshipped 'the sun and the other stars'. Tacitus here follows the practice common to Greeks and Romans alike of identifying deities of other peoples with one of their own

with similar attributes. In ch. 43 he refers explicitly to this 'Roman interpretation' of other peoples' religion. The German Mercury was Wotan, Wodan, or Odin, as shown by the coincidence of Wodan's Day, Wednesday, with the *dies Mercurii, mercredi*, etc. The messenger of the gods in the classical system had not all that much in common with the somewhat awesome god of wind and storm. But Odin also conducted the spirits of the dead, a role which Mercury acquired from his Greek counterpart Hermes.

on fixed days, human . . . victims: probably at the spring equinox, perhaps at the summer and winter solstices. Cf. on human sacrifice in chs. 39, 40.

Hercules: not the same as the hero of ch. 3 above, or 34 below; evidently the Germanic Donar or Thor, whose hammer would suggest Hercules' club. Cf. *Ann.* 2. 12. 1, a forest consecrated to 'Hercules' beyond the river Weser. Later Donar/Thor was identified with Jupiter, hence Thursday, *German Donnerstag*, is the *dies Iovis, jeudi*, etc.

Mars: certainly Tiu or Ziu, the original sky-god of the Indo-Europeans, who becomes Zeus to the Greeks, Jupiter (*Ju-pater*) to the Romans. But identification of Tiu with Roman Mars is clear from Tuesday, German *Dienstag*, equivalent to *dies Martis, mardi*, etc. German auxiliaries at Housesteads on Hadrian's Wall worshipped Mars Thincsus, Tiu, as the god of the *Thing* or assembly of warriors, *RIB* i. 1593.

part of the Suebi . . . Isis: the description of the Suebi begins in ch. 38. Yet in ch. 40 the northern Suebi, with access to the sea, are portrayed as worshippers of Nerthus rather than of Isis, who was, by definition, because of the ship symbol, brought in by sea. In any case, as Lund (138) notes, Isis is not a case of 'Roman interpretation'; Tacitus has apparently heard that the original goddess is worshipped by some of the Suebi, which would contradict his portrayal in ch. 2 of no immigration to Germany.

to confine them within walls or to portray them in any human likeness: a common feature of primitive peoples in classical literature, cf. Herodotus 1. 131 on the Persians; and it was the same with the early Romans according to Varro, quoted by Augustine, *City of God* 4. 31. Cf. ch. 43 below, on *the name is 'the Alci'*, of whom 'there are no images'.

10 *a nut-bearing tree*: the word 'frugiferae', lit. 'fruit-bearing', at first sight contradicts ch. 5, Germany 'will not grow fruit-trees'. Anderson (78 f.) explains the term here as trees that have nuts, such as beech, hazel, oak, which were thought to be lucky.

the call or flight of birds: unlike the Romans, to whom the direction of the birds' flight was all important, to the Germans the mere appearance of certain birds meant good or evil, according to species: Anderson, 81.

horses: cf. Herodotus 3. 84, 86 on the Persians, for whom neighing of horses could be an augury.

the priest or king or chief of the state: cf. n. on *Their kings* in ch. 7 above. The 'chief' here is one of the 'leading men' in states without a monarchy.

10 *the common people . . . the nobles and priests*: a contrast is probably intended
with Rome, where the élite no longer believed in augury, cf. e.g. Cicero,
Divination 2. 51.

They . . . take prisoner: as Anderson (82) notes, there is no parallel for this
practice and 'there may be some misconception here'.

11 *the chiefs*: or 'leading men' are either the aristocracy or the elders, who form
a kind of senate.

they do not reckon time by days . . . but by nights: this was because their calen-
dar was based on the moon, with lunar months, rather than on the sun. The
same practice was followed in Gaul, Caesar, *BG* 6. 18. 2; traces still survive
in expressions such as 'fortnight'.

Their freedom of spirit: the freedom Germans enjoyed, even in states which
had kings (cf. ch. 44), is stressed particularly in ch. 37 below, cf. n. on *The
freedom of the Germans*.

carrying arms: cf. the beginning of ch. 13.

they clash their spears: i.e. on their shields, also a Gallic custom, Caesar, *BG* 7.
21.

12 *those who have defiled their bodies*: 'corpore infames' presumably means
sodomites, cf. the same expression in *Ann.* 1. 73. 2 and 15. 49. 4, where the
context makes this clear.

are plunged into a boggy mire: confirmed by numerous finds of bodies of
persons who had evidently been executed, preserved in bogs, notably in
Denmark, see P. V. Glob, *The Bog People* (London, 1969).

a hundred assessors chosen from the people, as an advisory body: it has been
argued that Tacitus misunderstood the subdivision of German states into
'hundreds', as in later German and Anglo-Saxon practice, cf. n. on *that is
exactly what they are called . . .* in ch. 6 above, and on *a hundred cantons* in ch.
39 below; but see Anderson, pp. lviii ff. 'comites', here translated 'assessors',
is the same word for the members of the retinue, below, ch. 13. Tacitus is
appplying Roman terminology here, as with 'advisory body', 'consilium':
Anderson, 89 f.; Lund, 148.

13 *equivalent of our toga*: the *toga virilis*, 'toga of manhood', assumed at a formal
ceremony, when the boy (*puer*), usually aged between 14 and 16, became a
young man (*iuvenis*).

can gain the approval of a chief even for boys in their teens: this rendering
makes better sense than the alternative, 'the status of a chief', even though
the former sense of *dignatio* is not normal in Tacitus' other writings.

the chief's companions. There are grades of rank, indeed, within the retinue:
much has been made of Tacitus on the 'retinue', taken to refer to a funda-
mental Germanic institution, which it certainly was, cf. the two hundred
'comites' of the Alamannic king Chnodomar, who expressed loyalty to the
death to their lord, Ammianus 16. 12. 60. But similar customs existed among
the Gauls, Caesar, *BG* 3. 22, etc.

14 *If the country . . . is stagnating in a long period of peace*: a typically Roman attitude; cf. *Agr.* 11, 'the Britons display more ferocity [than the Gauls], having not yet been made soft by prolonged peace.'

the generosity of their chief: Anderson (96) notes that in Anglo-Saxon poetry the word for throne, *gifstol*, 'gift-chair', reflects the importance of giving 'among the obligations of the *princeps comitatus*'.

they think it tame and spiritless to accumulate slowly by sweat what they can get quickly by losing some blood: sweat and blood are often coupled, cf. Pliny, *Ep.* 2. 7. 1, here they are contrasted.

15 *they occupy a little of their time in hunting but a good deal more is spent without occupation*: Tacitus is still describing the way of life of the chiefs and their companions.

embossed discs, and necklaces: *phalerae* and torques were standard Roman awards for valour: V. A. Maxfield, *The Military Decorations of the Roman Army* (London, 1981) 86 ff.

They have now been taught to accept money as well—by us: cf. n. on *with notched edges or stamped with . . . chariots*, ch. 5 above. This sentence, concluding a section, is a typical epigram. It is not clear whether Tacitus means 'to accept bribes', or simply 'to accept money in payment'.

16 *none of the German peoples live in cities*: a statement borne out by archaeology. Cf. also *Hist.* 4. 64. 2, the Tencteri in AD 70 demanding that the Romanized people of Cologne tear down 'their walls, the ramparts of servitude—even wild beasts forget their courage if you keep them shut in!'; or Ammianus 16. 2. 12, the Alamanni in AD 357 'avoid towns as if they were tombs encircled by nets'.

or because they lack skill: a standard characteristic of primitive peoples in classical ethnography.

They employ timber for all purposes: 'materia' can mean building materials generally, but the sense 'timber' is clear from the context. Cf. also two contemporary documents, *TV* ii. 215 and 309.

digging underground caves: as well as subterranean refuges, underground storage pits were of course used: Anderson, 104 (cf. Varro, *De re rustica* 1. 57). Tacitus clearly meant the former.

manure: Anderson (104 f.) notes that the old German word for underground storage pits was *tunc*, i.e. dung.

17 *a cloak fastened with a brooch or . . . thorn*: the *sagum*, a thick woollen garment, also called *sagulum*, was worn by Celtic and other peoples as well; it is regularly mentioned in the Vindolanda tablets, *TV* ii. 192, 207, 255, along with the *sagacia*, also 184, 521.

the Sarmatians and Parthians: cf. n. on *Sarmatians* in ch. 1 above; for the Parthians nn. on *The freedom of the Germans . . .* , on *Crassus*, on *Pacorus*, and on *Ventidius* in ch. 37 below. Both are thought of as wearing baggy trousers.

17 *fits tightly and shows the shape of each limb*: the Germans are generally portrayed wearing trousers, *bracae*, 'breeches'. Tacitus may have avoided this word, or the adjective *bracatus*, because they had pejorative associations, cf. A. N. Sherwin-White, *Racial Prejudice in Ancient Rome*, 2nd edn. (Oxford, 1970), 58 f.

fur from the beasts found in the outer Ocean: i.e. sealskin and the like, from Scandinavia.

women's clothing is no different from the men's: this gives the impression that German women wore trousers, which does seem to have been the case on at least one stone relief, from Mainz (illustrated by Anderson, fig. 17, opposite p. 108), and with the personified Germania on coins. However this may be, most Roman depictions of German women show them wearing a long gown, and, exactly as Tacitus here describes them, 'their arms are bare . . . parts of their breasts are also exposed'.

18 *Nevertheless, the marriage code is strict*: with a skilful transition, Tacitus turns to a new topic, marriage. In spite of having their arms bare and part of their breasts exposed, which would lead Romans to expect something quite different, German women are very chaste. This is a very idealized picture of marriage among simple but morally far healthier people: the contrast—at first implicit, but soon with explicit comparisons—is with the situation in Rome.

almost the only barbarians . . . with a single wife: the Romans evidently assumed polygamous tendencies among their auxiliaries, since the formula legalizing marriage with a non-Roman woman after twenty-five years' service regularly states, 'one wife each', 'singuli singulas', *CIL* xvi, *passim*.

except for a very few . . . courted with numerous offers of marriage: e.g. Ariovistus, Caesar's opponent, had two wives, one a fellow Suebian, the other the sister of the Norican king, Voccio, *BG* 1. 53. 4.

The dowry: Tacitus has misunderstood the situation. What he describes is the payment of the 'bride-price', which actually went to the bride's parents.

The parents: here supposed just to be in attendance. In fact the bridegroom was by these gifts purchasing control over his bride from her family.

she herself in turn brings her husband some weapons: or rather, the bride's father gives the groom a sword to symbolize the control that the groom has purchased.

19 *sheltered chastity*: editors compare *Ann.* 4. 12. 2, the 'impenetrable chastity' of the widowed Elder Agrippina, a great rarity in early imperial Rome.

clandestine letters: cf. e.g. Juvenal 6. 277, to the duped husband: 'you have no idea what you would find in her letters, if you ever unlocked her desk.' Tacitus did not need to explain that Germans, men and women alike, could not read or write letters of any kind.

Considering the great size of the population, adultery is very rare: cf. ch. 4, 'so large a population'. As is clear from what follows, 'adultery' here refers, as in

the harsh Augustan legislation, to a married woman being unfaithful—a married man was only guilty if involved with another man's wife: Lund, 164.

To limit the number of their children . . . is regarded as a crime: Tacitus was evidently mistaken in his idealistic view that the Germans did not practice abortion or infanticide: Anderson, 114 f.

Good morality is more effective there than good laws elsewhere: the thought was often expressed, cf. e.g. Sallust, *Catiline* 9. 1, 'Good morals were cultivated at home and abroad . . . thanks not so much to law as to nature.' Tacitus here contrasts the sanctity of custom among a primitive people with the ineffective provisions of Roman law, referring by implication to the *lex Papia Poppaea* (of AD 9); cf. *Ann.* 3. 26 ff., his historical survey demonstrating the futility of attempts to regulate morality by legislation, from King Minos to Caesar Augustus.

20 *naked and dirty*: cf. chs. 6, 17, 24, for nakedness; and for 'sordidi', 'dirty', cf. ch. 46 where 'sordes', 'dirtiness', is rendered 'squalor', there said to be characteristic of all Germans.

Each mother breastfeeds her own child: Tacitus and his contemporaries had strong feelings about this, cf. *Dial.* 28. 4, yearning for the good old days when 'every son born to a chaste mother was reared at her bosom and in her lap, not in the lodgings of a hired wet-nurse', and A. Gellius, *Attic Nights* 12. 1. 17, the philosopher Favorinus denouncing 'the corruption of a new-born infant by alien and degenerate nourishment from another's milk, especially if the wet-nurse is a slave or foreign and barbarian'.

master and slave: i.e. 'future master and slave'; but contrast ch. 25, where slaves are stated not to belong within the household.

slow to mate: thus also Caesar, *BG* 6. 21. 4, 'those who reach puberty latest win the greatest praise . . . some think their size, strength, and sexual potency are thereby increased . . . it is a disgrace to have had knowledge of a woman before the twentieth year.' Cf. Lund, 167 f.

The sons of sisters: there are historical examples in Tacitus' other works: in *Hist.* 4. 33 and 5. 20 Civilis gives commands to sons of his sister(s), and in *Ann.* 12. 29 f. the deposed Suebian king Vannius is succeeded by two sons of his sister. Tacitus' point is just that the Germans did not, as the Romans did, give privileged status to patrilineal or agnatic descent: Lund, 169.

hostages: cf. ch. 8 with n. on *girls . . . among their hostages*.

There is no worth attached to childlessness: again, a contrast with Roman society to end the section. Cf. e.g. Horace, *Satires* 2. 5, advice for the 'legacy-hunter' on how to ingratiate himself with the childless rich man, for whose high status at the time Tacitus was writing Pliny, *Ep.* 4. 15. 3 is sufficient testimony.

21 *feuds and friendships*: the Romans were accustomed to hereditary 'guest-friendship', 'hospitium', but not to the formally inherited blood feud.

21 *fixed number of cattle or sheep*: cf. ch. 12, for 'horses or cattle' being paid as compensation. In later German practice, money, *Wergeld*, was paid for homicide on a scale determined by the victim's rank.

It is . . . a sin to turn away any person: cf. Caesar, *BG* 6. 23. 9 on German open-handedness, 'they protect from harm and regard as sacred those who have come to them for any reason; everyone's houses are open to these men and food is shared with them.' The last comment is echoed by Tacitus.

They take delight in gifts but expect no repayment: the contrast at the end of the section is again with Roman practice, for which Lund (172) cites Servius, the commentator on Virgil, on *Aeneid* 8. 166 and 9. 358. The Roman laws of *hospitium* involve *remuneratio*, a return gift; the Germans, as a sign of their free spirit, *libertas*, reject any such commitment.

22 *each one having a separate seat and table*: in the Latin the alliteration, here 'separate seat', is even stronger, 'separatae singulis sedes'. This preference again underlines the German freedom of spirit, or individualism, as well as being a contrast to the Roman custom of reclining on the couch round a shared table. Anderson (121 f.) notes that German *Tisch*, 'table', originally also meant 'dish' (and derived from the Latin *discus*): i.e. the early Germans dispensed with plates and ate their food straight from the table.

No one thinks it disgraceful to carry on drinking all day and all night: German drunkenness is also reported in *Hist.* 4. 79. 2, Civilis' Germans occupying Cologne rendered incapable by wine, and *Ann.* 11. 16. 2, 'vinolentia', 'intoxication', is approved of by the barbarians (Cherusci). It was less common with Romans, although Tiberius (Suetonius, *Tiberius* 42. 1) and Trajan (Dio 68. 7. 4) were notorious topers.

23 *they have a liquid made out of barley or other grain*: i.e. beer. The Celtic name for this was *cervesa*, which was drunk in large quantities by the Batavian and Tungrian troops in garrison at Vindolanda at this time, cf. *TV* ii. 182, 186, 190, 482; and in a letter to the prefect of the Ninth Cohort of Batavians a *decurio* (commander of a cavalry squadron) writes that 'the comrades have no beer, please have some sent': *Britannia*, 27 (1996), 323 ff.

Those who live nearest to the river-bank buy wine as well: Caesar, *BG* 4. 2. 6, reports that the Suebi refused to allow wine to be imported. Over 150 years later things had changed a great deal. The 'river-bank' probably refers here just to the Rhine. Lund (175) comments that amphorae have not been found in the interior, which might seem to confirm Tacitus' view that only those near the Rhine had taken to wine. But, as he notes, wine could have been transported in wooden barrels, and Anderson (124) refers to finds of 'wine ladles (*trullae*) far beyond the frontier'.

Their food is plain: in line with their general simplicity of life (cf. Lund, 28 ff.), and in contrast to the notorious excesses of the Roman table. Tacitus only mentions items of German diet which differ markedly from the Roman.

they will be as easily defeated by their vices as by force of arms: a typical epi-
grammatic remark to conclude the section. The idea is a commonplace, cf.
n. on *Agr.* 21, *The Britons . . . called it 'civilization'*. Lund (176) compares
Justin, *Epitome* 1. 8. 7, 'the Scythians were defeated by drunkenness before
they were defeated in war.'

24 *only one kind of public show . . . a dance between swords*: again, German simplicity is illustrated, as with their food, so with their shows—in contrast to
the Roman amphitheatre and circus. This is the oldest description of the
sword-dance. The Roman *Salii*, the dancing priests of Mars, may have
performed something not dissimilar. The Greek 'pyrrhic dance' with
weapons, approved of by Plato, *Laws* 815, was often performed at Rome
when Tacitus wrote. But it had changed its character (females often
performed); Athenaeus was to complain that it had degenerated,
Deipnosophistae 14. 631a.

They play at dice when sober: by contrast the Romans generally diced after
dinner, although it was officially prohibited (*Digest* 11. 5, etc.; cf. Horace,
Odes 3. 24. 58) except during the Saturnalia.

The loser goes into voluntary servitude: Seneca, *Letters* 41. 17, commented that
'nothing is more shameful than voluntary servitude'. Once again, among
these primitive northerners things were the other way about. This statement
provides the transition to the next subject, 'normal' slavery.

25 *Their ordinary slaves*: i.e. unlike those won through gambling, the ones
they kept. Tacitus says nothing about the source of such slaves. Presumably
prisoners of war or the like, cf. *Agr.* 28, the fate of the Usipian mutineers; or
Ann. 12. 27. 3, Romans enslaved by the Germans after Varus' disaster of AD
9. These slaves are more like medieval serfs or villeins. Tacitus insists that
the Germans' slaves only work the land.

not employed, as ours are, for . . . the household: cf. *Ann.* 14. 42 ff., the four
hundred slaves in the household of a rich senator at Rome. In spite of this
denial, in ch. 20 slave children are said to grow up side by side with their
future masters.

Freedmen are not much superior to slaves: this may well be accurate, cf. Anderson (130) on emancipation of slaves in later times among the Franks, Lombards, etc. But Tacitus' remark is clearly intended as a contrast with the
position of freedmen at Rome, not least in the obvious allusion to imperial
freedmen that follows.

*rarely have any influence . . . in the state, except in monarchies, in which they rise
not only higher than freemen but higher even than nobles*: cf. e.g. *Ann.* 14. 39, the
Britons astonished and scornful at the power of the freedman Polyclitus,
whom Paulinus (cf. *Agr.* 5 and 14 ff.) had to obey.

26 The transition from slavery to the new subject, moneylending and
then agriculture, is not immediately obvious. But Tacitus moves from
one form of property, slaves, to another, land. In between come these
remarks:

26 *The practice of lending out capital and stretching it out into interest is unknown*: the Latin term, *faenus agitare*, originally meant using the 'yield' of the harvest (cf. *faenum*, 'hay'), and hence 'interest' from any business activity. 'faenus' generally means 'interest', here 'interest-earning capital', as elsewhere in Tacitus, e.g. *Hist.* 1. 20. 1, *Ann.* 6. 17. 1; 'interest' in the present passage translates 'usuras'.

ignorance is a surer protection than any prohibition: an epigram, but 'rather absurd': Anderson (132), who notes that the thought had been better expressed at the end of ch. 19, 'Good morality is more effective', etc. Anyway, in ch. 46, the Fenni are apparently not ignorant of moneylending but actually prefer their primitive life to 'civilization' which includes 'speculating with their own and other people's money'.

Lands are occupied by the whole people to be cultivated, the quantity determined by the number of cultivators: it is often assumed that Tacitus took a similar view to Caesar, *BG* 4. 1. 7 ff. (on the Suebi), 'they have no private or separate landownership, nor are they permitted to stay more than a year in one place', etc., or 6. 22. 2 (on the Germans in general), 'no one has a fixed amount of land or his own estate; every year the magistrates and leading men assign to families and clans as much land as seems good to them, in a place they fix on', which is changed every year. This attribution of primitive communism to the early Germans has provoked passionate support and denial. But archaeological evidence makes it highly unlikely that cultivable land was held in common: Lund (180 f.), whose emendation of 'in vicem', 'in turn', which does not make good sense, to 'in usum', 'for cultivation', is followed here. Thus the Germans were subsistence farmers: they only produced what they could use themselves, not for a surplus. In any case Timpe (169 ff.) has shown that Tacitus here is simply describing an original take-over of land by a people on the move (like Caesar's Suebi); and that in the next sentence, 'They then divide the lands out among themselves according to rank', private ownership is meant.

They plough different fields every year: cf. Caesar's account, quoted above, and Horace, *Odes* 3. 24. 11 ff., for similar comments about the Getae of Thrace (modern Bulgaria), who never cultivate one piece of land for more than one year. But not because they are 'nomads': the 'great extent of their land' makes this possible, as would not be the case within the empire.

there is still spare land available: even if the Germans neglect to make intensive use of it. Timpe (196 ff.) shows that the viewpoint implied here, that the Germans do not take agriculture seriously—cf. ch. 14, 'you cannot so easily persuade them to plough the soil'—and Caesar's statement, 'the Germans are not keen on agriculture', *BG* 6. 22. 1, are misleading. Numerous passages in Tacitus' other writings show that the Germans were, if primitive, none the less basically a peasant-farming people.

the name of autumn is completely unknown, as are its blessings: as Anderson (137) notes, the words spring, summer, and winter all come from Anglo-

Saxon, while 'autumn' is taken from Latin; and the German word for autumn, *Herbst*, originally meant 'harvest'.

27 *There is no ostentation about their funerals*: by contrast, Roman attempts to cut down ostentation at funerals went back to the Law of the Twelve Tables, of the mid-fifth century BC.

famous men are cremated with particular kinds of wood: Anderson (137) lists 'oak, beech, pine, and juniper'. But Lund (182, with further references) doubts the validity of Tacitus' statement.

Only the dead man's weapons . . . in some cases his horse too, are cast into the flames: Caesar, *BG* 6. 19. 4, describes elaborate Gallic cremations at which 'everything, even living creatures . . . dear to the departed during life' were added to the funeral pyre. The simpler but warlike Germans need only their weapons and their war-horse, 'to serve their needs in Valhalla': Anderson, 138.

They disdain a lofty and elaborately constructed monument: the contrast is with Roman specimens such as that of Augustus, sixty feet (18 m.) high. Many of the larger tumuli, 'turf mounds', in the Rhineland and southern Germany were in fact of Celtic chieftains from the La Tène period.

They soon leave off weeping and lamenting . . . It is the honourable thing for . . . men to remember the dead: cf. *Agr.* 29, 46.

which peoples have migrated from Germany into the Gallic provinces: Tacitus seems to avoid saying 'which Germans have migrated into the Gallic lands', Lund, 184: he is about to point out that not all the peoples in Germany are of German origin.

28 *That the Gauls were once more powerful is recorded by . . . the Deified Julius*: 'than the Germans' has to be understood. Tacitus is referring to Caesar, *BG* 6. 24. 1, 'there was once a time when the Gauls were superior in courage to the Germans', etc., a passage he had already cited in *Agr.* 11 (cf. n. on *We are told . . . that their courage has been lost*), but without naming Caesar as the source.

migrations of Gauls into Germany: these included the Volcae Tectosages, who, according to Caesar, *BG* 6. 24, 'seized the most fertile places of Germany, round the Hercynian forest' (cf. below) and were still there when he wrote. The name 'Volcae' is reckoned to be the origin of the name applied to all Celtic- and Romance-speaking neighbours of the Germans: 'Welsch', e.g. 'Welschland' for Italy—or 'Welsh' for the neighbours of the Anglo-Saxons.

Helvetii: Caesar, *BG* 1. 1 ff., supplies great detail on their attempted migration, which he blocked, southwards into Roman territory from their home between Lakes Constance and Geneva.

the land between the Hercynian forest and the rivers Rhine and Main: that the Helvetii had previously lived further north is only attested here. It is assumed that they were driven out, or chose to leave this area, at the time of the Cimbric invasions, when some of their people joined the Cimbri, Strabo

7. 2. 2, cf. Caesar, *BG* 1. 7 (107 BC). The 'Hercynian forest' was the originally Celtic name for the vast tract of wooded country between the Rhine and the Carpathians, including Bohemia, which divides the northern German plain from southern Germany. The part referred to here is not entirely clear, perhaps the Swabian and Franconian Jura, if not the Bohemian forest, but at any rate different from that in ch. 30: Anderson, 140.

28 *Boii*: a Celtic people which *c.*60 BC left their original home in Bohemia.

Boihaemum: now Bohemia. Many of the Boii joined the Helvetii in Gaul, Caesar, *BG* 1. 5, 28, 29, others settled for a while in Pannonia before being wiped out by the Dacians, Strabo 5. 1. 6, etc. The remnant in Bohemia were driven out *c.*8 BC by the Marcoman(n)i, on whom cf. n. to ch. 42 below.

Aravisci: spelt Eravisci in most inscriptions and in Pliny, *NH* 3. 148. One of their main centres was Aquincum (Budapest): A. Mócsy, *Pannonia and Upper Moesia* (London, 1974), 155 ff.

the Osi . . . same language: Tacitus supposed that the Eravisci and the Osi spoke the same language, viz. 'Pannonian' or Illyrian. But both Eravisci and Osi were probably Celtic, cf. n. to ch. 43 on *the Osi speak Pannonian*.

Treveri . . . Nervii: there is still dispute as to whether the Treveri (sometimes spelt Treviri) and the Nervii were Celtic or 'Germanic'. Both joined the German side in the Batavian Revolt, the Treveri being led by Julius Classicus and Julius Tutor, equestrian officers as Civilis had been, *Hist*. 4. 55 f. But they and their allies the Gallic Lingones then sought to create a 'Gallic empire', 'imperium Galliarum', ibid. 59, a different aim from that of Civilis, restoration of German liberty. Cf. ibid. 66, the Nervii, Tungri, and Baetasii, all went over to Civilis' side together.

Vangiones: their chief town was Borbetomagus, modern Worms. According to Lucan, *Pharsalia* 1. 430, they wore baggy trousers, like the eastern Germans, perhaps indicating that they had migrated from the east: Anderson, 144. In *Hist*. 4. 70. 3 their defection to the side of Classicus' rebel Treveri is briefly mentioned, together with that of the Caeracates (otherwise unknown).

Triboci: also joined Classicus in AD 70; they inhabited the area round Breucomagus, modern Brumat, and Strasbourg, and rapidly became Celticized; indeed, their name is Celtic.

Nemetes: this is also a Celtic name. The chief town of the Nemetes was Noviomagus, modern Speyer. They are not known to have joined the Batavian Revolt.

Even the Ubii . . . prefer to call themselves Agrippinenses: the Ubii were still beyond the Rhine in Caesar's day, when they came under Suebian pressure and sought his protection, *BG* 1. 54, 4. 16. In 38 BC Agrippa resettled them on the left bank. Their chief centre, modern Cologne, which was chosen for the *Ara*, altar for the worship of Rome and Augustus, developed into a thriving city, with very Romanized inhabitants. It was given further settlers, legionary veterans, and the rank of *colonia* in AD 50 by Claudius, who named

it after his wife, the Younger Agrippina, Agrippa's granddaughter, *Ann.* 12. 27. 1. The *colonia*'s inhabitants, now all Roman citizens, were at great risk two decades later: in the eyes of Civilis' forces they had betrayed their German roots, *Hist.* 4. 28 ff. The city was besieged (ibid. 59 f.) and forced for a time to join the rebellion (63 ff.), but before long the people killed the German garrison and reasserted their Roman allegiance (79).

29 *Batavians*: their main centre was Noviomagus Batavorum, modern Nijmegen in the Netherlands; Betuwe near Arnhem preserves the ancient name. Cf. Introduction (pp. xv f.) for more detail on this people's history.

they are on their own bank: the chief place of the Mattiaci was just across the Rhine from the legionary fortress of Mogontiacum (Mainz), by its confluence with the Main, at Aquae Mattiacae (Wiesbaden). By the time Tacitus wrote, it had long been under direct Roman control. As to their 'allegiance', some of them did join the rebels in AD 70, *Hist.* 4. 37. 3.

I should not reckon among the peoples of Germany: Tacitus' motive here is transparent. Although dealing with territory 'on the far [i.e. German] side of the Rhine and Danube', he refuses to count it as part of Germany. This is precisely the area annexed by Domitian in AD 83 after the campaign against the Chatti for which he held a 'sham triumph', and called himself 'Germanicus', conqueror of the Germans (cf. *Agr.* 39 with n. on *his recent sham triumph* . . . , and ch. 37 below, n. on *In recent times . . . objects of triumphs rather than victories*). Tacitus' point is that there were and are no Germans in the territory Domitian conquered, the 'Ten-Lands'.

'Ten-Lands': the name, 'decumates agri', is controversial—the first word is not found elsewhere. Many favour a connection with *decumana*, 'tithe'; or it might refer to 'ten districts': J. G. F. Hind, *Britannia*, 15 (1984), 187 ff. The area in question was not necessarily or not merely that bounded by the Main, Rhine, and Danube (Anderson, 148), but also the Wetterau plain, previously a 'no-man's land' between Rome and the Chatti. This best matches the 'projection', below.

frontier line: 'limes' is generally taken to refer, at latest shortly after Tacitus' time of writing, to the fortified frontiers around the empire, especially the continuous barriers such as Hadrian's Wall, the palisade in Upper Germany and Raetia, with the ditch and running mound later added, or the 'Fossatum Africae'. Tacitus is presumably referring to the chain of signal-stations established under Domitian on the edge of the 'Ten-Lands', where Hadrian was to have the palisade erected some twenty-five years later.

projection: 'sinus' this refers to the 'protuberant' shape of part of this territory, viz. the fertile plain of the Wetterau, cf. also above, on ch. 28, *migrations of Gauls into Germany*.

30 *Beyond them, from the Hercynian forest onwards, the territory of the Chatti begins*: who 'them' refers to is not clear. It should, strictly, mean the inhabitants of the 'Ten-Lands' (thus Lund, 191). The Chatti occupied the hill country drained by the upper arms of the river Weser, the Werra and Fulda,

and its tributary the river Diemel; their name survives in the modern Hessen, whose people were called 'Hassi' in the seventh and eighth centuries. 'Hercynian forest' (cf. ch. 28) here refers to the heavily wooded Spessart, Vogelsberg, and Rhön hills, and their northern outliers. The Chatti were frequently engaged in war with Rome from 11 BC onwards. Domitian's campaign against them in AD 83 and their own incursion into the newly garrisoned Wetterau in January 89, made them very topical when Tacitus was writing (cf. n. on *his recent sham triumph . . .* in *Agr.* 39 and on *In recent times they have been the objects of triumphs* in ch. 37 below). This perhaps meant he had eyewitness informants, though the Elder Pliny, who probably served against the Chatti in AD 50, could well be his source here. The Chatti crop up only occasionally in later Roman history.

30 *For Germans they have a great deal of judgement and shrewdness*: contrast ch. 22, on the Germans in general: 'This people is neither cunning nor subtle.'

Speed and timidity go together; deliberate action . . . goes rather with steadfastness: a Tacitean epigram, here contrasting, by implication, not just slow but steady foot soldiers with fast but cowardly horsemen, but also Roman steadfastness with impulsive barbarian tactics: Lund, 195.

31 *they let their hair and beard grow long*: Germans usually had long hair, but kept it well combed, cf. esp. n. on the Suebian hair-knot, in ch. 38 below, *they comb their hair back . . .*

an iron ring like a manacle, a mark of dishonour among that people: to wear an iron finger-ring was quite normal for Romans, for the Chatti it was a symbol of bondage: Lund, 198. As 'like a manacle' sounds rather large for a finger-ring, some render 'anulum' as 'arm-band', but there was another normal word for this, *armilla*.

even when their hair is now grey: Tacitus does not explain how these fierce old heroes, who liked to keep their long unkempt locks, could be distinguished from aged cowards.

32 *the Usipi*: also called 'Usipetes', e.g. by Caesar, this people and the Tencteri (below) first crop up in 55 BC. Driven from their original homes by Ariovistus, they tried to cross the Rhine, to be repulsed by Caesar near Coblenz, *BG* 4. 1 ff. Drusus (cf. n. on ch. 37 below, *Drusus and Nero [Tiberius] . . .*) fought them in the lower Lippe valley, 12–11 BC, Dio 54. 32 f.; they attacked Germanicus in AD 14, *Ann.* 1. 51. Some time after 58, when they were still in the north, *Ann.* 13. 55, they moved to the area opposite the Rhine gorge, on both sides of the Lahn valley. Tacitus does not mention here that they came under Roman rule at latest following Domitian's campaign in AD 83. The cohort of Usipi that mutinied in 82, cf. the first two notes on *Agr.* 28, had been 'conscripted in the Germanies' before their territory had been annexed. (The plural, 'Germanies', there used is particularly appropriate: the Usipian territory was opposite the point where Upper and Lower Germany met.)

Tencteri: neighbours and allies of the Usipi, cf. above, they evidently took over the land opposite Cologne when the Sugambri were transplanted to the

left bank by Tiberius in 8 BC (Suetonius, *Tiberius* 9. 2). They tried to get the Ubii (cf. n. on ch. 28 above, *Even the Ubii . . .*) to join them against Rome in AD 70, *Hist.* 4. 64 f.

over and above the general military distinction: 'general', i.e. of all the Germans.

the art of horsemanship: eight hundred Tencteran and Usipian cavalry scattered five thousand of Caesar's Gallic horse in 55 BC, *BG* 4. 12.

A son inherits them, not necessarily the eldest: the implication that in other respects primogeniture prevailed is certainly mistaken (it applied to inheritance of property neither in Rome nor in later Germanic law codes). Lund (200 f.) suggests that 'the eldest' may be a later insertion and proposes further emendation.

33 *the Bructeri*: were divided into Greater and Lesser. Some lived between the rivers Ems and Weser, Strabo 7. 1. 3, also mentioning Drusus' naval victory against them on the Ems, others in the upper Lippe valley. They joined the attack on Varus in AD 9 (see n. on *Varus* in ch. 37 below): *Ann.* 1. 60, the eagle of the Nineteenth legion recaptured, AD 15. They were active in the Batavian Revolt (cf. n. on *our dissensions and the Civil Wars* in ch. 37 below), not least through their prophetess Veleda (see n. on *Veleda* in ch. 8 above). Some of them spread southwards, as far as the area opposite Cologne, where they were in the late fourth century, Gregory of Tours, *History of the Franks* 2. 9, as were the Chamavi.

Chamavi: previously neighbours of the *Batavians* (on whom see n. in ch. 29), they moved close to the Bructeri and the *Frisii* (see n. in ch. 34) under the impact of Drusus' measures. The name is supposed to survive in the modern *Hama*land in the Deventer area of the Netherlands. Tacitus may exaggerate the extent to which Bructeran land was seized by the Chamavi and the Angrivarii.

Angrivarii: there was a frontier dyke between them and the Cherusci, *Ann.* 2. 19. 3 (remains of which exist between the river Weser and the Steinhuder Meer north-west of Hanover); they were defeated by Germanicus, ibid. 2. 41. They reappear in the eighth century as the Angrarii, part of the Saxon federation.

Over sixty thousand were killed, not by Roman swords or spears, but, what was far more splendid, to gladden Roman eyes: this was apparently a very recent event, surely connected with the story in Pliny, *Ep.* 2. 7: his friend Spurinna had 'installed the king of the Bructeri in his kingdom by force of arms and by the mere threat of war had completely subdued an extremely fierce people'. Cf. Introduction (p. xviii) for further discussion.

Long may the barbarians continue, I pray, if not to love us, at least to hate one another: 'barbarians' here renders 'gentes', here used in the sense of 'barbarae gentes', 'barbarian peoples', as e.g. in *Ann.* 2. 88. 3. (On *barbari*, not actually used here, cf. n. on *as is usually the case with barbarians* in *Agr.* 11, and on *A human victim is slaughtered . . .* in ch. 39 below.)

33 *as fate bears remorselessly on the empire*: these words, in Latin 'urgentibus imperii fatis', are among the most discussed in Tacitus' works. For a full discussion, cf. Introduction (pp. xviii f.). They have mostly been understood as an expression of pessimism, as in this version. But 'remorselessly', not in the Latin, perhaps makes the pessimism too strong—'bears down on' would suffice. On discord among Rome's enemies cf. also n. on *nothing . . . helps us more . . . than their lack of unanimity* in *Agr.* 12.

34 *Dulgubnii*: this spelling is more plausible than 'Dugulbini', as Koestermann (see Select Bibliography), cf. 'Dulgumnii' in Ptolemy 2. 11. 9, the only other place they are mentioned. They probably lived between the Cherusci (ch. 36) and Langobardi (ch. 40): Anderson, 163 f.

Chasuarii: also little known. Ptolemy, 2. 11. 11, puts them south of the Suebi (ch. 38) and west of the Chatti (chs. 30–1). Tacitus' 'on the far side' would put them round Osnabrück, their name surviving in the river Hase: Anderson, 164.

Frisii: for them Tacitus specifies that there were 'Greater' and 'Lesser' (which he omits to do with *the Bructeri*, cf. n. on ch. 33, and *the Chauci*, cf. n. in ch. 35). They inhabited the country on the North Sea coast still called Friesland, part in the Netherlands, part in Germany. They were won over to Rome by Drusus in 12 BC and were in Roman service continuously until AD 28, when oppressive treatment caused a revolt, *Ann.* 4. 72. 1. They were restored to allegiance by Corbulo in 47, ibid. 11. 19. 1, but not long after this their territory ceased to be part of the empire. They joined the Batavian Revolt in 70, *Hist.* 4. 15 and 4. 79, but supplied troops again thereafter, cf. n. on *wedges* in ch. 6 above.

Pillars of Hercules still remained to be explored: some natural feature similar to the original 'Pillars' in the Straits of Gibraltar must be meant. Anderson (166) suggests that it could have been 'the twin red and white rocks of Heligoland . . . washed away by a great storm in 1721'. Cf. also notes on *Hercules visited . . .* and *dedicated by Ulysses* in ch. 3 above. 'still remained' refers to the situation just before the expedition by Drusus.

Drusus Germanicus: Augustus' stepson, named as 'the first Roman commander to sail the northern Ocean' by Suetonius, *Claudius* 1. 2. Drusus campaigned between Rhine and Elbe from 12–9 BC, and was given the name Germanicus, 'conqueror of Germany', posthumously. It is not usually applied to him, but rather to his elder son, Germanicus Caesar; it was also borne by his younger son, Claudius, grandson Caligula, and great-grandson Nero.

the Ocean resisted research: Anderson (166) aptly cites the poem on Germanicus' voyage in AD 16 (*Ann.* 2. 23 ff.) by his officer Albinovanus Pedo, partly preserved in the Elder Seneca's *Suasoriae* 1. 15: 'the gods call us back and forbid mortal eyes from getting to know the end of the world'. This voyage and indeed that of Tiberius in AD 5, who got even further than Drusus, Velleius 2. 106. 2 f., are apparently overlooked by Tacitus in view of the next sentence.

Subsequently no one has made the attempt: but 'navigated by Roman fleets', above, was doubtless intended to include these. He presumably meant that no one after Drusus attempted to find the Pillars.

more religious and reverent to believe in the deeds of the gods than to know the facts about them: Lund (204) suggests Tacitus was alluding to Pedo's poem here (see n. on *the Ocean resisted research*, above). Anderson (167) regards the epigram as 'perhaps ironical', a contrast between the feebleness of the present day with the great achievements of the Augustan age, cf. n. on *the Elbe . . .* in ch. 41 below.

35 *it falls back with a huge bend*: this must refer to the Jutland peninsula, which was supposed to begin further west than it actually does, and then, some way northwards, to turn abruptly to the east, cf. Mela 3. 1. 8.

the Chauci: inhabited the coastal region between the lower Ems and Elbe, in two sections, 'Greater' and 'Lesser', Pliny, *NH* 16. 2, not mentioned here, but cf. *Ann.* 11. 19, 'Chauci maiores'. They were conquered by Drusus in 12 BC, Dio 54. 32; and paid homage to Tiberius in AD 5, Velleius 2. 106, an eye-witness, who stresses their 'infinite numbers and massive physique'. Rome still had a base in their territory under Tiberius, *Ann.* 1. 60 and 2. 24, but it was soon withdrawn. Gabinius fought them in AD 41, and in 47 their ships attacked the Gallic coast; Claudius forbade Corbulo from responding, *Ann.* 11. 18 ff. They joined the rebellion in the Rhineland in 70, *Hist.* 4. 79, 5. 19, but thereafter virtually disappear from view.

the noblest people among the Germans: their 'righteous dealing' ('iustitia') is what earns the Chauci Tacitus' praise.

even when they are at peace, their reputation remains just as high: a Tacitean epigram.

36 *the Cherusci*: occupied both sides of the middle Weser, on the north side towards Hanover, on the south as far as the Harz mountains. They are first mentioned, briefly, by Caesar, *BG* 6. 10, as divided by dense forest from their enemies the Suebi. They were separated from the coastal *Angrivarii* (cf. n. on ch. 33 above) by a dyke. The Cherusci submitted to Drusus in 11 BC, Dio 54. 33, and renewed their loyalty in AD 4, Velleius 2. 105. Their main claim to fame was that their leader Arminius, after years as an officer in Roman service, led the forces that massacred Varus' three legions in AD 9 (cf. n. on *Varus*, ch. 37 below). Arminius continued to fight Rome until in 19 he was killed by his own people for attempting to make himself king: *Ann.* 2. 88, where he is called 'unquestionably the liberator of Germany'. Weakened by internal conflict, the Cherusci even requested Claudius to send them Italicus, a nephew of Arminius brought up at Rome, as king in 47, *Ann.* 11. 16 f.; they were also affected by warfare with the Chatti, lasting into the 80s (cf. notes on chs. 30–1, above), after which they are scarcely heard of again. Tacitus' explanation of their decline seems rather unfair.

the Fosi: nowhere else mentioned. But the name may survive in the valley of the river Diemel, where the inhabitants are still known as 'Diemel-Fossen'.

37 *the Cimbri, now a small state, although their renown is enormous*: Tacitus is
unable or unwilling to give any more details about this people, based in the
Jutland peninsula, the first Germans with whom Rome had come into conflict. Nor does he mention their main allies in this invasion, the Teutoni or
Teutones, who also inhabited Jutland (Mela 3. 32). The remains of the
Cimbri were discovered by Tiberius' fleet in AD 5, and petitioned for Rome's
and the emperor's friendship, as Augustus proudly registered in his *Res
Gestae*, 26. 4, where he also names the Charydes (Harudes) and *Semnones* (on
the latter cf. n. on ch. 39 below).

vast encampments . . . by the size of which one can still gauge: 'still' suggests a
recent eyewitness. Tacitus might have seen them himself, but probably
relied on the Elder Pliny. Presumably the Celtic hill-forts in the Rhineland
and adjacent areas, some extremely large, e.g. the Glauberg on the edge
of the Wetterau, seat of a La Tène prince in the fifth century BC, and
half a kilometre (550 yards) long, were attributed to the Cimbri.

Our city was in her 640th year: 113 BC, reckoned from what became the
'canonical' date, 21 April 753 BC, for the foundation by Romulus.

the second consulship of the emperor Trajan: i.e. AD 98. Trajan, already Caesar
and adopted son of Nerva, opened the year as consul with him. When Nerva
died on 27 January, Trajan became emperor, officially the next day.

For all this time have we been conquering Germany: 'conquering' is clearly
intended in a sarcastic sense, with particular reference to Domitian's claims.

*Neither the Samnites nor the Carthaginians nor Spain nor Gaul nor even the
Parthians have taught us more frequent lessons*: the Samnites of the southern
Apennines fought three wars against Rome in the fourth and third centuries
BC, inflicting many defeats, notably at the Caudine Forks (321). Of the three
'Punic Wars' between Rome and Carthage, 264–241, 218–202, and 149–146
BC, which ended in Carthage's destruction, the second, Hannibalic war was
particularly damaging. Rome took two hundred years to subdue the Iberian
peninsula (218–19 BC), with severe losses in the 'Fiery War' (154–133),
including the disaster of Numantia, 137. (Tacitus actually writes 'the
Spains' and 'the Gauls', plural—both referring to the lands rather than the
people, i.e. 'Galliae' not 'Galli'—because both countries were divided into
several provinces.) The best-known disaster inflicted by the Gauls was the
sack of Rome itself *c.*386 BC by Brennus. Rome fought several wars against
the Parthians after the disaster incurred by *Crassus*: cf. below on him, also on
Pacorus, and *Ventidius*.

*The freedom of the Germans does indeed show more aggression than the despo-
tism of the Arsacids*: Although some German peoples had kings, these were
less despotic than eastern monarchs (cf. n. on *Their kings* in ch. 7 above, and
on *the Gotones* in ch. 44 below). This was a prophetic comment: the Arsacids
were the reigning dynasty of Parthia, which indeed was to last only until AD
226, whereas the 'free Germans' went on to overthrow the Roman empire in
the west. Tacitus' point is the contrast between freedom and slavery: the
subjects of the Parthian king are in effect slaves, hence docile, the Germans,

by contrast, being free men (cf. e.g. on an aspect of this 'freedom' ch. 11 above) are more aggressive (for this meaning, Lund, 208).

Crassus: Marcus Licinius Crassus, consul 70 and 55 BC, ally and rival of Pompey and Caesar, set out to conquer Parthia but was killed at Carrhae in 53, losing several legionary standards in one of Rome's worst reverses. The Parthians invaded Roman territory in 41–40 BC, led by the renegade Roman Quintus Labienus.

Pacorus: the favourite son of the Parthian king, who controlled part of the Roman east for two years with Labienus (see n. immediately above), but was defeated and killed in 39 BC.

Ventidius: the humbly born general Publius Ventidius had served in Gaul with Caesar, was made consul in 43 BC by the Triumvirs, and then given command against the Parthians, whom he crushed in 38 at Mount Gindarus. He celebrated a triumph over the Parthians, the only Roman to have done so at the time Tacitus was writing. Tacitus implies that to have been defeated by a man of Ventidius' origins was humiliating for the Parthians. Augustus regained the lost standards by diplomacy in 20 BC. The long war under Nero, led by Corbulo, resulted in a compromise settlement, which lasted until Trajan's attempted conquest, AD 114–17, initially successful but ultimately a disastrous failure.

Carbo: Gnaeus Papirius Carbo, consul 113 BC, defeated by the Cimbri at Noreia (in modern Carinthia).

Cassius: Lucius Cassius Longinus, consul 107 BC, defeated and killed by the Tigurini, allies of the Cimbri, at Tolosa (Toulouse).

Scaurus Aurelius: Marcus Aurelius Scaurus. Tacitus has inverted his two main names, an archaizing fashion, as with Mallius, below, for variation. Scaurus had been consul in 108 and in 105 BC served as legate under one of the consuls of that year, Mallius, and alongside the proconsul Caepio.

Servilius Caepio: Quintus Servilius Caepio had been consul in 106 BC. As proconsul he failed to co-operate with the consul Mallius.

Maximus Mallius: his normal style was Gnaeus Mallius Maximus, cf. above on *Scaurus Aurelius*. The quarrel between Caepio and Mallius contributed to the disaster of 105 BC at the battle of Arausio (Orange) against the Cimbri, at which the legate Scaurus (above) was killed. Caepio was later convicted and sent into exile for stealing the Gallic treasure from Tolosa (Toulouse) the previous year.

five consular armies: although the five generals had all been consul, only three were consuls commanding consular armies when they were defeated; Caepio was proconsul, Scaurus only a legate.

Varus: consul in 13 BC and son-in-law of Agrippa, Publius Quinctilius Varus had governed Africa and Syria before commanding in Germany. In AD 9 he and his army were trapped by the Cheruscan Arminius (cf. n. on *the Cherusci*, ch. 36 above), long a trusted commander of native troops, who suddenly

switched loyalty. The Seventeenth, Eighteenth, and Nineteenth legions were destroyed in marshy land near Osnabrück: the battlefield has at last been identified through extensive finds of Roman equipment and coins at Kalkriese, *Germania*, 70 (1992), 307 ff. Varus, who committed suicide, was made the scapegoat for this disaster, which resulted in Rome's abandonment of Germany between Rhine and Elbe, cf. *Agr.* 15—the rebellious Britons know that the Gemans had liberated themselves—and ch. 41 below, Tacitus' comment on 'the Elbe, a river that was famous . . .' with accompanying note.

37 *Gaius Marius*: consul each year 104–100 BC; defeated the Teutones at Aquae Sextiae (Aix-en-Provence) in Gaul in 102 BC and the Cimbri at Vercellae (near Rovigo) in northern Italy the next year. No Germans invaded the Italian peninsula again until *c.* AD 170 (the Marcomannic Wars).

the Deified Julius in Gaul: this refers particularly to his victory over the Suebian Germans under Ariovistus in 58 BC, Caesar, *BG* 1. 30 ff.

Drusus and Nero [Tiberius] and Germanicus in their own country: Drusus, younger stepson of Augustus, campaigned beyond the Rhine for four years, 12–9 BC, reaching the Elbe, but died in the latter year after a fall from his horse. He was posthumously given the name Germanicus, 'conqueror of the Germans', assumed by his sons and descendants. Cf. also n. on *Drusus Germanicus*, ch. 34 above. Drusus' elder brother Tiberius, by his full names Tiberius Claudius Nero, was often called 'Nero', as here, before his adoption by Augustus (AD 4), when he became Tiberius Julius Caesar. Tiberius was transferred from his command in the Balkans to take over Drusus' role in Germany. He campaigned there in 8–7 BC, again in AD 4–6, and finally, to restore Roman credit after the Varian disaster, from 10 to 13: Syme, *RP* iii. (1984), 1200 ff. Germanicus, Drusus' elder son, served under Tiberius in AD 13, and took command from 14 until recalled in 16. Tacitus has full details on AD 14–16 in *Ann.* 1 and 2.

the grandiloquent threats of Gaius Caesar: cf. n. on *Gaius Caesar* in *Agr.* 13, on Caligula's apparent plan to invade Britain as well, on his northern expedition, begun in AD 39 but suddenly aborted the following spring.

our dissensions and the Civil Wars: the downfall of Nero in AD 68, which began with an uprising in Gaul, and the confused events that followed, and the Civil Wars of 69, the 'Year of the Four Emperors'. The Batavians and other peoples in the Rhineland and close by launched a major uprising in 69, at first ostensibly against Vitellius, not suppressed until late in 70. Cf. Introduction (pp. xv f.) and n. on ch. 28, *Even the Ubii . . .* , and on ch. 29, *Batavians*.

In recent times, certainly, they have been the objects of triumphs rather than victories: a sarcastic reference to Domitian's two triumphs over the Germans, of AD 83—on which *Agr.* 39 has an even fuller and more hostile comment (and cf. *Ger.* 30 with n. on *Beyond them . . . the territory of the Chatti begins*)—and of AD 89.

38–45 After the digression summarizing Roman relations with the Germans, triggered by the mention of the Cimbri, Tacitus turns to the remaining peoples, in effect those who were still outside the empire when Drusus had extended it to the Elbe, or who moved away in reaction to Rome's advance, see ch. 42 on the Marcoman(n)i and Quadi. Most of these Tacitus classifies as Suebian.

38 *Suebi, who do not, like the Chatti or Tencteri, constitute a single nation*: see ch. 2, where the Suebi are one of the alternative main groupings of Germans.

they occupy the greater part of Germany: all the peoples of the east and north except those dealt with in the last chapter (46) are treated as Suebian. Apart from the religious rites in chs. 39 and 40, the chief common characteristic is their hair-style.

they comb their hair back . . . and tie it in a knot: this is treated in some Roman writers as a general German characteristic, e.g. Juvenal 13. 165, 'a German's sky-blue eyes and greasy blond curls which he twists into a horn'. But Juvenal may in fact be referring to the Suebian chiefs' particular variety (see next note).

even more elaborate hair-style: they used greasy soap to make their hair stand on end, Pliny, *NH* 28. 191. Anderson (fig. 25) illustrates a bronze figure of a German chief, wearing trousers (*bracae*), and with a horn-shaped tuft of hair.

It is not for lovemaking or to inspire passion: once again the contrast is with Rome, where, of course, it was women who went in for elaborate hair-styles to attract men.

39 *Semnones*: first mentioned when Tiberius' campaign of AD 5 reached the Elbe, 'which flows past the territory of the Semnones and Hermunduri', Velleius 2. 106; they, like the Cimbri, then sought Rome's friendship through envoys, *Res Gestae* 26. 4. Their territory stretched from the middle Elbe to the river Oder. They were in the confederacy of *Maroboduus* (on whom see n. in ch. 42) but switched allegiance to Arminius in AD 17, *Ann.* 2. 45. 1. Their king, Masyus, and prophetess, Ganna, paid court to Domitian *c.* AD 93 (Dio 67. 5. 3), shortly after his war against the Marcoman(n)i (on whom see ch. 42 and note). The Semnones are last named in literary sources *c.* AD 179, Dio 71. 5. 3. It was assumed that they re-emerged as the Alamanni in the third century. But it turns out that they were the same as the Juthungi, western neighbours of the Alamanni, on the left bank of the upper Danube: a new inscription from Augsburg, *AE* 1993. 1231b, records the defeat of the 'barbarian people of the Semnones or Jouthungi' as they returned from a raid into Italy in 259–60.

sanctified by their forefathers' auguries and by ancient dread: the Latin here translated forms a line of hexameter verse, reminiscent of Virgil, *Aeneid* 7. 608, cf. 7. 172. Accidental, according to Anderson (182), but poetic language fits the solemn tone here.

39 *A human victim is slaughtered . . . barbarous ritual*: for human sacrifice cf. ch. 9 and n. to ch. 8, on *Albruna*. Tacitus uses 'barbari' here in a negative sense, 'inhuman', as also in *Agr.* 16, 'savagery common to barbarians'—elsewhere 'barbarian' is more or less neutral, meaning 'primitive'. As Timpe (132ff). stresses, the description is much less detailed than that of the Nerthus cult in the next chapter, probably because Tacitus' informant had only witnessed what went on among the Semnones as an outsider.

bound with a chain: cf. ch. 31 and n. on *an iron ring* which was a mark of dishonour among the Chatti.

the god who reigns over all dwells there: Anderson (183f). cites the view that as 'the later Swabians were entitled *Ziuwari*, worshippers of Ziu or Tiu', cf. n. on *Mars* in ch. 9 above, the god of the Semnones must have been Tiu, the original Germanic equivalent of Zeus or Jupiter, not yet ousted by Wodan. Yet as he points out, Tacitus ought to mean Wodan or 'Mercury', cf. n. on *Among the gods . . .* in ch. 9, where he is clearly called the principal German god and the only one to receive human sacrifice, on fixed occasions. Still, it is curious that he does not use the name here, and others think the tone of the passage, e.g. 'the belief that from this wood the people derives its origin', suggests rather that the deity was the ancestor of the people, called e.g. 'Semno', cf. Lund (217) and Timpe (132ff., with copious references).

a hundred cantons: cf. n. on *that is exactly what they are called . . .* in ch. 6 above. Ariovistus' Suebi were said by Caesar, *BG* I. 37. 3, to have had 'a hundred cantons ("pagi")', each of which could annually put a thousand men in the field while the same number remained at home, ibid. 4. I. 4. Some kind of misunderstanding was probably behind the statements in both Caesar and Tacitus. But it may well be that the Semnones were indeed numerically the largest Suebian people (cf. *Agr.* 17 with n. on *the Brigantes*, numerically the largest of the British states), or at least that e.g. when their king Masyus visited Domitian shortly before Tacitus wrote, Dio 67. 5. 3, it became known that they claimed to be 'the chief people of the Suebi'.

40 *Langobardi*: i.e. the Lombards, whose name, 'long-bearded', is thought to have been applied to them by their short-bearded neighbours the Saxons: Anderson, 184f. Their first home was in Scandinavia, from which they moved first to the southern Baltic coast between the rivers Oder and Vistula, then westwards to the lower Elbe, Paul the Deacon, *History of the Lombards* I. I. They were in Maroboduus' confederacy (cf. n. on *Maroboduus* in ch. 42 below) until AD 17 when, like the Semnones, they deserted him for Arminius, *Ann.* 2. 45, whose nephew they supported in 47, ibid. 11. 17. Then, apart from an attempt to cross the Danube in 166, Dio 71. 3. 1a, they disappear from view until late antiquity. After a long stay just north of the Danube they conquered northern Italy in 568, where their kingdom lasted until 774.

the Reudigni: and the six peoples that follow made up a religious 'league' that worshipped the goddess Nerthus. Their position seems to be listed from the

Elbe northwards, in Schleswig-Holstein and Jutland, although the final two perhaps lived in Mecklenburg. As Tacitus does not mention the Saxons (whose name referred to their short sword, *sachs*), placed by Ptolemy, 2. 11. 7, in Holstein north of the Elbe mouth, the Reudigni (probably correctly 'Reudingi') are thought to be Saxons under another name: Anderson, 185 f. Unlike the Angles (below) with whom some of them crossed for good to Britain in the fifth century, the Saxons are mentioned a good deal in ancient literary sources from the late third century onwards, when they began terrorizing the north-west provinces of the empire and became a byword for savage ferocity.

Aviones: as the name evidently means 'islanders' they are thought to have inhabited the northern Frisian islands off the Schleswig coast; they are not mentioned in any other classical writer, but are presumably the Eówan of Anglo-Saxon poetry: Anderson, 186.

Anglii: or Angles, placed east of the Langobardi on the middle Elbe by Ptolemy, 2. 11. 8, which is assumed to be a mistake, as they are the ancestors of the English, who left the Angeln district of Schleswig for Britain in the fifth century, Bede, *Ecclesiastical History* 1. 15. But they might have moved northwards a little in the course of three hundred years.

Varini: thought to be the same as Pliny's 'Varinnae', *NH* 4. 99, whom he assigns to the Vandal group of Germans, cf. n. on *Vandili* in ch. 2 above. In the early Middle Ages the 'Warni' appear in Thuringia with a group of Angles. They may originally have lived in Scandinavia, but their name might have survived in the river Warnow, which flows into the Baltic at Rostock: Anderson, 186.

Eudoses: perhaps the same as the 'Eudusii' in Ariovistus' army, Caesar, *BG* 1. 51, and probably connected with the Jutes, 'Iutae', also called 'Eutii', etc.; evidently a people of south Jutland: Anderson, 186 f.

Suarines, and Huitones: both names are unknown; the latter is read as 'Huitones' by Anderson (187), followed here.

Nerthus: clearly a fertility goddess, whose name is connected with a Celtic word meaning 'power', cf. Welsh *nerth*, and with the name of the Norse fertility god Njordh, whose son and daughter, Frey and Freyja, Frija, or Frigg, goddess of love, took over some of Njordh's functions. In western Germany Frija became the consort of Wodan and was equated with Venus, hence *Freitag*, Friday, *dies Veneris*: Anderson, 187 f.

female cattle: following the practice of Roman religious formulae, Tacitus writes 'bubus feminis', rather than just 'vaccis', 'cows'. They doubtless symbolized fertility.

41 *the Hermunduri*: the second element of this name, *-duri*, survives as the first part of modern *Thur*ingen (Thuringia). The Hermunduri were resettled by Lucius Domitius Ahenobarbus, not long after Drusus' death, in the lands vacated by the Marcoman(n)i (cf. n. on ch. 42), from Thuringia as far east as near Regensburg: Wells, 149 ff. Cf. *Ann.* 13. 57, their successful battle with

the Chatti for the control of salt springs, thought to be at Bad Salzungen on the river Werra or Bad Kissingen on the river Saale.

41 *Raetia's splendid* colonia: Augusta Vindelicum (Augsburg), founded by Drusus, the chief town in Raetia (cf. n. on *the Gauls, Raetians, and Pannonians* in ch. 1); seat of the governor, an equestrian procurator. This seems a curious error by Tacitus: Augusta Vindelicum had no charter at all, let alone that of a *colonia* (cf. Glossary); it first gained the (lower) status of a *municipium* under Hadrian. Perhaps Tacitus was using the word *colonia* in a non-technical sense. The Vindelici, whose chief place it was, were subjugated with the Raeti in 15 BC: Wells, 87 ff.

the Elbe, a river that was famous and well known once. Now it is known only from hearsay: Drusus reached the Elbe on his last campaign, 9 BC; Ahenobarbus (cf. n. on *the Hermunduri* above) was there *c*.2 BC, *Ann.* 4. 44, and Tiberius in AD 5, Velleius 2. 106: Wells, 149 ff. Augustus mentions 'the mouth of the river Elbe' as the limit of territory pacified in his time, *Res Gestae* 26. 2. Tacitus evidently regrets the good old days of glorious expansion.

42 *Naristi*: often spelt 'Naristae', lived between the Hermunduri and Marcomanni (cf. next note), i.e. on the borders of Bavaria and Bohemia, cf. Ptolemy 2. 11. 11. They may, however, have moved further east, for a remarkable inscription, *AE* 1956. 124, found at Diana Veteranorum (mod. Zana in Algeria), records how a Roman officer, who had killed their chief ('dux'), then commanded a contingent of this people, listed between the Marcomanni and Quadi, suggesting that they were east of the Marcomanni by the 170s, at the time of the great war named after the Marcomanni (cf. A. R. Birley, *Marcus Aurelius*, 2nd edn. (London, 1987, esp. 249 ff.).

Marcomani: whose name, 'the men of the marches', is generally spelt with double *n* in inscriptions. They are first mentioned by Caesar, *BG* 1. 51. 2, supplying troops for Ariovistus. They were defeated by Drusus in 9 BC and shortly afterwards migrated to Bohemia, probably accompanied by the Quadi.

Quadi: they are first mentioned in AD 19, cf. n. on *Tudrus* below. The Marcomanni drove out the remnants of the Boii.

Boii: see notes in ch. 28 on *Boii* and *Boihaemum*. In their new home the two peoples were built up into a formidable force by Maroboduus.

Maroboduus: he could supposedly muster 70,000 infantry and 4,000 cavalry: Velleius 2. 108 ff., who describes the massive campaign launched by Tiberius, with a force of twelve legions, in AD 6, which would have completed the conquest of Germany. But the great Pannonian revolt forced the abandonment of this operation. Maroboduus refused to join Arminius against Rome after the slaughter of Varus' legions in AD 9 (see n. on *Varus* in ch. 37 above); Arminius attacked him some years later, *c*.17; he was ousted and given refuge by Tiberius at Ravenna, *Ann.* 2. 44 ff.

Tudrus: otherwise unknown. He was presumably a king of the Quadi, a people first mentioned when Tiberius appointed the Quadian Vannius king over

both Marcomanni and Quadi in AD 19, *Ann.* 2. 63; Vannius reigned until 50, after which the kingdom was divided again, ibid. 12. 29 f.

they submit to ones from outside too: Tacitus' precise meaning here is unclear, but it is plausible that Domitian, who had fought the Marcomanni and probably Quadi too in his 'Suebian War', may have imposed a king from another Suebian people such as the Semnones—some such plan may have been behind his receiving the Semnonian king, Masyus, Dio 67. 5. 3 (cf. n. on *Semnones* in ch. 39 above). Alternatively Nerva may have imposed a new ruler in AD 97, the year before Tacitus wrote, cf. Pliny, *Pan.* 8: Anderson, 196.

They are occasionally backed up by our armed forces, more often by money, which is equally effective: a cynical epigram. In due course the system broke down, with the outbreak of the Marcomannic Wars (A. R. Birley, *Marcus Aurelius*, 2nd edn. (London, 1987), 249 ff.), in the course of which the Marcomanni and Quadi actually invaded Italy, the first Germans to get this far since the Cimbri nearly three hundred years earlier.

43 *Marsigni*: nowhere else mentioned. The name was probably in fact Marsingi and they may have been an offshoot of the *Marsi*, on whom cf. n. in ch. 2 above.

Buri: placed by Ptolemy, 2. 11. 10, on the borders of Moravia and Silesia. The Buri played a minor role in Trajan's First Dacian War, Dio 68. 8. 1, and in the Marcomannic War, id. 71. 18.

The Cotini speak Gallic: they were clearly a remnant of the Celtic population driven out by advancing Germans and others (cf. the Boii, chs. 28, 42): Anderson, 196 f., who suggests locating them south of the Quadi. Some Cotini were incorporated inside the province of Upper Pannonia, probably soon after Tacitus wrote, the remainder were resettled inside the empire by Marcus Aurelius: A. Mócsy, *Pannonia and Upper Moesia* (London, 1974), 57.

the Osi speak Pannonian: i.e. Illyrian, cf. ch. 28. On the language, which would presumably be 'Illyrian', see J. Wilkes, *The Illyrians* (Oxford, 1992), 67 ff. But A. Mócsy, (*Pannonia and Upper Moesia* (London, 1974), 59 ff.) argues that both the Osi and the Eravisci (cf. n. on ch. 28 above, *Aravisci*) were Celtic. The Osi inhabited the Hungarian plain, across the river from Budapest.

tribute . . . levied on the one by the Sarmatians, on the other by the Quadi: i.e. the Osi paid tribute to the Sarmatians, the Cotini to the Quadi: Anderson, 197 f.

The Cotini, more to their shame, have iron-mines: i.e. they should be able to make weapons to make themselves independent. For the iron-mines, probably in the mountains north of the river Thaya, a tributary of the March (Morava), see Anderson, 197.

Lugii: a collective name for the southern group of eastern Germans, the northern group being Goths (Gutones), Rugii, and Lemovii. They are evidently the same as Pliny's 'Vandili', *NH* 4. 99, although the constituent

peoples he names cannot be accurate; cf. n. to ch. 2 on *Vandili*. Tacitus mentions 'Vandili' there as a group name but omits it here. 'Vandili' was probably 'an extended ethnic name', while 'Lugii' was 'probably a cult-title'. The Vandals were later divided into Silingi, whose name perhaps survives in Silesia, and Hasdingi (cf. below, notes on *Harii* and on *Naharvali* . . .). The Lugii are first mentioned as members of Maroboduus' confederation, Strabo 7. 1. 3, and helped to expel Vannius (cf. n. to ch. 42 on *Tudrus*) in AD 50, *Ann.* 12. 30; they were supported against the Marcomanni and Quadi by Domitian, Dio 67. 5. 2, after which the name lapses: Anderson 198 f.

43 *Harii*: unknown under this name but perhaps the same as the Charini in Pliny, *NH* 4. 99, and the Hasdingi, the most prominent division of the Vandals, involved in the Marcomannic War, Eutropius, *Breviarium* 8. 13, Dio 71. 12.

Helvecones: clearly the 'Aelvaeones' in Ptolemy 2. 11. 9, where they are placed north of the Burgundians, a people curiously omitted by Tacitus, who then lived between the Oder and Vistula.

Manimi: probably the 'Omanoi', whom Ptolemy, 2. 11. 9, places south of the Burgundians. The real name may lie somewhere between the two versions.

Helisii: otherwise unknown, unless connected to 'Kalisia', a 'town' listed by Ptolemy, 2. 11. 9, in a position between modern Wrocław and Warsaw.

Naharvali . . . grove of ancient sanctity: the name of the people is also given as 'Nahanarvali'. They are otherwise unknown under this name, but their grove has been identified with a prominent wooded hill south-south-east of Wrocław; hence the suggestion that this people were the same as the Vandal Silingi, whose territory included this place: Anderson, 199.

priest . . . dressed in women's clothes: i.e. a long robe and a head-veil: Anderson, 200.

according to the Roman interpretation: cf. n. on *Among the gods Mercury* . . . in ch. 9 above.

Castor and Pollux: twin brethren who help warriors in battle and sailors in storms, similar to the Greek and Roman Dioscuri, were widely worshipped from Gaul to Scandinavia and as far as India (the *ásvins* in the Sanskrit Vedas): Anderson, 200.

the name is 'the Alci': the Latin text has *Alcis*, assumed to be dative of *Alci*, although it might be indeclinable or a nominative plural in *-is*. *alces* meant 'elk', Caesar, *BG* 6. 27. 1, Pliny, *NH* 8. 39, but this divine 'name' quite probably meant 'gods': Anderson, 201, comparing Gothic *alhs*, 'sanctuary', and Lettish *elks*, 'idol'.

army of ghosts: what Tacitus portrays as a military tactic was perhaps really some kind of religious rite. It suggests that the soldiers of this people played the part of the 'host of spirits of the dead which rages through the air under the leadership of Wodan': Anderson, 201 f. Cf. *Ann.* 14. 30. 1: Mona (Anglesey) defended against Roman attack by torch-bearing women dressed in

black like the Furies and by Druids howling imprecations; on Wodan cf. n. to ch. 9 above, *Among the gods Mercury* . . .

44 *the Gotones*: the Goths, who at this time lived east of the lower Vistula. Their own tradition (Jordanes, *Getica* 4) was that they had come there from Göta-land in southern Sweden. In AD 19 a Marcomannic noble, Catualda, was in exile among them, *Ann.* 2. 62. They later migrated to the Black Sea coast and from there into the Roman empire: H. Wolfram, *The Goths* (London, 1990).

under the rule of kings . . . *not inconsistent with freedom*: even in the German states that had kings the people enjoyed relative freedom (but not among the Sviones, cf. n. on *even respect wealth* . . . *absolute right to obedience*, below).

Rugii: in Pomerania, west of the lower Vistula, cf. Ptolemy 2. 11. 7 and 12. The Baltic island of Rügen is thought to have derived its name from this peo-ple, not mentioned again until the fifth century, when they were established in the Danube area. They are last heard of in AD 541, Procopius, *Gothic War* 3. 2.

Lemovii: otherwise unknown. Some MSS read 'Lemonii'.

The peoples of the Sviones: the ancestors of the Swedes, for whom the Anglo–Saxon name was *Swéon*.

in the midst of the Ocean itself: i.e. they lived on islands, or rather, surely, in Scandinavia, which was for Mela, 3. 54, and Pliny, *NH* 4. 96, an island 'of unknown size' and 'another world', inhabited by the people of the 'Hille-*viones* [surely a corrupt version of *Sviones*] in five hundred districts'.

They do not use sails: i.e. unlike the Romans, a state of affairs among the German peoples that continued until at least the fourth century if not longer: Lund, 229 f.

even respect wealth, which is why a single ruler is in power whose authority is now unrestricted, with an absolute right to obedience: this need not contradict ch. 5, the Germans' lack of interest in silver or gold. Tacitus adds there that 'cat-tle are their sole . . . wealth', 'opes', using the same word as here. If this is what he meant, the king of the ancient Swedes would have been the biggest cattle rancher in the land. But the thought may be that these seafarers were also traders, cf. Anderson, 204 f. To have to obey 'a single ruler' with unre-stricted or absolute authority was clearly not desirable. Tacitus' words would remind his hearers or readers what they had just escaped with the murder of Domitian. However this may be, the royal power probably did not derive from wealth: it was rather based on religion, the king being 'also priest of the national god Frey . . . from whom the royal house traced its descent': Anderson, 206, citing Olaf's Saga and Adam of Bremen.

Weapons . . . *are kept locked up*: a striking contrast to the general German practice, cf. chs. 11, 'carrying arms', and 13, 'no business . . . except under arms'.

in peacetime armed men can easily become indisciplined: this repeats with slightly different wording the comment on the army in Britain under the lax

command of Trebellius, *Agr.* 16: 'the soldiers, who had been accustomed to campaigning, were growing unruly through doing nothing.'

45 *another sea, sluggish and almost motionless*: a similar description to *Agr.* 10 on the waters north of Scotland.

the sound of the sun's emergence from the sea: Greek and Roman writers report the popular idea that the setting sun hissed as it dropped into the sea. None except Tacitus connect the rising sun with a noise, but in German folklore 'day-break' (*Tagesanbruch*) was associated with a sound: Anderson, 208.

the Suebian Sea: i.e. the Baltic. This is the only place where it is given this name.

the Aestii: said to be a Germanic name, thought to have been applied by the Germans to the speakers of a Baltic Indo-European language, ancestors of the Lithuanians and Latvians, who lived on the east coast of the Baltic. The name has been inherited by the modern Estonians, who are, however, descended rather from the Fenni (ch. 46 and n.): Anderson, 209.

their language is closer to British: in spite of this linguistic divergence, i.e. the failure to fulfil one of his criteria for belonging to an ethnic group (cf. esp. ch. 46 on the Bastarnae, with n. on *The Peucini, whom some call the Bastarnae*), Tacitus still includes the Aestii among the Suebian Germans. The idea that the language was 'closer to British', a form of early Celtic, cannot have been based on serious evidence. (Tacitus seems unaware of non-Celtic inhabitants of Caledonia, i.e. 'proto-Picts', cf. n. to *Agr.* 11 on *the inhabitants of Caledonia . . .*) It may have derived from Roman traders to whom the Aestians sounded more like Britons than Germans. Pliny, *NH* 37. 45, tells of a Roman knight who visited Baltic trading-posts in Nero's reign, a possible source for Tacitus: Anderson, 210.

the Mother of the Gods . . . wild boar: presumably in fact *Nerthus* (for whom see n. on ch. 40) or a similar deity; 'the Roman interpretation' (ch. 43) is again involved, for Tacitus' expression must mean the goddess Cybele, whose devotees wore amulets in the form of animal figures, although not of a wild boar—this was sacred in Sweden to the deities Frey and Freyja, and Scandinavian (and Anglo-Saxon) helmets were often decorated with the boar: Anderson, 210.

They seldom use iron weapons, clubs frequently: cf. the opening of ch. 6, 'Even iron is not plentiful', and n.

Grain and other crops they cultivate with a perseverance unusual among . . . Germans: cf. Tacitus' remarks on German laziness in chs. 4, 14, 15, 26. In ch. 26 the Germans' only crop is corn, 'seges'. Here 'grain' is 'frumenta'; the 'other crops' are presumably vegetables.

amber: Tacitus uses the Latin word 'sucinum' (from *sucus*, 'sap') rather than the Greek *electron*, which also means 'electrum', a compound of silver and gold. Amber was already valued by the Greeks in Homeric times. It was imported into the Po valley from the fifth century BC and became prized at Rome in the late Republic. The 'Amber Road' from the Baltic via Carnun-

tum on the Danube and on across the Julian Alps to the Adriatic became a major trade route. Pliny, *NH* 37. 30–51, has a lengthy account.

which they themselves call glesum: a Germanic word meaning something like 'shine', cf. Anglo–Saxon *glaes*, English 'glass'. The Romans learned the word during Germanicus' North Sea voyages, Pliny, *NH* 37. 42, cf. 4. 97, and renamed an island after it, 'Glaesaria'.

it just lay among the other jetsam . . . until our luxury gave it a reputation: this is a moralizing comment contradicted by the evidence for the long-standing trade in amber, cf. above and Lund, 235. But it fits Tacitus' picture of the uncorrupted Germans, uninterested in gold and silver (ch. 5), then led astray by the Romans, cf. ch. 15, 'taught to accept money . . . by us', and ch. 42, 'more often by money'.

Sithones: neighbours of the Sviones, and so presumably also living on their 'island(s)', i.e. in Scandinavia: Lund, 237. Since the preceding lines deal with the Aestii, some understandably favour transposing this short section back to ch. 44 or the beginning of 45 (where, however, 'Beyond the Sviones' would then have to be altered to 'Beyond the Sithones'). The name 'Sithones', spelt in some MSS without an *h*, is found nowhere else for a German or northern people, although there were Thracian Sithones in the Balkans, cf. e.g. Ovid, *Fasti* 3. 719. The name of the northern Sithones is supposedly a Germanic translation of the old Finnish name, *Kainu-laiset*, 'Lowlanders', of a people in north-west Finland, the Norse *Kvaenir*, now the Kvaens: Anderson, 214 f.

ruled by a woman. To this extent they have fallen lower not merely than free men but than slaves: female rule over the Sithones is supposed to have been an inference made by Germans from the name *Kvaenir*, associated with Old Norse *kvaen*, cf. English 'queen': Anderson, 215, who cites early medieval legends of a northern Amazon monarchy, associated, however, with the 'Sviones' rather than the Sithones. The theme of 'degeneration', here spiritual, is taken up in the next section, the physical degeneration of the Bastarnae. Tacitus is less misogynist in *Agr.* 16, on Boudicca as leader of the Britons. But cf. *Ann.* 12. 37. 4, on a shocking innovation, a woman (the Younger Agrippina) presiding at a military ceremony (the display of the captured Briton Caratacus); and shortly afterwards the Brigantes are 'ashamed at being ruled by a woman' and rise in rebellion, ibid. 12. 40. 3. Tacitus may here have written 'virtute', not 'servitute', as Lund (238), suggests. If so, this would mean something like 'they have lost not only their freedom but their manhood (or even, "their virility") too'. Cf. *Agr.* 11 for this thought: the Gauls have lost their 'virtus' (translated there 'courage') along with their liberty.

46 *the Peucini, whom some call the Bastarnae, are certainly like the Germans in their language, way of life, and in their type of houses*: the Bastarnae were already known under that name to the Greeks by the early second century BC, as allies of King Philip V of Macedon, Polybius, *History* 26. 9, Livy 40. 5, 57 f., etc. Strabo, 7. 3. 17, calls them a people 'of Germanic origin' who live on the

island of Peuce in the Danube delta. Their territory stretched along the north of the eastern Carpathians from Galicia southwards to the mouth of the Danube. The Elder Pliny (*NH* 4. 100) classified them as one of the five great groups of Germans, cf. n. to ch. 2 above, *some assert that the god had further offspring* . . .

46 *and all of them are characterized by squalor. But, as a result of mixed marriages, their lofty physique is to some extent taking on the misshapen appearance of the Sarmatians*: Tacitus uses four main criteria to identify the Peucini-Bastarnae as Germans, together with a further general characteristic of all Germans, dirt or squalor (cf. opening of ch. 20); the fourth criterion, their large physique, is being debased by intermarriage.

The Venethi . . . are on the whole to be classified as Germans: the correct form is evidently 'Venedi': Anderson, 216; cf. also the Veneti of the northern Adriatic. The Venethi were probably not Germanic, in spite of Tacitus, but the ancestors of the Slavs. The name could, however, have been transferred to the early Slavs when they moved into the area, between the rivers Oder and Vistula. At any rate, the Slavonic peoples generally were all labelled 'Wenden' by their later German neighbours.

The Fenni: neighbours of the Aestii on the east coast of the Baltic. This is the only mention of 'Finns', apart from Ptolemy 3. 5. 8 ('Phinnoi'), until late antiquity. The Fenni, whose name may be related to the Gothic *fani*, 'marsh' (thus 'Fenni' would be a Germanic name for this people), were apparently the ancestors of the modern Estonians rather than of the modern Finns.

remarkably savage . . . They have no weapons, no horses, and no homes: in other words they have nothing in common with either Germans or Sarmatians. 'homes' here translates 'penates', lit. 'household gods'. This description is a climax: the Bastarnae, as a result of intermarriage with Sarmatians, are to some extent inferior to other Germans, the Venethi have taken over many Sarmatian customs, but the Fenni are utterly primitive. Anderson (219 f.) suggests that Tacitus was again drawing on the Roman knight who travelled to the Baltic in Nero's reign, Pliny, *NH* 37. 45; cf. on ch. 45, *their language is closer to British*.

a shelter made from interwoven branches: Tacitus fails to note that the description applies only to summer conditions: Anderson, 221, who compares Herodotus 4. 23. 6, Scythian tents.

they think this is a happier lot: an ironic allusion to the Stoic and Epicurean doctrine that freedom from material needs is the highest good.

than . . . speculating . . . with their own and other peoples' money: the Fenni are supposed to be familiar with moneylending but deliberately to abstain from it, which conflicts with the remark in ch. 26 that 'ignorance [of capital and interest] is a surer protection than any prohibition'. But the conclusion of the work naturally has to highlight the advantages of the primitive life, summed up by an epigram.

Having nothing to fear at the hands of men or gods, they have reached a state that is very difficult to attain: they do not even need to pray for anything: Anderson (222) compares Justin, *Epitome* 2. 2. 10 on the Scythians, who spurn gold and silver, live on milk and honey, and wear animal-skins rather than woollen clothing.

The Hellusii and Oxiones are said to have human faces and features, the bodies and limbs of animals: neither name is elsewhere recorded. No doubt the characteristics of seals and sea-lions are behind these stories. Anderson (222) notes that the second name might be related to the Irish *oisin*, 'young seal'; he cites Mela 1. 48, 3. 56, 88, and 103, and Pliny, *NH* 4. 95 and 5. 44, for similar stories of monsters on the edge of the world. Tacitus himself relates how Germanicus' soldiers, shipwrecked in the North Sea, some of them on the coasts of Britain, brought back stories of having seen 'sea monsters and creatures which could have been either human or animal'.

GLOSSARY

ala plural *alae*; lit. 'wing'; a cavalry regiment, most of which were approximately 500 strong, Lat. *quingenaria*, in practice probably 480, made up of sixteen squadrons (*turmae*) of 30 men, each commanded by a decurion; there were also a few double strength *alae*, called *milliariae*, '1000-strong', exact organization not certain.

auxilia lit. 'assistant' or 'auxiliary (forces)', a general name for the non-citizen troops organized in *alae* (see above) and cohorts (see below), as opposed to the legions (see below).

Board of Three Lat. *tresviri*. There were various such boards, but in the imperial period the name refers mostly to two groups of young future senators within the 'vigintivirate' (see below), the three Mintmasters, *monetales*, and the *capitales*, whose duties included supervising the infliction of capital punishment and other police functions (e.g. book-burning in *Agr.* 2).

centurion officer commanding a 'century' or company, originally 100 strong but in practice by the time of Tacitus long since 80 strong. Centurions generally rose from the ranks and were professional military men, who often served for life.

civitas can mean 'citizenship' or, as in several places in the *Agr.* and *Ger.* 'community', 'state', etc. It is often employed with reference to 'native states', i.e. native communities that do not have a Roman charter as *colonia* or *municipium* (see below). The translation 'tribe' was often favoured in the past. It is avoided in the present version.

cognomen the third element in the Roman name, e.g. 'Caesar' in the case of Gaius Julius Caesar, or Agricola with Gnaeus Julius Agricola. See also *praenomen* and *nomen* below.

cohort either one of the ten subdivisions of a legion (see below) or (as in this work) an independent infantry regiment of the *auxilia*. There were several kinds of auxiliary cohort. The basic '500-strong' infantry unit in practice probably had 480 men, in six centuries of 80, each with a centurion. The commanding officer was a prefect, a man of equestrian rank. Some small cohorts also had a cavalry element, evidently 120 men, four squadrons (*turmae*) of 30, each commanded by a decurion, making their total size 600 men. They were called *cohortes equitatae* and were also commanded by a prefect. At latest during the Flavian period 'double-strength' cohorts, *cohortes mil-*

liariae, began to be used, in practice not really twice the size of the others but either 800 strong, ten centuries of 80 infantrymen, or 1,040 men in 'double' *equitatae* units, which would have 240 cavalry as well. These 'double cohorts' were generally commanded by equestrian officers with the rank of tribune, equal in status to an equestrian legionary tribune. (However, for some special reason which can only be guessed at, the Batavian and Tungrian cohorts, even when 'double' sized, were still commanded by prefects).

colonia, **colony** a Roman 'chartered town'. Originally only established within Italy, but in the imperial period increasingly outside Italy. Up till the early second century AD still founded as new settlements for legionary veterans. Meanwhile the status, involving full Roman citizenship for all inhabitants of such towns, was also conferred on existing communities.

Comitium the area north of the Forum (see below), at the foot of the Capitol, which was the main place of political assembly in the Republic. It retained only symbolic importance under the empire.

Commonwealth this translates *res publica*, which has this literal meaning (hence the English Commonwealth in the seventeenth century). The word continued to be used of the 'state' after the end of the Republic.

consul the original pair of chief magistrates of the Republic, elected every year. Under the empire the consuls elected for the start of the year, known as the 'ordinary consuls', were regularly replaced after a month or two by a new pair, known as 'suffect consuls'. By the Flavian period there were sometimes as many as half a dozen pairs of consuls in one year. The 'ordinary consuls', whose names were given to the year, had more prestige than the 'suffects'. The minimum age, the forty-second year, laid down in the Republic, seems to have been retained by Augustus, with exceptions.

consular an ex-consul. The term soon came to mean 'governor' of a province (eventually even if the governor in question had not been consul).

decemvir stlitibus iudicandis one of the Board of Ten Men for judging lawsuits. Under Augustus' reforms future senators were supposed to hold, for a year, one of the four posts in the vigintivirate (for which, see below). Half the 'twenty' were the *decemviri*, who, in spite of their youth (between 18 and 24), presided over civil courts at Rome.

Deified Julius, Augustus, Claudius, Vespasian, Nerva following the precedent set in the case of Julius Caesar, who became 'Divus

Julius' not long after his murder in 44 BC, the emperors (but not Tiberius, Caligula, Nero and his first three successors, or Domitian) were formally declared to be gods after their death and subsequently referred to as 'Divus Augustus', etc.

denarius the commonest silver coin in circulation, worth 4 sesterces (see 'sesterce' below). Roman legionaries were paid 300 *denarii* per year.

equestrian, *eques Romanus* often translated 'Roman knight'. There was a property qualification, 400,000 sesterces (see 'sesterce' below). Men of this status belonged to the 'second order' in society, after the senatorial, and could serve as army officers, prefects and military tribunes, and as procurators. Equestrians were entitled to wear a purple stripe on their tunics, but a narrow one; the broad senatorial stripe was more distinguished, see *latus clavus.*

Forum properly called the 'Roman Forum'. The chief public square in Rome, surrounded by important public buildings such as the senate-house.

freedman an ex-slave. A small number of imperial freedmen, i.e. ex-slaves of the emperor, wielded immense power as heads of palace secretariats which were practically 'ministries', of finance, etc. At the time that Tacitus was writing the role of these high-ranking 'officials' was being phased out, and the departments they had presided over were given new, equestrian chiefs.

gentilicium see *nomen.*

knight, Roman see 'equestrian'.

latus clavus the broad purple-coloured stripe on the tunic which only members of the senatorial order could wear. 'To confer the *latus clavus*' on a young man thus meant to make him eligible for membership of the senate. Each legion (except for those in Egypt, a province barred to senators) had one young man of this rank as an officer; see 'tribune, military', below.

legate originally 'envoy', 'delegate', or 'deputy', the legate was assistant to e.g. a proconsul or also, in the imperial period, deputy of the emperor, *legatus Augusti*, either as commander of a legion, sometimes called 'praetorian legate', or with the additional title *pro praetore*, 'acting praetor', a governor of a province. (Even men who had already been consul, informally called 'consular legate', see 'consular' above, were officially 'pro-praetorian legates of the emperor'.)

legion the largest unit in the Roman army, with a paper strength of between 5,000 and 6,000 men, all Roman citizens, subdivided into ten

cohorts. At the time Tacitus was writing *Agricola* and *Germany*, there were three legions still in Britain (there had been four from AD 43 until *c*.87) out a total strength in AD 98 of twenty-eight legions. The commanding officer of each legion was called the legate, by this date a man who had already been praetor. The other officers were the six tribunes, the camp prefect, and sixty centurions.

limes a word originally meaning 'cleared strip' or the like, which gradually came to mean 'boundary line'; from the end of the first century AD onwards it was used to describe the frontier of the empire, particularly where it was a fortified land boundary.

municipium a Roman chartered town, with a somewhat different form of constitution to a *colonia* (see above). Originally confined to Italy, *municipia* were revived by Julius Caesar. Romanized communities in the provinces with this title had 'Latin' status, in accordance with which only the annually elected magistrates and their families acquired full Roman citizenship. Many such towns were later promoted to be *coloniae*.

nomen also called the *nomen gentilicium*. The second element in the basic Roman 'three names', it was the main or family name, e.g. 'Cornelius', for Publius Cornelius Tacitus or 'Julius' for Gnaeus Julius Agricola. See also *cognomen, praenomen*.

patricians the original Roman aristocracy, supposedly descended from the earliest senators, from the foundation of the Republic or even earlier. As the number of patrician families (whose role included certain ancient religious rites) had dwindled, Caesar and Augustus were authorized to create new patricians, and subsequent emperors did likewise.

pontifex member of one of the four main colleges of 'priests', all in fact normal senators who had certain religious functions to perform, including oversight of the state cults. All emperors held the office of 'chief pontiff', *pontifex maximus*.

praenomen the forename, first of the basic 'three names' borne by Roman men. See also *cognomen, nomen* above. The number in use was very restricted, hardly more than a dozen. In some areas, notably Gaul, each son long continued to be given a separate forename. But by Tacitus' day it was not uncommon for a single forename to be used by one family, with brothers having the same one. Thus, of the two sons of Vespasian, whose full names were Titus Flavius Vespasianus, the elder, Titus for short, had exactly the same three names as Vespasian, the younger, Domitian, was called Titus Flavius Domitianus.

praetor annual magistrate at Rome, one of the traditional Republican office-holders retained under the empire, second in rank to the consuls. The minimum age had been reduced by Augustus to 30 or in effect 29 (the thirtieth year). The number of praetors gradually increased. By the end of the first century AD there were eighteen praetors each year. Their duties at Rome included presiding over law-courts and they were obliged to put on games at their own expense.

praetorian a senator who had been praetor but not yet consul. Men of this status could undertake a wide range of functions at Rome and in the provinces, notably as legate—of a legion, or of an imperial province, or to a proconsul.

prefect, of cohort, *ala,* **fleet** a word meaning 'commander', applied particularly to officers of equestrian rank (or even governors in a few cases), commanding regiments of *auxilia*, or naval units such as the *classis Britannica*, the British fleet.

proconsul governor of a province, 'with the powers of a consul', the title held in the imperial period by governors of ten urbanized and peaceful provinces (most of them were Greek-speaking). These were still governed in the Republican fashion by a senator chosen by lot—from the ex-praetors in the case of eight of them, e.g. Macedonia, Sicily, or Cyprus; from the ex-consuls in the case of Asia (western Turkey) and Africa (Tunisia and Tripolitania). The proconsul's staff included a quaestor and a legate (more than one legate in the case of Asia and Africa).

procurator officials of equestrian rank (there were also freedmen procurators). In the majority of cases their duties were financial, in charge of tax-raising, but in military provinces they functioned as army paymaster as well. Their sphere of duty often spanned more than one province, e.g. a single procurator was responsible for both Gallia Belgica and the two German army districts, later the two provinces of Upper and Lower Germany. A few provinces had procurators as governor, e.g. Raetia and Noricum.

quaestor the most junior of the traditional 'Republican' senatorial magistrates. The minimum age was reduced by Augustus to 25, effectively 24 (twenty-fifth year). Twenty took office each year, thereby formally entering the senate. Ten served in Rome (two attached to the emperor), the other ten in the provinces as assistant to a proconsul.

quindecimvir sacris faciundis the *XVviri,* 'fifteen men for carrying out sacred duties', like the *pontifices* (see *pontifex* above) formed one of the four main colleges of 'priests', all in fact normal senators who had

certain religious functions to perform, in this case including the supervision of foreign religious cults and, theoretically only once every 110 years, presiding at the 'Secular Games'.

Secular Games a religious celebration to mark the end of one century, *saeculum*, and the beginning of a new one. The *saeculum*, the longest span of a human life, was later fixed at 110 years when Augustus held a revived form in 17 BC—he had perhaps planned to hold them in 23 BC. (Claudius' Games, in AD 47, followed a different calculation, and marked the eight hundredth anniversary of Rome's founding.) Domitian's Games of AD 88 were supposedly on the Augustan model but if so were presumably timed from the originally intended date, 23 BC, 110 years earlier. The three days of sacrifices and games were organized by the *quindecimviri sacris faciundis* (see above).

senate the old high council of state of the Roman Republic, with six hundred members. It continued to have great prestige and responsibility under the empire and its members and their families constituted the imperial aristocracy. Entry was gained by becoming quaestor (see above). The qualifications, for those from non-senatorial families, included possession of property worth a minimum of 1,000,000 sesterces (250,000 *denarii*) (see entries on 'sesterce' and *denarius*) and the conferment by the emperor of the broad stripe, *latus clavus* (see above). This was usually followed by tenure of one of the preliminary posts (see 'vigintivirate') and often a military tribunate (see 'tribune, military').

sesterce Lat. *sestertius*, a large base-metal coin, worth one quarter of a *denarius*. It was used to express certain values, e.g. the property qualification for senate membership was 1,000,000 sesterces, for the equestrian order 400,000.

squadron Lat. *turma*, a subdivision of a cavalry regiment, *ala* (see above), or of the cavalry detachment in a part-mounted cohort (see above). The squadron was commanded by a decurion.

suffect consuls see 'consul'.

tax-farmer the *publicani* or 'publicans' classed with sinners in the New Testament were the businessmen who contracted to collect taxes and tolls for the Roman state. They still existed under the empire although less powerful than in the Republic, since imperial procurators (see above) could now oversee them.

toga the woollen robe which was the traditional main garment of the adult Roman male, assumed for the first time at a special ceremony which marked the transition from childhood to youth. It was officially

worn only by Roman citizens, who were thus sometimes called 'toga-wearers'.

tribune, military one of the senior officers in the Roman army. Each legion (see above) had six, of which one was the 'broad-stripe' tribune (see *latus clavus* above), a young man aged about 18 to 24; the other five were equestrian officers (see 'equestrian'), for whom the tribunate marked the second grade, the first being the prefecture of a cohort (see above), the third the prefecture of an *ala* (see above). (Commanders of 'double-strength' cohorts were also equestrian tribunes, of equivalent rank to legionary tribunes, who would serve for between one and three years).

tribune of the plebs originally officers elected annually to protect the humbler section of the population against maltreatment by patrician magistrates (see 'patricians'), the ten tribunes acquired an important political role in the later Republic, particularly as initiators of legislation. Under the principate the tribunes survived, but with virtually nothing of their old functions: the post was simply a qualifying stage in the senatorial career between quaestor and praetor (see above).

triumph, honorary triumph the triumph was the victory procession, including prisoners of war, booty, etc., led by a Roman general through the streets of Rome to the temple of Jupiter on the Capitol. The honour was restricted to cases where at least 5,000 enemy had been killed. Under the empire the honour was restricted after 19 BC to emperors and their close relatives; for other commanders a substitute was created, the 'honorary triumph' or 'triumphal decorations', *ornamenta triumphalia*. The holder of this award had the right to wear special costume and certain other privileges.

vigintivirate the collective name for the twenty young men who served on the four boards of minor annual magistrates at Rome, 10 of them as *decemviri* (see *decemvir stlitibus indicandi*), 6 in the two groups of *tresviri* (cf. also 'Board of Three' above), and the 4 *quattuorviri*. The duties were minimal but Augustus evidently laid down that all would-be senators should hold one of these four posts before being quaestor (see above). It is not known how strictly this rule was applied.

INDEX OF PEOPLE AND DEITIES

Romans are in most cases listed under their family name or *nomen*

INDEX OF PEOPLES AND PLACES

GENERAL INDEX

Terms in the Glossary have for the most part been omitted

A SELECTION OF OXFORD WORLD'S CLASSICS

THOMAS AQUINAS	Selected Philosophical Writings
GEORGE BERKELEY	Principles of Human Knowledge and Three Dialogues
EDMUND BURKE	A Philosophical Enquiry into the Origin of Our Ideas of the Sublime and Beautiful Reflections on the Revolution in France
THOMAS CARLYLE	The French Revolution
CONFUCIUS	The Analects
FRIEDRICH ENGELS	The Condition of the Working Class in England
JAMES GEORGE FRAZER	The Golden Bough
THOMAS HOBBES	Human Nature and De Corpore Politico Leviathan
JOHN HUME	Dialogues Concerning Natural Religion and The Natural History of Religion Selected Essays
THOMAS MALTHUS	An Essay on the Principle of Population
KARL MARX	Capital The Communist Manifesto
J. S. MILL	On Liberty and Other Essays Principles of Economy and Chapters on Socialism
FRIEDRICH NIETZSCHE	On the Genealogy of Morals Twilight of the Idols
THOMAS PAINE	Rights of Man, Common Sense, and Other Political Writings
JEAN-JACQUES ROUSSEAU	Discourse on Political Economy and The Social Contract Discourse on the Origin of Inequality
SIMA QIAN	Historical Records
ADAM SMITH	An Inquiry into the Nature and Causes of the Wealth of Nations
MARY WOLLSTONECRAFT	Political Writings

The Oxford World's Classics Website

www.worldsclassics.co.uk

- Information about new titles
- Explore the full range of Oxford World's Classics
- Links to other literary sites and the main OUP webpage
- Imaginative competitions, with bookish prizes
- Peruse *Compass*, the Oxford World's Classics magazine
- Articles by editors
- Extracts from Introductions
- A forum for discussion and feedback on the series
- Special information for teachers and lecturers

www.worldsclassics.co.uk

American Literature

British and Irish Literature

Children's Literature

Classics and Ancient Literature

Colonial Literature

Eastern Literature

European Literature

History

Medieval Literature

Oxford English Drama

Poetry

Philosophy

Politics

Religion

The Oxford Shakespeare

A complete list of Oxford Paperbacks, including Oxford World's Classics, OPUS, Past Masters, Oxford Authors, Oxford Shakespeare, Oxford Drama, and Oxford Paperback Reference, is available in the UK from the Academic Division Publicity Department, Oxford University Press, Great Clarendon Street, Oxford OX2 6DP.

In the USA, complete lists are available from the Paperbacks Marketing Manager, Oxford University Press, 198 Madison Avenue, New York, NY 10016.

Oxford Paperbacks are available from all good bookshops. In case of difficulty, customers in the UK can order direct from Oxford University Press Bookshop, Freepost, 116 High Street, Oxford OX1 4BR, enclosing full payment. Please add 10 per cent of published price for postage and packing.